EREC
by
HARTMANN VON AUE

Translated, with an introduction and commentary, by
MICHAEL RESLER

EREC

by

HARTMANN
VON AUE

EREC

by
HARTMANN
VON AUE

*Translated, with an Introduction
and Commentary, by*
MICHAEL RESLER

UNIVERSITY OF PENNSYLVANIA PRESS · PHILADELPHIA

upp

UNIVERSITY OF PENNSYLVANIA PRESS

MIDDLE AGES SERIES

Edited by

EDWARD PETERS

Henry Charles Lea Professor
of Medieval History
University of Pennsylvania

A complete listing of the books in this series
appears at the back of this volume

Frontispiece: The two unnamed "heroes" from the title
illustration of the Ambras Manuscript. From the facsimile edition
of the Ambras Manuscript (Codex Vindobonensis S. N. 2663 of
the Österreichische Nationalbibliothek in Vienna), vol. XLIII of
the series Codices Selecti, Akademische Druck- und
Verlagsanstalt, Graz, Austria, 1973.

Library of Congress Cataloging-in-Publication Data

Hartmann, von Aue, 12th cent.
    Erec.

    (University of Pennsylvania Press Middle Ages
series.)
        Bibliography: p.
        Includes index.
        1. Arthurian romances.   I. Resler, Michael.
    II. Title.   III. Series.
    PT1534.E8   1987b   831'2   87-12419
    ISBN 0-8122-8074-1
    ISBN 0-8122-1247-9 (pbk.)

Designed by Adrianne Onderdonk Dudden

CAROLO MAGNO

CONTENTS

Acknowledgments ix
Introduction 1

EREC

ACKNOWLEDGMENTS

I should like, first of all, to express my enduring gratitude to the National Endowment for the Humanities, which lent indispensible initial support to this project through a fellowship which enabled me to devote the entire academic year 1980–81 to Hartmann von Aue's *Erec*. I am also most grateful to Boston College for providing a generous subvention to offset the publication costs of this book.

In addition, a number of friends, colleagues and others have contributed in various important ways to the final form of this book. Special thanks are due to Lorraine Canavan, who typed the original version of the translation; to my father, Richard Resler, who patiently read aloud from the translation and offered numerous stylistic suggestions; to Professor Laurie Shepard of Boston College, whose thorough knowledge of the Middle Ages was instrumental in clarifying numerous points of difficulty; and to two different classes of students in my course on the German literature of the High Middle Ages, whose suggestions ranged from the nuts-and-bolts of typographical errors and punctuation to more substantive stylistic issues.

I reserve my most heartfelt thanks for Professor Charles Lutcavage of Harvard University, whose help and encouragement were willingly offered at virtually every stage of my work on *Erec*. If this book should at all be judged positively by its readers, then such success is due in no small measure to his lucid sense of style and to his unfailingly sharp editorial eye. Indeed, without his constant and ubiquitous input my efforts could hardly have come to final fruition.

Finally, I should like to acknowledge my considerable indebtedness to the editors at the University of Pennsylvania Press—most especially to Mr. Zachary Simpson, who offered a steady guiding hand at so many critical junctures, and to Professor Edward Peters for his numerous suggestions for the introduction.

INTRODUCTION

INTRODUCTION

HISTORICAL AND CULTURAL BACKGROUND

At Pentecost in the year 1184 the Holy Roman Emperor Friedrich I—known as Friedrich Barbarossa—hosted a great festival along the banks of the Rhein at Mainz to celebrate the knighting of his two sons Heinrich and Friedrich.[1] A graphic documentation of the splendor and pageantry of this remarkable *Hoftag* (or imperial gathering) can be found in the Latin *Chronicle of Henne-gaus*,[2] which was written twelve years later—in 1196—by Gislebert of Mons, one of the participants at Mainz. Gislebert reports that the festival was attended by some 70,000 knights and by hundreds of bishops, archbishops, princes, dukes and counts; in addition, we know from other sources[3] that a number of important poets journeyed to Mainz as well. Over the course of three days' time, Gislebert discloses, enormous stores of food and drink were provided the participants, along with entertainment and knightly tournaments. Indeed, Barbarossa erected on this site what appeared to be a veritable city of tents and pavilions to house the throngs which came to Mainz to take part in the festivities.[4] Not only in the view of many modern historians, but already in the minds of contemporary, twelfth-century chroniclers,[5] the emperor's *Hoftag* came to epitomize most succinctly the coming of the chivalric age to Germany. In Barbarossa's time, for instance, the 1184 festival was already being hailed as an extraordinary event[6] and as an external expression of the alliance of the emperor and the knights.[7]

So spectacular, in fact, was this assembly that it was recorded not only by historians, but was also treated—indeed, raised virtually to the level of myth—by numerous poets. For example, the Frenchman Guiot de Provins, himself in attendance at the festival, consciously alludes to the parallels between this chivalric spectacle at Mainz and the celebrated pageants hosted by Alexander the Great and by King Arthur.[8] One of the German poets present, Heinrich von Veldeke, in his romance *Eneit*, reports of Virgil's wedding feast for Lavinia and Aeneas, and likens this event to the great spectacle at Mainz: "I never heard of such a festival, unless it was that at Mainz, when Kaiser Frederick knighted his sons."[9] Hence, by the late twelfth century in Germany, both history and literature seem to have intersected in a common fascination with knighthood.

At virtually the same time as Barbarossa's *Hoftag*—farther to the south of Mainz, somewhere in present-day Swabia—yet another German poet by the name of Hartmann von Aue was composing in the Middle High German language the story of Erec, a member of King Arthur's fellowship of the Round Table. Although the rich pageantry of the Arthurian world had by this time already gained great popularity in France, Hartmann's romance was the very first account in the German tongue of the adventures of an Arthurian knight. Far from being an isolated or ephemeral literary phenomenon, the tale of Erec's quest for knightly fulfillment was to launch a new and immensely popular form of literature within Germany. Following directly in Hartmann's footsteps, the next several generations of German-speaking poets would draw frequently upon the colorful Arthurian mythology in their works.

Scholars generally believe that Hartmann's *Erec* was composed around the year 1185, give or take perhaps a half decade. This would make *Erec* almost exactly contemporaneous with the fabled events at Mainz. To be sure, we possess no evidence whatsoever to suggest that Hartmann was among the poets in attendance at the festival in Mainz, or even that this festival, in any direct way, occasioned Hartmann to write *Erec*. Yet these two phenomena of late twelfth-century Germany—one of them a literary fiction and the other a historical fact—have one very important thread in common: the primacy of knighthood. In a real sense, the chivalric ethic, which had rapidly overspread large parts of Europe during the eleventh and twelfth centuries and which seems to have taken on such palpable form in the celebration at Mainz, provided the cultural soil in which the works of Hartmann von Aue and his fellow Arthurian poets would soon take root and come to full blossom. To a great extent, the seeds of new literature in Germany were nurtured by the larger cultural and political forces—most especially the rise of knighthood—that were shaping life in Western Europe.

A major factor in the development of the chivalric order during the eleventh and twelfth centuries was the advent of the Crusades. Indeed, it was during the age of the Crusades that knighthood reached its zenith. A long series of wars waged by European Christians between the eleventh and fourteenth centuries, the Crusades promoted the development of a new order of fighters, the knights. Through the deployment of large armies of warriors in the Middle East, the Crusaders hoped—first and foremost—to recapture the Holy Land by force from the Muslims. Full absolution was promised to all who took up the cross to that end, and the mobilization of a fighting force was undertaken on a grand scale. Knighthood and the Church, the two mainstays of medieval Europe, were, at least on the surface and for a limited time, united in one common cause.

To be sure, the Church's attitude towards much of what constituted chivalry had been, prior to the Crusades, lukewarm. The Church, the preponderant social institution in medieval Christendom, continued throughout the high Middle Ages to proscribe such knightly activities as jousting.[10] On the other hand, a certain ecclesiastical ambivalence towards warfare was fundamentally ingrained in the medieval Church, for the bellicose streak rooted in the militant God of the Old Testament had long been intermingled with the predominantly pacific ethos of the New Testament.[11] At any rate, this tension within the Church between war and peace was sufficiently palpable to preclude any sort of wholehearted ecclesiastical embracing of the ideals of knighthood. However, a major shift in this attitude, which parallels the development of chivalry as a Christian calling,[12] came with the age of the Crusades. Now the Church began to preach the Crusading effort as a "positive transformation of the knightly way of life."[13]

An intriguing footnote to the interrelationships among chivalry, the Crusades, and the Church can be interposed if we return once more to Mainz and to Emperor Friedrich I. It is interesting to note that at the 1184 chivalric pageant at Mainz, the notion of the Crusade, although it had already contributed so much to the rise of chivalry, appears not to have been a motivating concern. Four years later, however, in 1188, Emperor Friedrich once again assembled a great host at Mainz—this time for the express purpose of taking up the cross and embarking upon the coming Crusade. Finally, now that the Crusading fervor had found full resonance at the imperial court, the Church would grant its full approval, indeed its blessing. The Church, which had remained largely in the background in 1184, now joined the constellation—formalized four years earlier—of emperor, knights and poets.[14] This second great festival at Mainz was no longer a vainglorious, self-indulgent, secular exercise, but rather a part of the concerted effort to retake the Holy Land. On the surface, at least, the *militia imperatoris* had now become the *militia Christi*.[15]

Seen from a strictly historical standpoint, the Crusades were ultimately unsuccessful. For one thing, individual motives for taking up the cross were— probably from the outset—very much mixed, the pursuit of worldly honor figuring strongly alongside the outwardly expressed religious priorities. In fact, the emperor himself was convinced that he was fighting "tam pro Deo quam pro honore temporali."[16] Furthermore, the Crusades, with their grandiose aim of capturing the Holy Land, may well have been, from a purely practical stance, unrealistic and thus doomed from the outset. By the twelfth century a certain disillusionment had already begun to set in.

Disenchantment with the Crusading movement may in some ways have been linked to the fact that the Church, far from being a monolithic institution acting with the full and unanimous consent of its many and diverse arms, was, during much of this period, torn by new currents of theology and by numerous heretical movements, most significantly in Southern France and in Northern Italy. By the late twelfth century, ever greater numbers of thinkers were beginning to pursue new religious practices and to embrace diverse moral values. Indeed, it is difficult to understand or to appreciate this age by looking for common denominators or universally held beliefs, for "it was the variety, not the reconciliation, which struck deepest root in the late twelfth and early thirteenth centuries."[17] In the broadest sense, the unity of purpose necessary for so huge an undertaking as the Crusades seems to have been lacking.

Yet whatever the reasons for their failure, the impact of the Crusades on medieval European civilization for long after the Middle Ages was profound, indeed virtually incalculable.[18] First of all, the Crusades served to stimulate trade and commerce. Along with this, new and exotic-sounding names came into the European languages to describe the various spices, fabrics, and medicines that were being brought back from the Middle East. The Crusades also served as the catalyst for a great cross-fertilization among European and Eastern institutions and nations. There began a broad influx of new ways of thinking into Western Europe.

On a lesser scale, this great intermingling of people and ideas caused by the Crusades helped to spark the literary growth experienced by the German tongue during the final years of the twelfth and the early decades of the thirteenth century. For not only merchants and the Crusading *milites Dei* journeyed to the Holy Land: poets and thinkers went as well. Among the important German-speaking poets of this age many (perhaps most) are thought to have been knights,[19] and certain of them—including, as we shall see, Hartmann von Aue himself—actually took part in the Crusades.

The Crusading experience supplied the subject matter for some of the literature composed in the Middle High German language, in particular portions of the song poetry. However, of far greater import for the literature was the newly enhanced role of knighthood. Whether or not the individual German poets actually left home to take up the cross and journey across the Mediterranean (and some apparently did), the important fact remains that many of these tellers of adventurous tales were first and foremost knight-poets. As such, their stories are thoroughly steeped in the ideals of chivalry, which was the driving force in Middle High German literature in the decades surrounding the year 1200.

While this period marked the first great literary age in the German tongue, it was not the first time that German culture, in the broader sense, had flourished. The late eighth and early ninth centuries had already witnessed—during the Carolingian renaissance—lofty cultural achievements on German soil. However, the chief literary and official language of Charlemagne's court was Latin, and not German. The vernacular was at that time not yet deemed a serious vehicle for the linguistic needs of the court.

By the late twelfth century, however—by the time of Hartmann von Aue—German had acquired significantly higher status as a literary language.[20] Perhaps the earliest memorable literary work of this period to resonate fully with the timbre of its age was the *Rolandslied*, an epic dating from around 1170 (at least a full decade before Hartmann's *Erec*). Ostensibly, the *Rolandslied* was composed as a retelling of the deeds of Charlemagne and his adjutant Roland in their battle against the Saracens, which had taken place four centuries earlier in Spain. It was no accident, however, that the recounting of this and other tales from the distant past came at the very time when the battle had just been resumed in the Holy Land against the same opponent. And insofar as the Church was the chief promoter of the Crusades, it is noteworthy that the *Rolandslied* was written by a priest of the Church, Konrad of Regensburg. Finally, given the need for at least some degree of popular support for the Crusading effort, it is significant that Konrad composed his work in German, and not in Latin, which—albeit the sole written language widely understood throughout the European Middle Ages—was chiefly learned and used only by the educated ruling classes.

To be sure, the ethos of the *Rolandslied* was still a half generation or more removed from that of the more refined courtly literature of Heinrich von Veldeke and Hartmann von Aue, for the *Rolandslied* still rings with the earlier barbaric conviction that the heathen masses are little more than cattle for the slaughter.[21] A more enlightened, tolerant attitude towards non-Christians would not fully find its way into the literature for another several decades, with Wolfram von Eschenbach's *Willehalm* (ca. 1215–20). Nonetheless, with the composition of the *Rolandslied*, the notion that the Crusade was "the adventure of the hour,"[22] regardless of individual motives or dogmatic preconceptions, had now taken on popular literary expression.

Within the literature of the Middle High German age—a period which followed close on the heels of the *Rolandslied*—the courtly romance and the heroic epic were the most important narrative genres. Above all else, the poets of these romances and epics (along with the earlier *Rolandslied* poet) clearly relished recounting the valorous deeds of a strong heroic central figure. The wondrous feats of Siegfried in the *Nibelungenlied* or the long and arduous quest by Parzival for the Holy Grail are but two examples of the propensity to glorify and mythologize the actions of a larger-than-life hero.

In this same vein, the literature can be seen as a mirror of its times. Great ages in history are marked by great leaders, and there was no shortage of imposing historical figures in Europe around 1200. This was the age of Saint Francis of Assisi and of Richard the Lion-Heart, of powerful popes and renowned kings. Within Germany itself, the Hohenstaufen family produced a dynastic line of Holy Roman emperors whose rule coincided with the very peak of Europe's knightly glory.

Emperor Friedrich I (ca. 1125–1190) was the most famous of the Hohenstaufen rulers. As we have seen, not only did Barbarossa encourage and foster Crusading, he took part in the Third Crusade and drowned in the year 1190 in Cilicia (in Asia Minor) while embarking upon this effort. Moreover, Friedrich I was an important patron of literature as well. In fact, one of the poets present at the 1184 *Hoftag* in Mainz, Guiot de Provins, expressly names Friedrich Barbarossa as his patron. Yet another French poet, Raimon Vidal, comments in one of his works that the emperor did much to encourage the poetry of the troubadours.[23] The German poet Friedrich von Hausen, who composed Crusading songs while in the company of Friedrich Barbarossa on the Third Crusade, is also named in certain documents as the *secretarius* and *familiaris*[24] of the emperor. It is possible that Friedrich's wife, the Empress Beatrix, whose ties to literature can be traced back as far as 1167, may have moved her husband to grant a willing ear to poetry.[25] At any rate, it is abundantly clear that poets were made to feel welcome at the imperial court and that the emperor's bonds with men of letters were quite strong.

While Friedrich Barbarossa was a dominant figure in European politics, it was his grandson, Friedrich II (1194–1250), who was perhaps the most brilliant member of the Hohenstaufen family. As a ruler, Friedrich II was, in the final analysis, flawed, for he was unable to halt the forces which ultimately brought down the Hohenstaufen dynasty. But like his grandfather and like numerous other political figures of the day (most notably Landgrave Hermann of Thuringia and the Babenberg dukes of Vienna), the younger Friedrich was a patron of art and poetry. Without such patronage it is questionable whether much of the great literature of the period would have been preserved for later generations, or indeed whether it would have been composed at all. Not only were the poets offered encouragement (in the form of commissions) and the necessary material conditions for writing, the wealthier patrons also saw to it that the tales and lyrics were permanently recorded in sometimes very costly and precious manuscripts. The role of the patrons was undoubtedly pivotal in passing on to us much of what we possess of the literary legacy of the Middle High German age.

While secular rulers such as the two Friedrichs left an indelible mark upon life and literature during this period, the religious leadership was certainly not without its impact as well. In fact, the papacy—that other ruling sphere within the dichotomy of the spiritual and the worldly—stood at the forefront of events. A strong, dominant, even heroic figure occupied center-stage, in the person of Pope Innocent III.

Generally acknowledged as the most powerful of medieval popes, Innocent was intimately involved in the power politics of his day. Innocent preached the notion of the papal monarchy, the idea that the pope was not only the ecclesiastical leader, but also the rightful political ruler of the world. Only months after assuming the throne of St. Peter in 1198, Innocent became embroiled in the so-called double election—a dispute within Germany over the successor to Barbarossa's son, the Holy Roman Emperor Heinrich VI, who had died unexpectedly in 1197. Because the imperial throne was technically not hereditary, and because Heinrich's son Friedrich (Barbarossa's grandson, later to become Emperor Friedrich II) was at that time only three years of age, the German princes had little choice but to turn to Heinrich's brother, Philip of Swabia, as the next Holy Roman Emperor. The Pope, wishing to maneuver events to his own political advantage, injected himself and his office into the now smouldering unrest within Germany. First, he backed the cause of a rival claimant, Otto of Brunswick, who presented an ostensibly lesser threat to papal prerogatives. Then, as events began to shift, Innocent threw his support behind Philip, only to revert later (following Philip's assassination) to Otto. In time, however, Otto's encroachments on various papal territories caused Innocent to turn from him again and to champion the accession of the young Friedrich, who was eventually crowned emperor in 1212 at the age of eighteen. As a result of these imbroglios, there was no single, universally recognized leader of the Holy Roman Empire for a period of approximately a decade and a half. For much of this time, Germany was mired in political uncertainty and periodic outbreaks of civil war. While much of this strife would likely have ensued even without papal intervention, clearly Pope Innocent had stirred up the embers of unrest and had played at least a supporting role in the unfortunate unfolding of events.

In this question of papal versus secular authority, we find yet another instance of the interplay between life and literature during the high Middle Ages.

In the political poems of Walther von der Vogelweide came swift and vociferous reaction to Innocent's mixing of politics and religion. Walther portrays the pope as laughing gleefully at the destruction and chaos he has generated by placing two Germans beneath the imperial crown. Depicted as a tool of the devil, Walther's Innocent is shown spreading heresy and expunging St. Peter's teachings from the books of Scripture.[26] Certainly it would be fundamentally wrong to label Walther as anti-*Christian* in his attacks upon Pope Innocent III, but often enough an unmistakably anti-*ecclesiastical* note is sounded in his works, as well as in the writings of certain of his fellow poets. In a broader sense—one which reflects the changing intellectual and social climate—the literature of this era was significantly more secular, and less religious, in spirit than it had been in the past.[27]

In view of the far-reaching cultural, political, intellectual and spiritual ferment which was current in Germany—and in Western Europe—around the year 1200, it is fitting that this age is commonly referred to as the "high" Middle Ages. Certainly it was a fertile period, one in which great transformations were taking place in the way men thought and lived, and one which "opened men's minds and broadened their vision."[28] As we have seen, it was a time when the full might of the Hohenstaufen dynasty coincided with the height of the medieval papacy. Alongside the cosmopolitan effects of the Crusades and the rapid influx of foreign culture, there arose that new elite order of fighters, the knights. The chivalric code and the knightly cult which developed around them, along with the deeds of valor they performed, became the stuff of legend. The final ingredient, the one component still needed to crystallize all the rich pageantry of this age into permanent verbal form, was a body of poets of true genius.

Previously in Germany there had always existed some impediment to a full flowering of vernacular literature. Either the literature itself had been inferior or it had been composed in Latin. Now there came onto the stage a small but especially gifted array of poets who were nurtured by the great events and transformations going on around them. The time was ripe for a blossoming of first-rate literature in the German tongue. Four names stand out in particular as the literary giants of this chivalric, or courtly age in Germany: Hartmann von Aue, Wolfram von Eschenbach, Gottfried von Strassburg and Walther von der Vogelweide. Whereas Walther's fame is rooted in his lyric poetry, the other three poets are noted chiefly for their courtly romances: Wolfram for his monumental *Parzival*, Gottfried for his courtly tale of love *Tristan*, and Hartmann for his two Arthurian romances *Erec* and *Iwein*.

To the extent we are able to judge, the stories and songs of these and other poets must have been enormously popular at courts throughout Germany. A public which probably did not extend much beyond the narrow circle of these courts appears to have listened enthusiastically and to have embraced whole-heartedly the ideals espoused by these highly class-conscious—and very elit-ist—knight-poets.[29] (Of the four poets, only Gottfried was almost irrefutably *not* a knight.) For a relatively brief period of approximately four decades, roughly between the years 1185 and 1225, German literature, set astir by the high-wrought events of the day, soared to lofty heights. The literary monu-ments of this era are as noble and enduring as the great Gothic cathedrals which were slowly inching to the heavens across much of Europe during that same age.

HARTMANN VON AUE

What little we know of the external details of Hartmann's life must be recon-structed from various indirect sources. This obtains for most poets of the age. Although the most eminent of them were well known during their lifetimes (and presumably Hartmann was a noted practitioner of his art), nonetheless they were not celebrated personalities in the modern sense. There was no one to act as their biographer, to record the events of their lives. As a result, only what they said about themselves in their works, implicitly and explicitly, and what their fellow poets wrote about them can be said to contribute to our knowledge of the lives of these poets.

As for Hartmann, we believe that he was born sometime around 1160–65 and that he died between 1210 and 1220–30. Both sets of dates, however, are only approximate. The birth date of 1160–65 is arrived at somewhat arbitrarily, by assuming that Hartmann must have been at least twenty or twenty-five years old when he began to write, and by then subtracting that number from what we think to be the year of origin (1185) of his first major work, *Erec*. At the other end, the evidence is a bit more convincing, albeit not overwhelmingly so. Gottfried, in his *Tristan*, makes mention of Hartmann as still alive, and since this passage in *Tristan* is dated (again, not with absolute certainty) around 1210, then our poet must still have been living in 1210. However, in a later work, Heinrich von dem Türlin's *Krône*, Hartmann is named among the de-ceased. Since Heinrich's *Krône* was probably composed between 1220 and 1230, Hartmann's death must have occurred sometime prior to this.

In the prologue to his superbly crafted courtly legend *Henry the Leper* (*Der arme Heinrich*), Hartmann tells us a bit more about himself. In fact, for a poet of this era, Hartmann sheds considerable light upon the circumstances of his life in this passage. Here he states that he is a knight, that he is an educated man, and that he is in the service of a lord in Aue. The first two assertions can be readily confirmed simply by a reading of Hartmann's works, for in them he betrays a familiarity with the full array of knightly terminology of his day and a thorough schooling in the art of rhetoric. What is more, numerous allusions scattered throughout his various tales clearly suggest that he was versed both in the Latin literature of antiquity and in contemporary French literature. His knowledge of Old French was demonstrably sound, for in several of his longer narrative romances (*Erec* included) he worked at least partially from an original text in French. That Hartmann was indeed educated (probably, as was common in those days for someone of his standing, in a cloister school) and that he was a member of the knightly class appear beyond question. As to the third piece of information which he offers concerning himself—that he served a liege lord in Aue—here too there is no reason not to take his claim at face value. The problem arises in locating just *where* on the map this Aue is to be found. Careful analysis of Hartmann's dialect (together with other intrinsic and extrinsic evidence) enables us to state with certainty that our poet's linguistic roots, and therefore his homeland, lay in present-day Swabia, in southwestern Germany. Unfortunately, "Aue" was a common place name, even within Swabia. Consequently, despite a plethora of conjectures and theories we are, in the final analysis, unable to assign Hartmann any more specific a geographical home than simply Swabia, itself by no means a small area.

A final word on Hartmann's social standing: in the same passage in which he reveals so much about himself (more than we ever hear from Wolfram, Gottfried, or Walther), Hartmann uses the word *dienstman*, or ministerial, to describe himself. An estate unique to medieval Germany, the ministerials developed during the twelfth century into a distinct class of "individuals of servile legal status, but of aristocratic life style."[30] Not all ministerials were knights, but it is abundantly clear, from what we have seen above, that Hartmann practiced the knightly trade. The ministerials, though originally unfree and in the service of the older nobility, had, by Hartmann's day, begun to acquire for themselves some of the privileges of their lords, and in fact gradually came to constitute the lowest ranks of the nobility. Functionally, the ministerials were nobles, although legally they remained serfs.[31] It was just such a middle position, then, that our poet must have held—a position not of lofty rank, but not, on the other hand, one of humble servitude.

A final brushstroke can be added to our still rather sketchy biographical portrait of Hartmann von Aue. Again, it is the poet Hartmann who offers us a glimpse of himself. In several of his lyric poems he alludes to the death of his overlord and to the profound psychological impact which this event had upon him. Just who this lord was, we shall perhaps never know. But the injection of so poignantly private a note into the generally impersonal song poetry of this age is unusual and testifies most likely to the real depth of loss which Hartmann experienced.

In one of the poems dealing with the death of his lord—the so-called "Third Crusading Song"—Hartmann appears to be telling us that he has been so overwhelmed by his lord's death that he plans to set out on a Crusade. Unfortunately, a crucial line in this poem can be punctuated in two different ways (there is virtually no punctuation, as we know it, in the manuscripts of this era), each yielding a significantly different reading. The more likely of the two possible interpretations tells of a man who has undergone an inner change, a sort of renewed or heightened faith in God. Had he not come face to face, Hartmann reports, with the reality of death, then Saladin and all his army could not have induced him to leave home on a Crusade. The reference to Saladin, the Sultan of Syria and Egypt and the Christians' chief opponent in the Third Crusade, would—if it were not for the punctuational uncertainty clouding this particular verse—enable us to determine precisely in which Crusade Hartmann was a participant.[32] As is so often the case with the biographies of these poets, we simply cannot be certain. At any rate, Hartmann must have joined either the Third Crusade, led by Friedrich Barbarossa in 1189–90, or the Crusade of 1197–98, an ill-fated adventure which was aborted at the death of its leader, Emperor Heinrich VI. Regardless, Hartmann seems to have undergone a personal religious experience at this point—an experience which caused him to turn away, in his writings, from the glittering, secular world of the court and to devote his poetic efforts, at least for a time, to the quest for spiritual fulfillment.

Of the major poets of the age, Hartmann von Aue was certainly the most prolific and the most versatile. We have works by Hartmann in virtually every common literary genre of the day, although his single most important service was probably the introduction of Arthurian romance into Germany. Prior to his religious experience, Hartmann wrote two such romances (*Erec* and at least part of *Iwein*), along with numerous courtly love songs and the *Lament* (often called the *Büchlein*), an allegorical dispute on the function of love. Then, in what may have been a response to his overlord's death, Hartmann renounced courtly love and worldly pursuits. From this period are often thought to come the Crusading songs and other poems of renunciation, as well as the two longer courtly legends (*Gregorius* and *Henry the Leper*), in which Hartmann deals at length with the question of how to please both God and the world. The presumably younger Hartmann had seen, particularly within the harmonious Arthurian realm, no insurmountable conflict between the secular and the spiritual. In what are often thought to be his later works, however, circumstances are quite different. Here, the pursuit of worldly glory is depicted as the root of man's downfall, and only through renunciation of the world and assumption of an ascetic lifestyle can he be assured of salvation.

The diversity among Hartmann's various works is certainly beyond question. We venture out onto considerably less secure ground, however, when we attempt to assign such thematically and philosophically different works to different "periods" in the life of a medieval poet. It may well be that Hartmann was more likely to celebrate the chivalric life and the secular world in his writings prior to the death of his overlord, and that, after having gone through that apparently devastating experience, he was more strongly inclined to praise the spiritual life. But it is just as likely that, in making such assumptions as these, we are following a typically modern (and not medieval) line of thinking. Much of medieval literature is non-confessional in origin. A medieval poet's private experiences do not necessarily surface in his fictional writings. While there may be a correlation between Hartmann von Aue's literary predilections at a given time and his grappling with certain spiritual questions, it is far too simplistic to assume a necessary correspondence between the two. In fact, there is a considerable body of evidence to suggest that *Iwein,* his second Arthurian romance, was composed in two parts, the first early in his career and the second much later. Are we to conclude, if Hartmann the *poet* returned late in life to complete this unfinished work of his youth, that Hartmann the *man* intended thereby to embrace once again the secular values of this knight's tale? Perhaps, but not necessarily. While we can attempt to construct a certain order in which Hartmann's works may have been composed, we are left, finally, with a good measure of uncertainty as to their actual chronology.

None of the many unanswered extrinsic questions concerning Hartmann von Aue detracts in any way from the intrinsic charm of his stories or from the beauty of his language. If there is one stylistic quality for which Hartmann is especially noted, it is his clarity of expression. In the famous literary excursus in *Tristan,* Gottfried von Strassburg comments—approvingly and disapprovingly—upon various of his contemporary fellow poets. In his encomium to Hartmann, Gottfried gives our poet his due when he says, "How clear and transparent [Hartmann's] crystal words are and ever must remain!"[33] The unadorned, lucid harmony of Hartmann's style is nothing more than the outward, verbal manifestation of an inner virtue which Hartmann extolled again and again in his works: moderation. The golden mean—that state of inward and outward balance and proportion—must first be discovered by Hartmann's protagonists before they can ever hope to achieve enduring bliss. So vital is this sense of moderation to Hartmann that it cuts thematically across the full range of his works, from the Arthurian romances (in which the ultimate happiness is of a decidedly secular tone) to the courtly legends (where a more clearly spiritual bliss is at stake). In the end, Hartmann's heroes succeed—usually after rigorous and perilous trials—in attaining moderation, the same moderation which finds formal resonance in Hartmann's crystalline verses.

ARTHURIAN ROMANCE

The tales of King Arthur and his knights of the Round Table first became popular in France soon after the middle of the twelfth century. These stories centering on King Arthur's court are not portrayed as contemporary events, for they are set not in the twelfth century, but rather at some uncertain, ahistorical point in the distant past. Indeed, the origins of the Arthurian legend, in their written form, can be traced back nearly four centuries, to ca. 800. The oral legend of King Arthur extends back even farther in time. However, it was a contemporary phenomenon—the rise of the knightly culture—which helped to enkindle the new courtly literature in Europe. The past (ancient Arthurian legend) and the present (the new chivalric vogue) converged, each supplying a vital ingredient for a form of entertainment which was to become enormously popular throughout large parts of Europe for the next several centuries.

It may be impossible to establish with certainty whether or not a warrior-king by the name of Arthur ever actually existed. To be sure, there is no reason for believing that this legendary Celtic figure did *not* live, but historians have been unable to identify him incontrovertibly with any specific historical king. At any rate, the familiar mythologized figure of the literature has taken on greater proportions than the historical King Arthur—if indeed he existed—could have assumed. For twelfth-century France (and later, for thirteenth-century Germany), King Arthur became both the symbol of the ideal courtly leader and the focal point of these new romances, in which the chivalric ethic and the full panoply of knightly glory were showcased for eager audiences.

The earliest written evidence of King Arthur as a historical figure stems from around 800, in the *Historia Brittonum*. This work is a compilation of material from numerous sources and is preserved in several divergent versions. Two passages refer to Arthur, and in the more significant of these he is depicted as the leader of the Britons in their battle against the Saxons. The origins of the legend, then, are rooted in England, and not on the continent.

In one of the battles attested in the *Historia Brittonum* (these campaigns actually took place ca. 500 A.D.), Arthur is reported to have slain 960 of the enemy single-handedly. Unfortunately, other historical sources closer to the period in question fail to mention such a figure. Nonetheless, the passage in the *Historia Brittonum*, taken together with a handful of other documents,[34] leads to the conclusion that there must have been a popular (possibly pre-medieval) tradition surrounding the figure of King Arthur, be that figure historical, quasi-historical, or mythological.

It was roughly three and one half centuries later, around 1135, that Arthur was first made accessible to a broader audience. This came at the hand of Geoffrey of Monmouth, whose *Historia Regum Brittaniae* portrays Arthur (in Books 8–10) as a British king so powerful that he even dares to challenge the hegemony of the Roman Empire. Unfortunately, Geoffrey's work (preserved in over 200 manuscripts and translated into several languages) abounds in fictional inventions and can make little claim to historical accuracy. Geoffrey's design was to glorify the British people and probably to curry personal favor among members of Britain's ruling family, whose ancestors he depicts here in glowing and heroic colors. In any event, the *Historia* is important to us not for its historical veracity, but rather for the fictional amplification which Arthur underwent at the pen of Geoffrey of Monmouth. Geoffrey created from this little-known Celtic hero a figure of great proportions, a ruler who might well be called—albeit with a blind eye towards historical fact—the British equivalent of Charlemagne.

So towering a character as Arthur was bound to become the fodder of poets. Around the year 1155 (just twenty years or so after Geoffrey's work), a Norman writer by the name of Wace composed the *Roman de Brut*, a verse adaptation of the *Historia* in Anglo-Norman dialect. Wace's achievements were two-fold. First, he embued the work with the new chivalric, courtly elegance of the day. King Arthur, for example, appears here more the noble feudal lord than the hardened warrior of old. Second, Wace introduced the concept of the Round Table to the Arthurian legend. It was in this literary form that the expanded and refined story of King Arthur was eventually passed on to the poets of the European continent, where it was later to flourish and take on the contours familiar to modern readers. Wace's *Roman de Brut*, therefore, marks the transformation of Arthurian legend into Arthurian literature.

In part because of the position occupied by Wace at the court of King Henry II of England, his *Roman de Brut* became very popular and widely read. Wace dedicated his work to King Henry's wife, the celebrated Eleanor of Aquitaine. Eleanor was among the most powerful and influential women of the Middle Ages. At the time of her marriage to Henry, she already ruled over Poitou and Aquitaine. For his part, Henry was also duke of Normandy and count of Anjou. Hence, the two of them not only governed as king and queen of England, but they also controlled most of Western France as well. Just as important for our purposes, both were enthusiastic supporters of the arts and patrons of literature. Eleanor boasted a brilliant circle of poets at her court: Thomas of Britain, Marie de France, and Benoît de Sainte-Maure, in addition to Wace. Prior to her marriage to Henry, Eleanor had been married to King Louis VII of France. After the annulment of her marriage to Louis in 1152, Eleanor came to England, bringing with her a predilection for the refined courtly tone of the new love poetry which had become so popular in her homeland. To the Norman rulers of England, this French taste must certainly have been more palatable than the older Germanic style of literature.

Eleanor's eldest daughter (from her marriage to the French king), Marie de Champagne, was, like her mother, an important patron of literature. Born in France, Marie lived for a time with her mother in England, but later returned to France and married the French Count Henri, whose court at Troyes was also a major cultural and intellectual center. It was here that the greatest of the French romancers, Chrétien de Troyes, lived and worked. While few concrete facts are preserved concerning Chrétien's life, it is known that he composed his most important works in Troyes at the court—and probably under the direct sponsorship—of Marie de Champagne. Although, as we have noted, the Arthurian legend is British in its origins, it is, in its ultimate literary embodiment, the invention of this French poet. Chrétien stands alone as the prime molder of the Arthurian story into Arthurian romance, and it was at the court in Troyes that Chrétien gave the legend its classic form as literature.[35]

Chrétien probably lived between about 1135 and 1190. Although the substance of the Arthurian saga reaches back, as we have seen, at least 350 years before Chrétien's time, nonetheless Chrétien brought a full measure of his own originality to the legend. To cite just one example, Chrétien portrays Arthur as a wise, older king whose own deeds of valor had taken place earlier, during his youth. Unlike his predecessors, Chrétien relates not the adventures of King Arthur himself, but rather those of the many fine knights who journey to his court in search of fame and honor. Chrétien depicts Arthur, in other words, as a magnetic, yet passive figure—not as the actively heroic figure of the legends. Also, the setting of Chrétien's works tends to alternate frequently between Britain and Brittany (in France), with little regard for geography. The chronological parameters of the stories are likewise vague, so that the reader never has a firm notion as to just when they are set in history.

While Chrétien's chief contribution was as an innovator, this is not to deny him his due as a skillful poet. Indeed, Chrétien is numbered among the greatest of the Old French poets. His works were very popular during his lifetime and were translated and adapted into English, Welsh, Norse and of course German.[36] It was Chrétien's *Erec et Enide* which served as the model for Hartmann von Aue's *Erec*. And with *Erec* (completed around 1185), the legend of King Arthur—now cast in the mold of refined courtly literature—finally reached a German audience.[37]

PROBLEMS WITH THE TEXT

If Chrétien de Troyes can be called the architect of Arthurian romance, Hartmann von Aue plays an equally pivotal role within the German tradition. It was Hartmann's *Erec* which first brought to the ears of large numbers of German listeners the chivalric tales of adventure of Arthur's men. In so doing, Hartmann opened the door to what would become, along with the poetry of lovesong, the predominant form of literary entertainment in Germany for the following century and a half.[38]

Both of Hartmann's Arthurian romances *(Erec* and *Iwein)* deal, typically, with the search for moderation, balance and proper proportion. In *Erec* the title hero becomes so amorously obsessed with his wife Enite that he ignores his responsibilities as a knight. *Iwein* stands in direct counterpoint to this. Here the protagonist inordinately pursues knightly adventures and neglects his duties at home. Both must atone at length for their immoderation, and both—characteristically for this optimistic genre—ultimately succeed in restoring harmony to their lives.

For literature written prior to the invention of the printing press, we are precariously dependent upon the survival of hand-copied documents; they are our only source for what Hartmann von Aue actually wrote eight hundred years ago. In general, Hartmann's works are poorly preserved from medieval times: most survive in very few manuscripts, many of which were copied well after the poet's lifetime. Only *Iwein* has been transmitted in a large number of manuscripts (thirty-two, of which seventeen are fragmentary). *Erec* survives in only one major manuscript, the well-known Ambras Manuscript. Unfortunately, the text of the Ambras Manuscript is seriously flawed. A major shortcoming is that it was written down more than three centuries after Hartmann originally composed his *Erec*. Consequently it contains numerous changes introduced by later scribes (in particular by the Ambras scribe, Hans Ried), so that Hartmann's precise wording is irretrievably lost. Moreover, there are two major lacunae in the Ambras text of *Erec*. The first of these occurs at the very beginning (where Hartmann would have written his prologue and the initial lines of the story) and the second at line 4629 (just after the passage in which

Erec defeats King Guivreiz and recuperates overnight at the little king's castle). Fortunately, the latter gap was neatly bridged by the discovery in 1898 of the fragment of a thirteenth-century *Erec* manuscript.[39] The loss of the prologue is very regrettable. For while the name of King Arthur was not entirely unknown in German literature before Hartmann,[40] nonetheless it was his task to introduce to a German audience the full dimensions of the Arthurian world: the Round Table, the court, the individual knights, the various stock characters; in short, the warm and brightly colored fabric of Arthurian conventions which had been, for the most part, invented or refined in France by Chrétien de Troyes. Because the prologue to *Erec* is lost, we shall presumably never know the method employed by Hartmann to present this richly woven mythology to his listeners. Scholars generally assume that as many as 150 verses are missing from Hartmann's text at this point. For this reason and in the interest of presenting a smooth and "complete" story, I have prefaced my translation with a brief summary (set off in italics) of the initial lines of Chrétien's *Erec et Enide*, up to the point where the Ambras Manuscript finally commences. Thereupon follows Hartmann's own story, beginning in mid-sentence, just as does the text of the Ambras Manuscript.

HARTMANN'S SOURCE

It is a mistake to regard Hartmann's *Erec* as a translation of Chrétien's *Erec et Enide*. In his *Iwein*, to be sure, our poet approaches more nearly the role of translator of Chrétien's *Yvain*, but even in this instance significant differences in the spirit and tone of the two romances ought to caution against such a label. A translation endeavors to render faithfully both the wording and the flavor of the original. Hartmann does neither. Hence the terms "adaptation" or "reworking" might be more aptly used to describe both of Hartmann's romances.

On the other hand, Hartmann's indebtedness to Chrétien in *Erec* must not be understated, and he is quick to recognize that debt. At one point (p. 15) he mentions Chrétien by name, and the several references to the "Master" (pp. 147, 149, 154, 158) are unequivocal allusions to the great poet of Troyes.

Undoubtedly, Hartmann owes the main body of his story to Chrétien, yet the numerous and significant points of divergence between the two versions are equally undeniable. So striking, in fact, are some of the dissimilarities that the question has been raised by scholars as to whether Hartmann might have also known and used other, separate versions of the Erec legend (for example, the Old Norse *Erex-Saga*) while composing his story.[41] Thus far, however, no convincing evidence has been presented either to prove or, for that matter, to dis-

prove the notion that many (perhaps most) of Hartmann's additions and alterations are anything other than the product of his own poetic fantasy.

One of the most striking differences is that Hartmann's *Erec* is significantly
longer than Chrétien's story, containing 10,192 lines versus 6958 in the French
version. But the differences encompass more than mere length. For example,
Hartmann displays a marked proclivity throughout to smooth out the rough
edges, to tone down the coarse or garish scenes in Chrétien. This difference in
tone is perhaps best expressed by the observation (made in reference to both
poets' versions of *Iwein*, but equally applicable to the two *Erecs* as well) that
Hartmann's story, "placed alongside Chrétien's work, appears as a carefully man-
icured and well-tended tree next to one which has grown in wildly with the
weeds and which sways in the wind."[42] Hartmann, in other words, strives for a
stylistic smoothness and orderliness not unlike the moderation which he so fervently espouses in his works.

Furthermore, Hartmann's purpose was not just to entertain his audience
with the tale of Sir Erec, but to offer occasional moral instruction as well. This
didactic tendency is much more difficult to discern in Chrétien, who was generally content simply to tell an entertaining tale. For example, after Hartmann's
Erec has triumphed against the knight Mabonagrin in the hidden arbor, Erec
expressly orders that the skulls of Mabonagrin's victims all be given proper
burial by priests of the Church. Lest this point be overlooked, Hartmann's narrator then adds his own personal approbation: "May God honor Erec for that!"
(p. 176). This is a minor detail, to be sure, but very characteristic of Hartmann,
and entirely missing in Chrétien's version of the story. Indeed, Hartmann's in-
structiveness at times seems to the modern reader to border on preaching. One
must bear in mind, however, that many (if not all) of these passages would
surely not have been judged quite so harshly by a medieval audience more accustomed than we to frequent social and religious constraints and precepts;
such moralizing is very "medieval" in character.

In addition to the quest for moderation and the characteristically didactic
orientation, Hartmann's story is distinguished from Chrétien's by a number of
other features. Hartmann appears, for one thing, to have been much enamored
of the many splendid trappings of the medieval court, for again and again he
pauses in his narrative to offer (sometimes tediously, even immoderately!) detailed descriptions of lovely ladies, of precious gems, of costly garments, of
knightly accoutrements, of stout-hearted horses, of marvelous medicines and
of dwarfs and giants. Once more, Hartmann steers the story along a different
path from Chrétien, who does not betray this urge to enumerate and describe.
The most famous instance in which Hartmann indulges himself in long de-

scription is his meticulously detailed account of Enite's horse and saddle. While this passage occupies just forty verses in Chrétien's *Erec et Enide*, Hartmann expands it to over twelve times this length, so that it encompasses roughly 500 lines of his story.

Not only does Hartmann alter the tale by enlarging upon certain features found in Chrétien; he also invents other elements by weaving entirely new threads into the story-line. The tale of the eighty widows illustrates this tendency. The widows are not mentioned at all in Chrétien's story and are presumably Hartmann's invention. Each of these ladies has lost her husband in battle against the Red Knight Mabonagrin, who dwells with his unnamed lady in the mysterious arbor. All of the eighty widows now live together in mournful sorrow at Brandigan, near the source of their grief. Their presence at the court evokes a general atmosphere of pathos and gloom. The effect of this episode is that, with one swift and deftly executed stroke, Hartmann has planted the haunting question in the minds of his listeners: will Enite, too, be left behind in their company, a widow bereft of her husband?

At the very end of the work can be found another of Hartmann's additions. While Chrétien's story concludes with the great festival at King Arthur's court, Hartmann extends the action at this juncture by sending Erec back to his homeland. Here he is crowned king and receives the full inheritance of his deceased father's kingdom. Hartmann then reports briefly on the ensuing festival (this one in Erec's land of Destrigales), the fate of Enite's parents, and the eventual heavenly reward granted Erec and Enite. In his studiously meticulous way, the poet seems intent upon accounting for all the final details of his story and upon giving voice one last time to his own didactic proclivities.

In addition to his role as expander and inventor, Hartmann takes upon himself the task of recasting certain facets of the story, of altering key details to suit his own poetic ends. For example, in the nettlesome question of Enite's guilt—a favorite topic among literary scholars—Hartmann is careful to place his own stamp upon the story. After Erec has become thoroughly neglectful of his responsibilities as a knight, it is Enite who first speaks to him (albeit unwittingly) of the shame which he has brought upon himself and his court. Angered by her words, he forces Enite to set out with him on a series of adventures through which he hopes to redeem his good name. In the course of their wanderings, Erec subjects his wife to harsh, even brutal treatment, both for her bluntly spoken words of lament and for the repeated breach of her forced vow of silence (she speaks up, however, only to warn him of impending danger). By any measure, Enite endures undeserved hardship at the hands of her husband. That is precisely Hartmann's point, i.e. that Erec's behavior is wrong. In fact, it is merely a further symptom of the underlying disease, Erec's loss of moderation. In both versions (Chrétien's and Hartmann's) Erec and Enite are reconciled after the testing period, but the reconciliations are vastly different. Chrétien's Erec forgives Enite (and not vice versa) for *her* misconduct: "if you have spoken ill of me, I pardon you and call you quit of both the offence and the word you spoke."[43] To Hartmann, however, this bizarre twist was clearly unacceptable. Erec was intended to embody the ideal knight who, through a process of guilt and atonement, finds his way to ultimate happiness. Unlike Chrétien, Hartmann felt obliged to grapple in this passage with two fundamental questions: how can guilt be atoned for if the offender does not first recognize and acknowledge his guilt? and how could such an offending knight be held up as a paragon of chivalric virtue? For Hartmann the only possible solution lay in reversing the two roles: in having Erec ask Enite's forgiveness (p. 141). Hartmann's transposition of the guilt not only restores Erec's lustre as a model knight, but also helps to mitigate the sense of indignation (shared most likely by medieval listeners and by modern readers as well) that Enite has been unduly punished.

Thus, while Hartmann is clearly indebted to Chrétien de Troyes both for the main trunk of his story as well as for countless details, he nevertheless allows himself a free hand in expanding, inventing and reworking the individual threads of the overall fabric. The specific points of difference between Chrétien's *Erec et Enide* and Hartmann's *Erec* are myriad and extend well beyond the few examples discussed here. Yet a thorough analysis of all of Hartmann's many alterations demonstrates that few of them are purely arbitrary, and that many of them in fact serve to render the tale of Erec more consistent, more engaging and more rich in detail.

THE STRUCTURE OF *EREC*

It is possible to delineate a common structural configuration for the so-called "classical" Arthurian romances. Among these are all five of Chrétien's works, both of Hartmann's romances, and Wolfram von Eschenbach's *Parzival*. Each of these romances can be subdivided into five distinct segments: (1) the exposition, which takes place at King Arthur's court and which contains an incident prompting the hero to leave the court; (2) the first series of adventures, during which the protagonist achieves a state of apparent happiness; (3) a catastrophe for the hero, in which he is accused of having committed a grave mistake; (4) the second series of adventures, during which the knight atones for this guilt; and (5) the conclusion, at which the hero attains a state of true happiness and reestablished harmony.

In the case of Hartmann's *Erec* these five sections can be outlined as follows. The exposition (pp. 57–59) depicts Erec at the Arthurian court, where he is struck by Iders' dwarf and sets forth to avenge his disgrace. During the first set of adventures (pp. 59–93) he does precisely this, defeating Iders and acquiring Enite's hand in marriage. The catastrophe follows (pp. 93–95) as Erec begins to lose sight of his knightly obligations and thereupon overhears Enite's lament. Then, during the second series of adventures (pp. 95–177), he survives assorted perils (culminating in the Joy of the Court adventure) and once again proves his knightly mettle. Finally, the conclusion (pp. 177–81) comes when Erec, now reunited with Enite, returns in great triumph to King Arthur's court (and later to his homeland of Destrigales).

As is obvious from this, *Erec* adheres closely to the structural norms set forth by Chrétien.[44] It is also interesting to note (and this is very typical of Arthurian romance) that the overwhelming bulk of the story is devoted to the two series of adventures. In fact, by simply counting the page numbers, one can quickly establish that these two segments occupy fully 116 pages, or nearly 93% of the work. By contrast, the other three parts (exposition, catastrophe and conclusion) constitute only a very small portion of the story. In light of this, it is evident that the knight Hartmann (along with his fellow Arthurian poets) must have taken especial delight in recounting the deeds of chivalric valor undertaken by his protagonist. By the same token, such accounts of knightly derring-do clearly found resonance among medieval audiences.

A further feature of the characteristic Arthurian structure is the presence or absence of the Round Table—the symbol of Arthurian society—at a given juncture in the story. Erec appears at King Arthur's court at four different points in the story: (1) at the exposition, where he is disgraced by the dwarf; (2) at the end of his initial adventures, when he is wedded to Enite; (3) during his second set of adventures, when Gawein lures him into Arthur's camp before he has yet succeeded in restoring his reputation; and (4) at the conclusion, where his success is celebrated at the festival hosted by King Arthur. At all other points Erec is on his own, absent from the Round Table.

Clearly, the Arthurian court (symbolized by the Round Table) provides the most visible yardstick for measuring a hero's acceptance or rejection by society. Scholars like to describe Arthurian romance as the tale of a hero's individual, solitary quest for his proper place within society. Erec's wanderings remove him from the scrutiny of his fellow knights for extended periods of time, but in the final analysis Erec is a social creature, for it is the periodic review by his peers that gauges the success or failure of his adventures. The function of the Arthurian court is to witness both the high-points and the low-points of the hero and thereby to measure and confirm his triumphs and defeats against the standards of a larger (Arthurian) society. Accordingly, Arthur and his knights observe Erec both when he is in adverse circumstances (after the dwarf's blow and again when he is unwillingly brought in to King Arthur's encampment at the edge of the woods) and when he is riding high with success (initially, at his wedding to Enite and finally, after he has proved his knightly prowess once and for all). While Erec's stays at the Arthurian court are quite brief,[45] nevertheless these visits afford him an external compass with which to measure his standing within the chivalric society.

All of this may be visually respresented by the following plot-line:

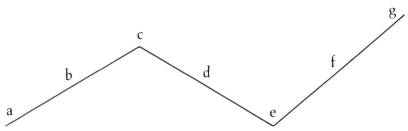

The upward and downward trends on the graph depict the various ups and downs experienced by Erec in the course of the story. At point *a* Erec is present at King Arthur's court and is brought to shame by the dwarf. This gives rise to *b*, the first adventures, which culminate in the apparent bliss of his marriage *(c)* to Enite. After becoming amorously indolent and incurring the disdain of his own court *(d)*, Erec ventures forth in disgrace to reclaim his good name. During his adventures he is tricked into appearing—still unredeemed of his shame—at the Round Table *(e)*. After meeting the challenge of his ensuing adventures *(f)*, Erec finally wins the permanent acclaim *(g)* of his king and fellow knights at the concluding festival. The low points *(a* and *e)* are witnessed by King Arthur and his company, just as are the high points *(c* and *g)*. Thus, while the enormous bulk of Hartmann's story is devoted to the individual adventures of the knight Erec, the scenes at Arthur's court, brief though they are, fulfill a crucial function—that of assessing and judging Erec's performance at critical junctures in his transformation into a worthy member of the society of knights.

THE NARRATOR

By the end of the twelfth century, Germany was witnessing a flourishing of written literature. Not only were the fashionable new fictional narratives such as Hartmann's *Erec* being written down and preserved in permanent verbal form, so too were many of the older works which prior to this age had been transmitted primarily by word of mouth. These literary texts were significant—as texts—not only in the sense that individuals could now read them privately, but also for the fact that the written word could now be read out loud, indeed performed, for groups of listeners.[46] Much of the literature of the Middle High German period was performed before a live audience, often at the courts. This is not to say that the individual reading of literature was nonexistent, for medieval Europe was becoming more and more oriented towards the written document from the eleventh century on. Nonetheless textuality did not surpass orality for most members of society during the high Middle Ages,[47] and most people (even at the major courts) were illiterate, in one sense or another. During the period prior to 1200, literacy was largely the monopoly of ecclesiastical circles in Europe.[48]

The simplest definition of literacy is the ability to read and write. Yet the term is more complex than this. For one thing, there are varying degrees of literacy. Furthermore, in medieval times literacy was characteristically gauged in terms of the Latin language. The *litteratus*—the common term for a person able to read and write—specifically designated one who possessed a familiarity with Latin grammar and syntax;[49] and the average person living in Europe during the high Middle Ages did not possess this familiarity. Even if the definition of literacy is expanded to comprise other languages, still only a small percentage of laymen living between the years 1000 and 1300 could be termed literate.[50]

In Hartmann von Aue's time, widespread literacy—by whatever definition—was still far from being the norm. Furthermore, the invention of the printing press was still another 200 to 250 years in the future, so that written copies of literary works were relatively rare and expensive. Hence, the most common means of dissemination of literature (and, as we have seen, a popular form of entertainment at the courts) was oral recitation, possibly by the poets themselves and certainly by independent, non-creative minstrels. While there is a considerable body of evidence[51] that textually fixed (i.e. written down) stories such as *Erec* were read both aloud in more or less public recitation and privately by individual readers,[52] it is quite likely that this written vernacular literature was more often *heard* than *read*.[53]

Because oral recitation was very common, the performing minstrel/poet assumed a crucial role. Hence, given the importance of this performer in reading aloud to the assembled courtiers, it is quite natural that, in many of the longer narrative romances of the age, there is a very strongly felt narratorial presence—a background voice which is implanted within the story itself, and from which the story seems to emanate. This is very much the case in *Erec*. Early on, the frequent narratorial intrusions in the first person singular establish themselves as a regular feature of the story. Again and again the narrator of Hartmann's first romance steps out of his role as teller of the tale in order to comment, summarize, tease, digress, or interpret. As a result, the listener/reader has, almost from the outset, a strong sense that this tale is not simply issuing forth from some anonymous source. Far from being a mere rhetorical device employed by Hartmann, the narrator is a figure very much parallel to the medieval poets and minstrels who performed such works as *Erec*. As such, Hartmann's storyteller is firmly rooted in the narratorial circumstances of the day, i.e. in what is assumed to have been the predominantly oral nature of the literature.

While the narrator is in many regards the literary equivalent of the real-life minstrel or performer, this same narrator cannot necessarily be equated with the poet. At times, to be sure, Hartmann and his narrator are clearly one and the same in outlook, and the poet uses the person of the narrator to express his (Hartmann's) views on a given matter. But it would be a mistake to assume that this is always so. In fact, the literature of the high Middle Ages is rarely the sort of *Erlebnisdichtung* (literature spawned by personal experience) that would allow us to assume a necessary unity of poet and narrator. When the narrator in *Erec* speaks to us of himself, we cannot safely interpret his personal opinions and prejudices to be those of Hartmann von Aue.

With this caveat in mind, it is worthwhile to explore some of the ways in which Hartmann's narrator establishes his presence. In one rather humorous instance (pp. 149f.), the narrator—here explicitly under the guise of Hartmann—engages in a spirited exchange with a supposed member of his audience. The two of them vie with one another to describe the little saddle on Enite's horse. After a playful stichomythy the narrator finally dismisses his listener's storytelling attempt as hopelessly inadequate, and proceeds to describe the saddle himself.

Similar narratorial digressions can be found in at least three other passages in which Hartmann's narrator fields questions, even anticipates interruptive comments from his audience. Hartmann includes among his cast of characters in *Erec* not only a storyteller, but also an audience.[54] Such devices as these are a clear reminder that in medieval times a congregation of courtiers sat and listened to the tale of Erec's adventures—and that this audience was not always as silent, attentive or respectful as it ought to have been. In effect, the performer and his public could readily become a part of the fiction because the social reality corresponded so closely to this fiction.[55]

The role of the narrator as a figure necessitated by the actual storytelling circumstances of the day is likewise reflected in the frequently recurring phrases "as I have already reported" and "as I have previously told you." Here we are reminded that *Erec* was much too long to have been performed in one single evening. Instead, one or more episodes were probably presented at each sitting, over a period of perhaps a week or more. Surely not everyone was present to hear all of the installments, and those who did hear it all were not able to recall everything they had heard.[56] Hence the necessity for summarization, in a manner akin to the brief synoptic capsules that precede each episode in a television serial.

What do these and other of the narratorial interjections tell us about the character of Hartmann's narrator? By and large, characterization in medieval literature tends to be, by modern standards, pronouncedly monochrome. Only rarely does one gain any psychological or personal insights into the various figures in Arthurian romance. However, the narrator of *Erec* acquires, by virtue of his frequent personal interspersions, somewhat more psychological depth than most of the bona fide characters within the tale itself. He is, for example, thoroughly modest regarding his poetic skills. "I would fain laud [Enite] as I ought to," he says at one point, "but I am not so artful a man as to escape failure in that venture. Such craft is not mine to know" (p. 77). Nor does he claim to know every detail of the story, which in any event he openly and candidly attributes to Chrétien de Troyes. Furthermore, the narrator makes no secret of his generally high opinion of Erec. On the other hand, he does not hesitate to remonstrate with Erec when chiding is in order. After the reconciliation of Erec and Enite at Limors, for example, he speaks of the "feigned cruelty and the strange dissimulation to which [Erec] had until that day subjected her without good cause" (p. 141).

Hartmann's narrator is also not averse to occasional good-natured teasing. Aside from his stichomythic exchange with the fictitious listener (cited above), he engages at another point (p. 151) in an almost self-parodying digression in which, characteristically, he says he would like to list in detail—if only he could—the names of all the various sea creatures depicted on Enite's saddle. In an *argumentum ad absurdum*, he instructs his audience how they might go about ascertaining such names. In the end, such a quest can only be accomplished "at great harm to you" (in other words, any would-be sea explorers among his listeners would be engulfed and drowned in the ocean waters) and "with little gain" (after all, Hartmann's narrator seems to be saying, who really cares about such an arcane catalogue of sea creatures?).

In a different vein, Hartmann consciously employs the person of his narrator to heighten the listener/reader's sense of suspense at various perilous junctures in the story. Just as Erec rides alone into the arbor to battle the fierce Mabonagrin, we hear, whispered, as it were, from behind the page: "How things turned out for [Erec], I do not know" (p. 166). In his next breath, the narrator hurriedly utters a prayer for Erec's safety and then exhorts his assembled listeners to do the same: "assist [Enite], all of you, in asking God that victory may fall to Erec!" (p. 166). The calculated effect of these narratorial utterances is to intensify the audience's sense of anticipation as Erec goes forth into danger. In several such passages the narrator abruptly switches into the present tense, again with dramatic effect: [57] "Lord God, vouchsafe to watch over King Erec! For he is going into battle with a warrior possessed of courage and strength, which enkindles in me fear for Erec's safety!" (p. 169). Far from being carelessness on Hartmann's (or the scribe's) part, this sudden shift into the present tense jolts the listener/reader into an uneasy illusion that this story is only now unfolding, that the outcome for Erec is anything but preordained.

On several occasions, Hartmann's narrator consciously abandons his normal storyline in order to anticipate future events. He tells us (p. 110), for instance, after Enite has warned Erec of impending danger, that this will not be the last time she breaks her vow of silence. And in the scene where Count Oringles compels Enite to become his bride (a union rendered automatically null and void by the fact that Erec is, contrary to all appearances, still alive), Hartmann's narrator divulges (p. 136) that Oringles will never realize his fantasy of possessing Enite. Such foreshadowings stand in direct counterpoint to the passages discussed above, where the narrator consciously fosters uncertainty, doubt, and even anxiety as to the outcome of certain events. In general, however, foreshadowing in *Erec* occurs only infrequently, and is not nearly so prominent a storytelling technique as it is in the older Germanic-heroic epics, such as the *Nibelungenlied.*

Another of the prominent qualities of Hartmann's narrator is a proclivity to wordiness. As mentioned previously, he indulges first in a lengthy and meticulously detailed description of Enite's first horse and then continues with an even more protracted account of her second horse and her saddle. Yet the narrator is not unaware of his inordinate loquacity. The convoluted *praeteritio* on p. 149 shows him in a remarkably hopeless struggle against his own verbose instincts: he knows he has already dwelled too long on the horse, and he would like to refrain from an all too lengthy account of the saddle. In the end, he succumbs to his penchant for minutiae. Not always, however, is his self-editing so unsuccessful. When he introduces King Guivreiz, for example, he claims to be able to relate wondrous things about this little dwarf. Yet a "large part of his tale we must pass over in silence," he avers, for otherwise "this story would then become too wordy" (p. 111).

Hartmann's narrator at times plays a pivotal role in rendering the audience more receptive to certain hyperbolic statements in *Erec*. Erec himself, for example, is repeatedly described in glowing terms: he is the "most excellent man who had ever come to that land" (p. 74); "[n]ever did a knight perform more admirably" (p. 88) than Erec; and "no man living in those days was as highly praised" (p. 179) as he. Similarly, Enite is said to be "the fairest maiden" (pp. 77 and 79); and never was there "a more comely page" (p. 67) than she. Not only does the story abound with such superlatives, but with all types of hyperbolic formulations as well. In the eyes of modern readers, the repeated occurrence of such overstatements may detract from the enjoyment of Hartmann's tale, but a similar reaction on the part of the medieval listener cannot be assumed. Such extravagance of expression was quite common in both the courtly and the heroic literature of the day. Moreover, based upon its ubiquitousness, it was most likely expected and generally tolerated by medieval audiences. Still, lest some of the more inordinate exaggerations strain his listeners' belief, Hartmann employs the voice of his narrator numerous times throughout the work to state unequivocally (often in the first person singular) that this is, despite all its fantastic proportions, a true story. At one point he states, bluntly and simply, "I am telling you the truth" (p. 151). And in a passage dealing with Guivreiz, he defends his incredible description of the little king with the words: "unless I have been told untruths" (p. 110).

The intended result of these repeated claims of truthfulness is that the listener/reader will be more likely to trust and believe Hartmann's storyteller. If there are any errors in his account, they cannot be attributed to the narrator, who is merely reporting what he has been told. It is significant that the narrator repeatedly cites his veridical source as the "story" or the "adventure." Moreover, as we have seen, he openly attributes his story on several occasions to the "Master," and at one point even mentions Chrétien by name. There are no fewer than twenty-four such instances, where Hartmann—through the medium of his narrator—explicitly claims to have obtained his story from an outside source. Clearly, he is very much concerned with convincing his public that he has not invented or in any way fabricated the tale of Sir Erec.

Why this dogged reluctance to engage in (or at least to own up to) freely invented fiction? The key to an understanding of this pseudo-historicity on the part of many medieval poets is the concept of *auctoritas*, or authority. To a large degree, medieval thinking was based upon the cautious appeal to established authority. Unguarded free thinking was somewhat rare in medieval times. Instead, one built upon the trusted authority of what had been handed down from earlier times by earlier sources. It was acceptable to place one or two new stones onto the growing pyramid of traditional knowledge, but to start constructing one's own pyramid was to build on uncharted and unsafe ground. Hence Hartmann's claim (through the voice of his narrator) of a source, and his invocation of the authority of that source—even in individual details where he differed from Chrétien and was in all likelihood engaged in the very fictionalizing which he so vehemently disavowed.[58]

This recurrent appeal to truthfulness was commonplace among poets of the age—so much so that it surfaces even in many works where not just isolated details, but the whole fabric of the story has been fictionally contrived. There is little doubt that, at some point in the history of medieval narrative, these repeated assertions of truthfulness began to assume the tone of mere formulaic phrases. Yet, as we have seen, their roots go much deeper, and the phenomenon is a larger one, which manifests itself not just in *Erec* or in German Arthurian romance, but in much of the narrative literature of the high Middle Ages. In Hartmann's case, the person of the narrator is the favorite and most prominent vehicle for upholding this virtually canonical pretense of verisimilitude in *Erec*.

In conclusion, it can be said that Hartmann succeeds in capturing the attention of his public in part by the appeal of the story itself and in part by the buoyant, sometimes sportive personality of his narrator. The powerful role of Hartmann's narrator within the story may be rooted in the fact that *Erec* was, in all likelihood, performed before courtly audiences. As we have seen, Hartmann is quick to seize upon the multifaceted narratorial possibilities which ensue from this circumstance. Far from being an anonymous, evanescent voice from which issues forth the tale of Erec, Hartmann's narrator assumes a robust presence throughout and can rightfully claim the rank of an independent character within the work. He carefully guides his reader/listener through the story—at times revealing in advance the outcome of certain situations, but usually keeping all his cards to himself so as to heighten the sense of suspense for his audience. Without question, he is a partisan of his hero Erec, but not blindly so, for he is sufficiently distant to recognize and frown upon Erec's faults. At times he is pedantic, and at times he becomes too verbose, but his is a self-conscious pedanticism and verbosity: he is aware that if he overtaxes our patience, he may start to bore us—and this he is mindful not to do. In short, he is a skilled and engaging raconteur.

SELECTED THEMATIC ISSUES

Courtly Love

Foremost among the issues addressed in Hartmann's *Erec* is the notion of love and its effects—beneficial as well as injurious—upon those it besets. This was a prevalent theme in much of the literature of the high Middle Ages. Indeed, the courtly, chivalric civilization of this era might well be called a love-sick culture. Particularly within the lyric song poetry of the day it was love that most occupied the attention (indeed, was the virtual obsession) of German song poets. While other branches of the literature were not so exclusively concerned with love as the paramount human emotion, nevertheless it plays a central role—for example, in the courtly romance—as a prime motivator of human action.

Like so many of his contemporaries, Hartmann von Aue saw human love as capable of showing two radically different faces. In its purest form, love could be ennobling, yet in wrong measure or in wrong circumstance love could be destructive as well. Even an "upright and good" (p. 103) man such as the unnamed count who desires Enite can be blinded and "robbed [. . .] of his good senses" (p. 103) by the power of love. And later, when the other count, Oringles, has the apparently widowed Enite at his court, he becomes so wholly overwhelmed by the desire to possess her as his wife that he subjects her to harsh language and to cruel treatment. It was likewise under the spell of love that Mabonagrin had sworn an oath to his lady to remain together with her in the hidden arbor. Only Mabonagrin's defeat at the hand of another knight could free him from that vow. Erec vanquishes Mabonagrin, and in victory he offers Mabonagrin words of advice that, ironically, he himself ought to have heeded earlier, as he lay about idly with Enite, incapacitated by an immoderate measure of love. "[O]ne ought, in truth, to escape upon occasion from the women," he states. "For it is so good to be out amongst other people" (p. 172).

Hartmann appears in *Erec* to prescribe two prerequisites, each of which must be met in order for love to become an edifying experience: love within the parameters of marriage and *mâze* (or moderation) in that love. Where neither is present, as with the two counts, love is pernicious. Where, as with both Erec and Mabonagrin, only one requirement (marriage) is met, love still assumes a corruptive character, for moderation in all things appears to be a *sine qua non* in Hartmann's world view.

The notion of *mâze* permeates the whole fabric of chivalric literature of this age. However, while moderation is more or less universally extolled in all forms of classical Middle High German literature, the role of marriage appears—from one genre to the next—to be considerably more ambiguous. Most striking in this regard is the discrepancy between lyric song poetry and Arthurian romance. In the lyric poetry the poet-knight expresses his unfulfilled longing for an already married and therefore unattainable lady. In Arthurian romance love is ultimately attainable and is nearly always cast within the happier dimensions of marriage. In the simplest terms, the lyric knight seeks a lover, and the Arthurian knight seeks a wife. The two genres impose differing demands upon the male in the love relationship. These apparently contradictory attitudes towards love and marriage assume a more puzzling dimension when one considers that the chief Arthurian poets—in particular Hartmann and Wolfram—also practiced the poetic art of lovesong.

Which view of love did they really wish to propound? Or were both conceits merely the appropriate posture to be assumed when composing within one genre or the other? Such questions are, in the final analysis, unanswerable. Yet these two depictions of love (in what were probably the two most popular forms of literary entertainment of the day) are not really so mutually exclusive. For in classical German lovesong there simply *is* no happiness to be found in love: the knight's obsession is invariably directed at a married lady whom he can never possess, and he is left pining for her. In Arthurian romance love has the potential for fulfillment, but only if it is practiced, as mentioned earlier, within the parameters both of moderation and of marriage. In effect, there is a certain consistency here, for the poets were actually playing by the same rules in both genres: love can engender happiness only in the context of marriage.

What, specifically, are some of the fruits of love when practiced temperately between a knight and his spouse? What salutary effects can love have upon its agents? For one thing, there is a calmness, a mental tranquility. An example of this can be seen when Erec must go off into battle against the fearsome Mabonagrin. Enite rightfully fears for his life, but Erec faces this peril with serenity and fortitude: "Whenever my thoughts turn to you," he comforts Enite, "my hand is blessed with victory, for your love is the fount of my strength, so that nothing can trouble me the whole day long" (p. 166). Indeed, along with a tranquil mind there also emanates from such love a fortified physical vigor. During the contest with Mabonagrin, when each man's grit is being tested mercilessly, Hartmann assures us of Erec: "whenever he thought of Lady Enite, her love imbued his heart as well as his senses with such vitality that he too fought with renewed strength, in pursuit of manly excellence" (p. 169). Love, then, while harboring a certain potential for intemperance, could—under the proper circumstances—yield not only bliss between the two lovers, but also a mental and physical resoluteness essential to the knight's success in battle.

The Role of Women

Hartmann appears most concerned with depicting love's effect upon the various male figures (Erec, Mabonagrin, the two counts). Such gender bias as this is symptomatic of the status of women in courtly literature—which was, after all, composed almost exclusively by men and which tends by and large to disregard the ennoblement of women through the force of love. With few exceptions, the female character in courtly literature "remains essentially an object, however adored."[59] For example, Hartmann has Enite meekly acknowledge that she is, in effect, the "property" of her husband: "I am at his command as his wife, his squire, or for whatever else he wishes me" (p. 104). The same sort of proprietary relationship between husband and wife is also struck by Count Oringles, as he tries to silence those who would criticize him for mistreating his "wife" Enite: "It is indeed no one's privilege to speak either ill or well of what a man does to his wife. She is mine and I am hers" (p. 138).

Women in general (and Enite in particular) are also portrayed as being much more subject to overwhelming emotions than are men. For instance, Enite blushes as she steps before the assemblage of knights (p. 78), and she swoons out of fear for Erec when he is about to venture forth into the arbor: "[Enite] turned pale and took on the appearance of death, falling unconscious with grief" (p. 165).

A persistent emphasis on feminine beauty is another important facet of this disparity between male and female characters. To be sure, outward, physical appearance tends—for both sexes—to be much more indicative of inner worth in medieval literature than in more modern works. Yet even within these parameters, women are more often described—and judged—in terms of their physical attributes than are men. For example, Hartmann first introduces Enite, the central female character in *Erec*, by recounting her great beauty, an attribute which is repeatedly praised throughout the work.

Nevertheless, Enite unquestionably displays certain more momentous, indeed quite laudable qualities as well—ones which transcend mere pulchritude. For example, Enite exhibits an admirable measure of cunning when, wishing to gain time to warn Erec, she lies to the count (pp. 105–6), who is about to seize her by force. Under the circumstances, she has no choice but to resort to some sort of subterfuge. For, realistically speaking, the count's superior strength would surely overcome any physical resistance on Enite's part, and would endanger Erec's life as well. A long-suffering fortitude likewise occupies a spot in Enite's heart. In the passage where Erec imposes upon Enite the harsh task of tending all eight of his horses, Hartmann leaves no question as to where his sympathies lie: "she endured it serenely and without discontent. Such was the teaching of Enite's goodness" (p. 100). Hers is a demeaning chore, to be sure, yet Enite's self-abasing submission stands in sharp moral counterpoint to Erec's illaudable hardness of heart. What is more, Hartmann explicitly praises "Enite's loyalty" (p. 111) to Erec and her courage (p. 96) in speaking up (and thus breaching her oath of silence) so as to warn her husband whenever danger awaits him along their journey. Enite displays this moral courage again later (p. 138), when she leaves herself open to the violent blows of Count Oringles. She would rather be beaten to death than become this man's wife.

Aside from Enite, there are no other important women in *Erec*, though many appear in minor roles. These secondary female characters are for the most part cast in terms of their physical beauty, and—as is the case with the eighty widows residing together in Brandigan near the arbor—they tend to be non-individuated and ultimately indistinguishable from one another. Moreover, Hartmann allows himself several unforgettable remarks about what women, in general, are or ought to be. They must be submissive to men, to the point where they learn to "prefer, whenever they might rightfully receive it, a sweet kiss over a beating" (p. 74)—either of which fate, Hartmann seems to imply, might fairly be imposed upon them by a man. Since they are weaker than men, Hartmann says, when faced with adversity, "they are wont to put their eyes and their hands to work, with tears and with beating" (p. 129). Aside from such emotional excesses, Hartmann's women also suffer from an uncontrollable curiosity about anything which has been placed under interdiction: "they have always been so attracted to precisely that thing which is emphatically forbidden to them," Erec complains to Enite, "that they could not help but try it" (p. 97).

However, positive qualities as well as certain prerogatives are ascribed to women. Hartmann makes frequent mention, for instance, of Queen Guinevere's goodness. Furthermore, women—precisely because they *are* women—deserve special treatment in Hartmann's view. Early on, when the dwarf Malclisier strikes one of Guinevere's maidens, he is severely scolded (pp. 70–71) by Erec for having committed such an act of ill-breeding against a woman. Later, Hartmann (through the voice of his narrator) underscores the special courtesy—indeed, courtliness—which he feels is due women: "may ill fortune bring down its curse upon any man (this I wish upon him!) who inflicts suffering upon women, for such is neither valiant nor good" (p. 129).

Both men and women in *Erec* possess virtues along with vices. If much of what is "bad" about women appears hopelessly prejudiced to the modern reader, then even the "good" ascribed to women by Hartmann must seem condescending at best. Their role, at any rate, is one of submission in virtually every regard. Many modern readers will, understandably, cast a harsh verdict against Hartmann von Aue for his lack of sophistication in this question. Yet the idea that women are inferior—physically, intellectually and morally—to men is not the invention of Hartmann von Aue, nor even of the Middle Ages, but harks back at least as far as Aristotle.[60] Much of what offends the sensibilities of the modern reader probably made little if any adverse impression upon the listener of medieval times.

For the social historian, it is a formidable task to frame any sort of reliable generalizations about the realities of women's lot during the Middle Ages. Courtly literature, which largely represents "escape into fable and fairy tale,"[61] is a poor source for facts about life in the Middle Ages, at least as experienced by any social group other than the nobility, by whom and for whom it was chiefly written. On the other hand, historians have produced ample evidence from non-literary documents to show that some women occupied positions of considerable responsibility during the Middle Ages, and that, in general, women were not faced with such wholly bleak prospects as we tend to assume. It was, for instance, not entirely extraordinary for a women to hold a fief;[62] and a number of these same women actually exercised ruling powers over their territories. Furthermore, medieval noblemen were often absent from home for extended periods of time (to engage in warfare, to participate in Crusades), and it was frequently their wives who took over the most important tasks.[63] Even when the husband was at home, the wife was commonly entrusted with important tasks,[64] especially the economic management of the estates.[65] Women of the nobility frequently learned to read, sometimes even to write, and—up until about the thirteenth century, when the universities began to flourish—there was no inordinate gulf between their level of education and that of men.[66] Finally, as we have seen, women such as Eleanor of Aquitaine and Marie de Champagne *inter alias* played an enormously important role as patrons of literature during the Middle Ages.

To be sure, the exceptions must not be confused with the rule, and despite the demonstrable impact of such spectacular medieval women as Eleanor or Marie or even Joan of Arc, it would be naive to harbor exaggerated misconceptions concerning the influence of the far more ordinary, less celebrated women. Still, it is clear that, in general, medieval women fulfilled a significant role in society. Some historians, however, see a gradual worsening in the position of women as the Middle Ages progressed. In part, this decline may be attributable to changes in the Church's opinion of women—changes signalled by the Gregorian reform movement of the late eleventh century.[67] Also, the establishment of the chivalric ethic, in which women played virtually no role except as passive objects of the knights' amorous endeavors, tended to diminish the importance of women.[68] The continued strengthening of the feudal system helped to attenuate further the role of women, for feudalism instated a direct link between landholding and military service, from which women were excluded.[69]

Going well beyond such social and historical realities, the courtly, chivalric literature of this era almost never depicts women in any of the practical roles which at least some of them did actually fulfill—albeit, as it appears, with decreasing frequency over the course of the Middle Ages. Instead, the romantic image of the woman is persistently nurtured in the literature—the image of the noble lady who initiates knightly suitors into the secrets of love, who imposes special tasks upon her lovers, and who engages in chess, falconry or embroidery.[70] Despite some notable exceptions[71] to this rule, the chief concern of the poets of this age was to recount the great deeds of valor performed by members of the exclusively male society of knights. In Arthurian romance, where one individual knight nearly always occupies center stage, it is particularly difficult to envision a female figure (other than the hero's wife) in any position of real prominence. Certainly this is very much the case in Hartmann's *Erec*.

The Chivalric Ethic

While *Erec* sheds rather little light on the real-life status of women in medieval times, it does offer a trenchant—and more nearly realistic—glimpse into the chivalric code of that most prominent order of warriors, the knights. By detailing the individual qualities extolled in Erec and his fellow knights, it is possible to assemble a compendium of the cardinal virtues of chivalry—virtues which, as we shall see, were actually demanded of knights living in Europe towards the end of the twelfth century. Even a short list of such virtues would include the following traits: generosity, courage, loyalty, good breeding, honor, strenuous striving, moderation and love.

The final two of these—moderation and love—are, as has been shown, inextricably connected. Excessive love threatens to be Erec's downfall, but once he has attained moderation in his longing for Enite, love becomes for him a virtual partner in battle. This quest for moderation is the focal point of Erec's tale, and indeed, moderation must manifest itself not solely in love, but in every other facet of a knight's existence. Early in the story, for instance, we see the inexperienced Erec on the eve of his first tournament. While others are indulging themselves in carousing and in celebration, Erec holds back from any extravagance, "squandering nothing in revelry" (p. 87).

This notion of moderation in all things serves to mediate, in the knight's mind, between the two extremes of abject fear and foolish daring, whenever a perilous situation arises. Of all the chivalric virtues, courage is certainly the most self-evident. Conversely, "timidity which is born of cowardice" (p. 163), Hartmann tells us, must be renounced outright by any man aspiring to the rank of knight. On the other hand, the precepts of moderation do not allow for foolhardiness in the actions of a good knight. For "[n]ever was there a heart so valiant that a proper measure of fear was unbecoming to it" (p. 163). Even the bold courage of a high-spirited knight, then, must be offset to a moderate degree by the sober recognition of peril.

Generosity likewise occupies a central position in any catalogue of chivalric virtues. Perhaps the most common forum in Arthurian romance for this particular quality is the (sometimes almost immoderately) bountiful hospitality typically shown by a host towards his guests. King Arthur hosts a two-week festival to celebrate Erec's marriage to Enite, and then, in a customary flourish, proclaims that the celebration shall be extended for yet another fourteen days. Later it is King Guivreiz who showers Erec with "lavish hospitality" (p. 115), though the guest is anxious to be off again on his journey. At the end, it is Erec who exercises great munificence, first by offering charity to the poor before departing King Arthur's court and then by hosting a great festival of six weeks' duration in his homeland: "a festival such that there never was, before or since, a celebration in that realm so delightful or attended by such mighty lords" (p. 180).

If miserliness is disdained in the knight, then infidelity likewise has no place in his heart. Beyond the fundamental loyalty which Erec shows Enite (his harsh treatment of her notwithstanding), there are numerous lesser instances of faithfulness, as practiced both by Erec and by others. After Erec has defeated Iders and won the sparrow-hawk for Enite, for example, the host Duke Imain is eager to have the victorious Erec as his guest. Yet in a poignant show of sensitivity Erec loyally refuses (p. 74) Duke Imain's offer of hospitality, for fear of offending Enite's father, Koralus. Of foremost concern to Erec at this point is that he not appear in any way disloyal to his impoverished father-in-law, who has already invited him to share his meager abode. In a different vein, Hartmann later expands upon this notion of loyalty and posits that it is the knight's duty to remain unswervingly true to a commitment once made, even when that commitment is essentially a misguided one. Such is the case with Mabonagrin's vow to remain together with his lady in the lovely arbor. Only a victorious intruder can set him free from that oath, and Mabonagrin waits faithfully until such time as Erec enters and defeats him in battle.

Equally indispensable to the character of the model knight is a sense of good breeding—a politesse and a gentility of spirit. Erec himself serves as the best model of this polished behavior. It is interesting to note that in many ways Erec's good breeding contrasts starkly with the generally rough and crude bearing of the older, Germanic heroes who had previously populated German literature. Indeed, this particular virtue (along with so much else of the chivalric culture) was not at all endemic to Germany, but was imported together with the courtly literature from France. It is no etymological accident that the words "courtesy" and "courtliness" derive directly from the French "courts" at which this polite gentility was so ardently practiced. Therefore, lest his German listeners overlook the fact that Erec is of the new school (new, at least, to Germany), and that he belongs to this refined and gracious society of knights, Hartmann says of his hero at one point that "his good breeding was most abundant" (p. 167). Conversely, any knight whose boorish behavior brings dishonor to that fellowship is open to the sharpest of scorn. Erec upbraids the first count (who had schemed to take Enite by various means) with just such disdain: "Your conduct towards me is a vile transgression against all courtliness," he cries out. "A vulgar court it was indeed at which you were schooled!" (p. 109).

Just as courtly behavior is indispensable in the knight's personal comportment, so too is an inbred code of honor requisite for chivalrous combat. It is not enough simply to defeat an opponent in battle; such triumph must be achieved with honor. Hartmann offers explicit instruction as to this particular clause in the chivalric code in the passage where he tells of Erec's defeat of Iders (whose dwarf had shamed Erec in the presence of Queen Guinevere). After a long and exhausting bout Erec finally manages to unseat his opponent. But as Iders lies vanquished before him, Erec steps back, and Hartmann interjects a brief lesson on knightly honor: "[Erec] refrained from pouncing upon him from his superior vantage point. This he did lest anyone could accuse him of the disgrace of slaying Iders as he still lay on the ground. It was a higher reputation which Erec desired to pursue" (p. 68). For this reason Erec comes forward once more and allows the duel to resume, instead of killing his downed opponent and thereby claiming a less than honorable victory. Similarly, Hartmann views it as unchivalric to take up the fight against an unarmed man. In the passage where Erec and the roguish Keii face one another in a duel, Erec is about to unhorse his attacker with the sharp point of his lance. Suddenly he notices that Keii has no weapon with which to defend himself. Quickly Erec reverses his lance and strikes Keii with the blunt end, knocking him to the ground "quite like a sack" (p. 117), but leaving him physically unharmed.

Perhaps the least self-explanatory among the various chivalric virtues is that of strenuous striving. Both components of this phrase "strenuous striving" are needed to render properly into English the Middle High German word *arebeit*. Not only must the knight be constantly in action (striving), he must also feel the fatiguing toll of that exertion and not allow himself to indulge immoderately in the languorous comfort of inactivity. At several junctures in the story the importance of such strenuous striving is underscored. First, King Arthur harshly rebukes (pp. 88–89) his sleeping knights for their slothfulness. Later in the tale, the count (who has schemed to seize Enite) curses himself for having slept too long, thus enabling Erec and Enite to escape during the night. The count's rhetorical question "What man has ever attained anything worthwhile without enduring some discomfort?" (p. 108) reflects his own woe for having failed to strive strenuously. Yet it is Erec whose inactivity brings him to the brink of ruin, and who must finally learn the value of *arebeit*. Indeed, Erec's protracted period of lethargy while under the spell of immoderate love for Enite stands in direct counterpoint to the notion of strenuous striving, and it is just such lethargy that causes boredom and disrepute to hang over his court. Once jolted (by Enite's lament) into an awareness of his shame, however, Erec sets out with his lady to pursue knightly adventure and thereby to rectify his past mistakes. By the time he reaches King Guivreiz' castle, the lesson has clearly taken hold, for despite his serious battle wounds, Erec remains obdurate in his refusal of Guivreiz' offer of hospitality and recuperation. Erec will stay no longer than the following morning, for, as he says, "it is not in search of comfort that I have embarked upon this journey. I pay little heed to whatever comfort comes my way" (p. 114).

Perhaps the single most comprehensive catalogue of knightly virtues is contained in Hartmann's extended praise of Gawein (p. 91), who is, in the German tradition, customarily set forth as the quintessential Arthurian knight. In these verses, Hartmann ascribes to Gawein many of the same qualities outlined above, along with certain others. For this reason, this passage serves as a good starting-point for enlarging upon the compendium of primary chivalric virtues. Courage and prowess in battle, for example, are obvious prerequisites for a successful knight. Yet not every goal can be reached through physical force alone. Frequently cunning, so often the province of women (cf. Enite's deceit of the count), also becomes the proper tool of knights. Gawein, for instance, resorts to cunning in the passage where he lures Erec into King Arthur's camp. At this point in the story (pp. 119–20), Erec has not yet fully restored his honor and is therefore intent upon not being seen among Arthur's company. Realizing that no other means will be of avail in bringing the reluctant Erec before King Arthur, Gawein contrives to delay Erec with artfully drawn-out conversation. Finally, enough time is consumed with such talk that the entire Arthurian court is able to station itself at the very point where Gawein and Erec are eventually to ride out of the forest. In general, cunning does not play the important role in classical Arthurian romance that it does, for example, in Gottfried's *Tristan* or in the *Nibelungenlied*. Nevertheless, as is quite evident from this passage in *Erec*, the Arthurian knight finds it necessary at times to resort to such mental agility as a complement to the physical prowess upon which he chiefly relies.

Further secondary characteristics from elsewhere in *Erec* can readily be added to the original list of chivalric virtues. A good knight must also be a God-fearing man, at least in a superficial sense. The Arthurian knight typically attends Mass before engaging in a tournament, as Erec does (p. 163) prior to the duel with Mabonagrin. God's assistance is invoked at several perilous junctures in the story, and Hartmann even has priests summoned to provide proper burial for the decapitated victims of Mabonagrin. In Arthurian romance, however, the external symbols of the Church are often little more than perfunctory ornamentation. For, as has been shown, the predominant tenor of these works is decidedly secular rather than spiritual.[72] Arthurian knights generally focus their energies upon winning worldly fame, despite the recurring but usually conventional presence of Church trappings. Nonetheless, Hartmann von Aue appears to be more genuinely concerned with the role of God than most of his fellow Arthurian poets, for whom such religious symbols frequently involve mere lip service.

Compassion, too, has its proper place in an expanded list of chivalric virtues. A concrete illustration of this can be seen in Erec's concern for the eighty widows at Brandigan—a concern which wholly precludes his enjoyment of the festival. So troubled is Erec by the continuing grief suffered by these ladies that he finally resolves to remove them from the source of their suffering and to conduct them to Arthur's court. Lest his audience overlook the importance of this particular virtue, Hartmann states directly that Erec's actions are characteristic of "men of compassion, whose eyes often well up with tears, in public as well as in private, whenever they behold something which rightfully awakens pity in their hearts" (p. 176).

Finally, Arthurian knights are possessed of an enduring optimism, even in the face of overwhelming peril. As Erec first rides up to the castle of Brandigan to seek out Mabonagrin's challenge, he is confronted with gloomy words of discouragement, with women weeping and beating their breasts. Yet throughout all of this "Erec contemplated things with a happy and certain mind, as should a brave man who cannot be easily unnerved by mere words" (p. 157). Again and again this particular trait manifests itself in Erec's thoughts and actions. Such cheerful optimism in the person of the protagonist finds a resonance in the overall optimistic timbre of classical Arthurian romance, in which, in the end, harmony is restored and the hero attains a lasting happiness.

In summary, the literary knight of Arthurian romance (be he Erec or Gawein or, for that matter, the title hero of any of the romances) presents a curious patchwork of variegated virtues. Certain of these qualities (courage, strenuous striving, fighting prowess, honor) are stereotypically "masculine." Some (good breeding, compassion, cunning, generosity) are frequently perceived as "feminine," while others fail to fit distinctly into either gender group. What emerges from the composite picture of this model knight of literature is a multicolored yet smoothly blended mosaic of diverse attributes. Such a man was stout-hearted and confident, yet at the same time gentle and refined.

What similarities, if any, exist between this set of literary chivalric values (as exemplified most specifically by Hartmann's fictional knight Erec) and the real-life chivalric code of the Middle Ages? As we have already noted, courtly literature is a highly precarious source of information for the social historian because of the simple fact that it moves within a realm of myth and fairy tale. Courtly literature does not necessarily reflect medieval life. Yet in the question of knighthood and knightly virtues, we possess compelling *extra-literary* testimony to suggest that Arthurian romance paints a somewhat realistic picture of what was expected of knights during the Middle Ages. Such evidence of common ground between "literary knighthood" and "historical knighthood" is provided, albeit somewhat indirectly, by Maurice Keen in his previously cited book *Chivalry*. Keen introduces his study with a detailed analysis of three separate non-literary documents—all of them treatises on chivalry written in the vernacular, expressly for the instruction of knights in the art of chivalry.[73] With Keen's findings as a starting point, it is a simple matter to codify a set of explicitly stated precepts for knightly conduct during the high Middle Ages: (1) the military virtues: loyalty to one's temporal lord, courage, hardiness, fitness of body (best achieved by hunting and jousting), and constant endeavor; (2) the virtues of nobility: courtesy, generosity, cleanliness, moderation, humility, cheerfulness of spirit, a readiness to honor and defend women and the helpless, and a commitment to justice and truth; and finally (3) the religious virtues: loyalty to God and the Church, regular attendance at Mass, awareness of one's own mortality, and the pursuit of heavenly salvation.

Despite some minor points of difference, the affinities between these real-life chivalric virtues and Hartmann's prescriptions for his fictional hero Erec are striking, to say the least. Indeed, the world of literary illusion appears here to mirror quite precisely those same traits which medieval society found most desirable in its practitioners of the knightly trade. To be sure, even within this realm of historical reality we are dealing by definition with an ideal—with what knights ought to be—and not necessarily with the actuality of what they were. Nonetheless, it is abundantly clear that the ideal medieval knight was virtually identical in the real world (regardless of whether the ideal was always effectuated) and in the realm of literature (where perfection typically *is* achieved). This consummate, exemplary knight—firmly rooted as he was in literary fiction and in real life—was a role model, an engaging figure that captured the imagination of courtiers throughout major areas of Europe during the most glorious days of chivalry. In him men glimpsed an image of what they strove to be, and in his idealized world they sought a reflection of their own less perfect, yet certainly vibrant and, for the time at least, rather optimistic world.

Hartmann's Sense of Humor

It would be a mistake to say that the tone of *Erec*—or of Arthurian romance in general—is fundamentally comedic. Yet by the same token, few would derogate Hartmann's tale as a dry and somberly intoned story. Indeed, the narrative circumstances of the Middle Ages largely precluded excessive gravity. Put simply, a poet or a minstrel of Hartmann's day could hardly expect an audience to appear, night after night, to hear a dull and soporific story. Throughout most segments of his tale, Hartmann von Aue masterfully commands the willing and eager attention of his listener/reader. This is accomplished in part through the lively persona of his narrator and in part through regular infusions of humor. Several instances of Hartmann's wit have already been noted. For example, when Erec reverses the tip of his lance in order to spare the unarmed and cowardly Keii serious injury, Hartmann has Keii end up ignominiously deposited on the ground: "much in keeping with what he deserved, but hardly in the fashion of a fine knight!" (p. 117). Then, following directly on the dry understatement of this passage, Hartmann resorts to the burlesque by having Keii "chas[e] full speed" (p. 117) after Erec in hopes of retrieving his horse.

Elsewhere, in the stichomythic bantering with a supposed listener (in which each competes to outdo the other in describing Enite's saddle) Hartmann is at his roguish best. "Quickly now, I am in a hurry!" (p. 149), the narrator snaps as this purported member of the audience stops to collect his thoughts. And at each attempt by this upstart to recount the details of the saddle, Hartmann's narrator dispatches a devastatingly critical riposte. Finally the listener protests such roughshod treatment: "you talk as though to mock me." Whereupon Hartmann's storyteller demurs, only to be pursued further by the listener: "In truth, your lips are curled with scorn." To this the narrator declares mischievously: "I always like to laugh" (p. 149). And indeed, he does like to laugh, and to evoke laughter in his audience as well.

Other passages come readily to mind in which Hartmann allows his sense of humor to step to the forefront. The account by King Guivreiz of how he pilfered the little horse from a dwarf must surely have amused medieval audiences. For although this tiny man has unquestionably been aggrieved by the theft and although he is utterly helpless to avenge his loss, Hartmann manages to depict the scene as grotesquely funny: the dwarf's "screaming and his weeping grew most loud indeed"; and once Guivreiz had refused his offer of ransom for the horse, "the little man, out of misery, raised so loud a din that the mountain resounded with his cry" (p. 148).

Certainly the most masterfully executed comic scene in *Erec* is the account (pp. 139–40) of the hero's unexpected appearance before Count Oringles' assembled court. Just as with the dwarf's horse, the jollity ought, by all rights, to be blunted by the fact that unfortunate circumstances accompany the laughter: Erec, thought by all to be dead, arrives in the hall and peremptorily slays Count Oringles along with two of his guests. Yet Oringles' behavior towards Enite has unquestionably been such as to merit him some sort of retribution. Furthermore, the sight of all the remaining courtiers fleeing in a panic—"slipping off into holes like mice"—is simply too droll not to pursue. And pursue it Hartmann does, at times with tongue-in-cheek understatement ("No one present heeded the dictates of good breeding"), at times with mock-heroic waggishness ("Many a fine warrior cowered underneath the benches, contrary to all the knightly code"), and at other times with outright burlesque farce ("they dropped over the wall in a throng thick as hail").

Hartmann adds his master's touch to this scene of panicked mass confusion by having his narrator confess that, under the same circumstances, he too would take to flight. After all, he says, these people suddenly see standing before them a man presumed dead. Hartmann's audience, of course, knows better, and it is precisely such disparity of information that gives rise to the ludicrousness of this episode. Oringles' courtiers wish nothing more than to flee from Erec (who has "bloody wounds" and is "already laid out for burial, head and hands wrapped in cloth") as he abruptly rushes in on them all, "brandishing a drawn sword." The narrator's comic interjection ("I too would have fled") places him within the parameters of his story, reminding his audience of the discongruity between reality and fiction, between their own secure circumstances and the abject fear that clutches Oringles' courtiers. In this fashion Hartmann relaxes the grip of suspense which he has imposed upon his audience, thereby allowing them to laugh, one and all, at this scene of farcical pandemonium. At Hartmann's skillful hand, danger and comedy can coexist, each complementing the other.

Joy and Sorrow

The humor with which Hartmann laces his story is merely another expression of the joy which so typifies the courtly literature of this age. Joy was a central catchword for Hartmann and many of his contemporaries. At Erec's wedding festival, for example, Hartmann speaks with an impassioned voice of the high-spirited exhilaration enjoyed by knights and their company. He tells of the jousting and dancing and of the great banquet, and he concludes his description of this lavish celebration with the words: "all sorrow [was] banished from sight there, and by the time they grew weary of their games, their joy had truly taken hold" (pp. 83–84). Of particular interest in this passage is the presence of the seemingly contradictory word "sorrow." However prominent the notion of joy was in this and other works of the day, seldom did joy fully overcome its companion sorrow. In fact, on the basis of this passage it appears that sorrow—not joy—is the pre-existent, perhaps even the more natural affect, and that the merriment of the festival is expressly contrived in order to dislodge that sorrow.

Again and again the two polar opposites of joy and sorrow are seen paired together, the one following inexorably on the heels of the other. Erec's most daunting task (and the one whose successful completion brings him final redemption as a knight) is to restore the "joy of the court" at Brandigan, and ultimately to reestablish the joy at his own court in Karnant. Beneath the brightly sparkling, optimistic mask of this courtly literature, there lurks a darker, more somber countenance—one which the knights must struggle incessantly to overpower. It is almost as though the zealous, even feverish pursuit of chivalric deeds could provide temporary diversion from a potential underlying tragedy, and that once such heroic feats cease, woe must once more inexorably come to the forefront. When Erec forsakes his knightly calling in order to be alone with Enite, Hartmann tells us that, at Erec's court, "Those people who had previously been filled with gladness were now drooped with deep gloom" (p. 94). All of this simply because Erec has refrained for too long from his quest for knightly glory!

As is the case in the above passage, Hartmann occasionally depicts joy and sorrow as mutually exclusive counterpoles. But more often than not they coexist in a delicate emotional equilibrium. When Enite hears tell of Erec's heroic performance in the tournament, she is "filled with both joy and sorrow at his valor" (p. 92). She is, of course, gladdened by the fact that he has acquitted himself so admirably; yet she is also aware that Erec's newly-won fame will now certainly expose him ever increasingly to the perils of battle. Later, after Erec finally wins victory over Guivreiz following a long and costly bout, Hartmann tells us that, once again, Enite "was filled with joy intermingled with sorrow" (p. 113). Here her gladness at Erec's victory is attenuated by the obvious severity of his battle wounds. Likewise, the wife of Sir Cadoc, whom Erec rescues from the two giants, is overcome by both emotions at the sight of her bloodied husband: "both joy and sorrow welled up in the shrine of her heart," Hartmann reports, "ill paired as these feelings are with one another" (p. 127).

Ill paired perhaps, but they recur in tandem with one another in a great many circumstances throughout the story. Just prior to the adventure in the mysterious arbor at Brandigan, King Ivreins welcomes Erec to his court with these same mixed emotions: "That Erec was his guest was a source of both joy and sorrow to him" (p. 157). The fear (indeed, the perceived certainty) that Erec will be added to the company of Mabonagrin's victims gives rise here to Ivreins' gloom—a gloom which stands in sharp contrast to the cheerfulness typically expressed by a medieval host in welcoming his guests. Later, at the conclusion of the fierce duel between their husbands, Enite offers her friendship to Mabonagrin's wife. The two ladies sit down with one another, Hartmann declares, and exchange "many tales back and forth, of joy as well as of sorrow" (p. 175).

The doublet of joy and sorrow is by no means peculiar to Hartmann's *Erec*. These two conflicting humors appear inextricably bound up with one another in much of the courtly literature. In one sense, an almost fatalistic negativism might be perceived in the concept that joy will ultimately end in sorrow. Yet at the same time a fundamentally optimistic world view manifests itself in the opposite notion, that sorrow will eventually give way to joy. In classical Arthurian romance, joy does invariably stand victorious in the final analysis.

In a larger sense, however, the juxtaposition of joy and sorrow in these works may be more than a common literary motif. It might, instead, be viewed as a statement on the perceived condition of medieval man. In fact, it might even be seen as a literary concretization of the philosophical shift away from the dualism which had dominated medieval thinking up to the time of the courtly period. According to dualistic thought, secular values and pleasures were transient and therefore to be rejected in favor of a later, permanent reward in the afterlife. The worldly realm was generally associated with suffering, and the heavenly domain with bliss. During the high Middle Ages the dualistic system of philosophy began slowly to give ground to a gradualistic world view, which recognized the secular realm as a legitimate, albeit inferior, component of the divine order.[74] According to gradualistic thinking, even though earthly pursuit occupies a lower position within this hierarchy than spiritual interests, the affairs of the here and now nonetheless command a sanctioned place within the larger order of things. No longer sorrow and suffering alone, but also a modicum of felicity—however fleeting—came to be expected from man's earthly existence. Hence, perhaps, the joy which is a hallmark of courtly literature in Germany.

The concomitant sorrow may have its roots in the residual effects of dualism (gradualistic thought was, to the extent we are at all able to measure such shifts, still in the early stages of establishing itself in the late twelfth century). Or it might be more efficacious, in looking for the foundations of sorrow in literature, to search among the real circumstances of life during this period. For the fact is that life was hard in the Middle Ages, even for the privileged few. In the simplest terms, there was much sorrow intermingled with whatever joy medieval man was able to extract from his life on earth. For one thing, average life expectancy in the thirteenth century is thought to have been thirty-five years. Furthermore, childbirth posed so great a danger to the life of a mother that, on average, men lived five years longer than women. Infant mortality was also very high: a child fortunate enough to survive his first ten years could expect to live to an age between forty and fifty (although forty was considered quite old in medieval times).[75] What is more, such estimates as these are based largely upon documents describing life among the nobility. For the peasantry—the overwhelming bulk of medieval European population—the numbers were almost certainly even more somber. Clearly, then, the very circumstances of life in the Middle Ages offer a convincing explanation for the frequent constellation, in literature, of sorrow and joy. Seen from this perspective the poets' feverish advocacy of courtly joy assumes the appearance of escapism from bleak reality into an idealized literary realm.

One of the most trenchant non-literary accounts of the inextricability of joy and sorrow in the medieval mind can be uncovered by returning one final time to the *Mainzer Hoftag* held at Pentecost in the year 1184. As we have seen,[76] the chronicler Gislebert of Mons renders a detailed account of the splendid array of knighthood at this marvelous festival hosted by Emperor Friedrich Barbarossa. On the final day of the tournament, however, Gislebert reports that a great storm came up and destroyed a number of buildings and tents, killing fifteen of the revelers. Many of those present, Gislebert discloses, interpreted this catastrophe as a sign from God that all of these thousands of men had become blinded by the splendid, but ultimately evanescent glitter of the pageant, and had lost sight of their own fundamental human frailty.[77]

In a sense, joy and sorrow had once again intersected in real life, just as they so often cross in the literature of the courtly epoch. Despite the optimisim and good cheer which pervade and dominate the tale of Erec, one can never fully elude (until the very end, where Hartmann affirms the irreversibly happy outcome of his story) the gnawing awareness that all of the splendor is fragile, and that, not unlike the Whitsun fesitval at Mainz, the joy of the court is anything but a permanent condition.

NOTES ON THE TRANSLATION

Unfortunately, an important dimension of any work is lost during the process of translation from verse into prose. However, after some unpropitious early attempts at casting Hartmann's work into English verse, I concluded that the spirit—if not the form—of Erec could be more faithfully preserved in a prose rendition. The formal exigencies of the original (rhymed couplets of four-beat lines) are so constricting as to force any translator (save perhaps the rare one who is a poet in his own right) to resort, finally, to prose. The only alternative, I found, would have been to sacrifice an unacceptable measure of precision and fidelity to the text. In opting for prose, moreover, I have followed the example of virtually all of the recognized translators of Middle High German literature.

No translation can presume to capture the full resonance of its original. Just as the most technologically advanced sound recording inevitably muffles some portion of the rich sonorousness of a live orchestral performance, so too is any translation—even the very finest—doomed to fall short, to a greater or lesser degree, of its prototype. It is my hope that such deficiencies in this version of Erec will be judged to be minimal. Where apparent flaws in the story occur, they are, in the main, a result of the process of translation, and not the fault of Hartmann von Aue, whose tale has gracefully withstood the judgment of countless generations of readers.

As is virtually always the case when eight centuries stand between poet and translator, certain passages in Erec are and will remain inscrutable. Hartmann's stylistic simplicity and "crystal little words" notwithstanding, numerous verses continue to confound the critics' attempts at clarification. In all such instances I have adopted in my text what I judge to be the most accurate rendition, while pointing out possible divergent readings in the footnotes.

As previously mentioned, the first 150 or so verses of Erec are missing in the Ambras Manuscript, the only document containing major portions of Hartmann's poem. In order to present a harmonious and intact story, I have prefixed my translation with three paragraphs (printed in italics) which summarize the introductory lines of Chrétien de Troyes' Erec et Enide.

One problem endemic to translating from Middle High German is the penchant of many of the poets, Hartmann included, to employ lengthy series of personal pronouns without intermittent reintroduction of their antecedents. The resulting uncertainties become especially pronounced in long passages (e.g. combat scenes) in which the actions or speech of two or more characters of the same gender are being recounted. For the sake of clarity I have therefore replaced, where necessary, selected personal pronouns with nouns, proper or common. Such minor alterations have not been individually recorded in the notes.

In many instances where Hartmann employs Old French words, particularly in proper names (e.g. Erec, fils du roi Lac), I have translated these into modern French, rather than into English.

For the convenience of the modern reader, I have divided the work into sixteen chapters, each of which marks a logical caesura in the progress of the story. Although such subdivisions are not present in the Ambras Manuscript, it is hoped that this will not represent too grievous a violation of the original format. *Erec* is of sufficient length that it must have been recited in numerous, individual installments (or "chapters") over a period of days.

Finally, I have followed closely the critical edition by Albert Leitzmann (Altdeutsche Textbibliothek 39). In the very few and very minor passages in which I deviate from the fifth printing of the Leitzmann edition, I have recorded this in the notes.

NOTES

Full bibliographic citations are to be found in the Selected Bibliography at the end of the volume; author-title references are used in these notes.

[1] I should like to acknowledge my indebtedness to the following scholars for many of the insights and facts incorporated into this introduction: Karl Otto Brogsitter, *Artusepik*; M. O'C. Walshe, *Medieval German Literature*; Peter Wapnewski, *Hartmann von Aue*; and Christoph Cormeau and Wilhelm Störmer, *Hartmann von Aue: Epoche— Werk—Wirkung*.

[2] Cited from Arno Borst, *Lebensformen im Mittelalter*, pp. 85–90.

[3] Particularly from what the poets say in their works about the gathering at Mainz.

[4] See Maurice Keen, *Chivalry*, p. 22.

[5] See Joseph Fleckenstein, "Friedrich Barbarossa und das Rittertum. Zur Bedeutung der großen Mainzer Hoftage von 1184 und 1188," p. 398.

[6] Fleckenstein, p. 392.

[7] Fleckenstein, p. 395.

[8] Cited from Fleckenstein, p. 395.

[9] Cited from Keen, p. 22.

[10] In 1130, Pope Innocent II, at the second Council of Clermont, officially condemned "those detestable markets and fairs, vulgarly called tournaments," while at the same time denying Christian burial to those killed in tournament (cited from Keen, p. 84).

[11] See Keen, p. 45.

[12] See Keen, p. 46.

[13] Keen, p. 48.

[14] Within the realm of literature, the "new" intermingling of Christianity and chivalry during this age was in fact nothing new at all: it had already come to the forefront, to name but one example, during the Carolingian era in the French *chansons de geste*. Earlier Germanic literature as well had already established a tentative link between Christianity and chivalry: the Old Saxon *Heliand*, for instance, depicts Christ and his apostles as a warrior band gathered about a noble leader. Yet in a significant way, the Church, by its advocacy of the Crusading effort, supplied a major boost to the rise of knighthood, thereby rejuvenating and intensifying chivalry as a subject matter for the German poets writing around the year 1200.

[15] Fleckenstein, p. 407.

[16] "as much for God as for secular glory"; Fleckenstein, p. 407.

[17] Christopher Brooke, *The Twelfth Century Renaissance*, p. 183.

[18] See Keen, p. 44.

[19] Up until recent years it was more or less assumed that virtually all of these poets belonged to the knightly order. However, recent research—in particular Joachim Bumke's study *Ministerialität und Ritterdichtung*—has exposed this notion as, at least in part, a romantic myth. Hence, while many of Hartmann von Aue's fellow poets surely practiced the knightly trade, scholars are nowadays considerably more cautious in their use of the term knight.

[20] This was a painfully slow process which had modest beginnings as early as the time of the Carolingian period, when a relatively small number of Old High German texts were produced, chiefly by monks of the larger monasteries. Most of these works, however, were based upon (and often directly translated from) Latin texts, and were intended specifically to further the Christianization of the Germanic tribes. For the most part, in other words, they did not constitute systematic, independent literary activity on the part of German writers. Then, following a period of over a century in which virtually nothing appeared in the German language, works such as the *Ezzolied* and the *Mementô morî* emerged from around the middle of the eleventh century. By a hundred years later—just prior to the great blossoming of the Middle High German era—major epics composed in the German tongue (among them so-called *Spielmannsepen* such as *König Rother* and *Herzog Ernst*) were already commonplace.

[21] See Brooke, p. 158.

[22] Brooke, p. 158.

[23] Both French poets cited from Fleckenstein, pp. 406 and 414 respectively.

[24] Confidential counsellor or secretary, and manorial dependent or member of the official household.

[25] See Fleckenstein, pp. 415f.

[26] According to one of Walther's contemporaries, these virulent attacks upon the pope, both for his role in the double election and for what Walther saw as Innocent's unremitting greed for alms money, were not without impact. Thomasin of Circlaria, an opponent of Walther, laments in *Der wälsche Gast* (ca. 1215–16) that these intemperate assaults on the pope had seduced a great many people into disregarding the commandments of God and of the pope. With this, we have for the first time in German literature evidence of the political effect of lyric poetry, directed as it was against a spiritual leader.

[27] In general, much of medieval thinking centered on a perceived dichotomy between worldly and spiritual strivings. For earlier medieval thinkers especially, the surest way to attain heavenly salvation had been to renounce all secular yearnings. Indeed, how to please both God and the world was a common dilemma. More often than not, the one seemed to preclude the other. Under the aegis of the Crusades, secular achievement and religious striving were, for a time, united in one common cause. The Crusading soldier of God could pursue heroic, even blood-thirsty deeds and still find favor in the eyes of God. In at least a limited, philosophical sense, the Crusades bridged the gulf between these two disparate realms.

[28] Brooke, p. 183.

[29] While we possess relatively little direct evidence concerning the contemporary reception of this literature, several important factors suggest that such genres as Arthurian romance must have been quite popular. For one thing, a large number of Arthurian romances were composed in the German tongue. Secondly, many of them (*Erec* being an anomaly in this regard) were copied—and are still preserved—in numerous manuscripts.

[30] John B. Freed, "Reflections on the Medieval German Nobility," p. 553, note 3.

[31] See Freed, p. 569.

[32] As indicated, the more probable reading of this passage is: "If my lord were living, then Saladin and all his army could not move me as much as a foot away from [Germany]." By this interpretation, Hartmann's lord is dead and Saladin is still alive. Since Saladin is known to have died in the year 1193, our poet must have participated in a Crusade prior to 1193, most likely the Third Crusade of 1189–90. The variant reading, however, yields an altogether different set of circumstances: "Even if my lord Saladin were still alive, he and all his army could not move me as much as a foot away from [Germany.]" Here, the word "lord" refers not to Hartmann's master, but rather to Lord (or Sir) Saladin, who clearly is depicted as deceased. By this reading, then, Hartmann must have set out on a later Crusading effort (in 1197–98), that is, after the death of Saladin in 1193.

[33] Gottfried von Strassburg, *Tristan*, trans. A. T. Hatto (New York: Penguin, 1960), p. 105.

[34] Especially the Cymric *Gododdin* (ascribed to the poet Aneirin and thought to have been composed ca. 600) and the *Annales Cambriae* (a chronicle dating from the late 900s).

[35] The exact route by which Arthurian legend first migrated from Britain into France and ultimately came to Chrétien's attention is not entirely certain. The most obvious path is suggested by the close connections between the court in England (where Wace's *Roman de Brut* had gained such popularity) and the court at Troyes

(where Marie, daughter of the English queen Eleanor, resided after leaving England). However, more recent scholarship leans towards the theory that the Arthurian legend first made its way across the English Channel and onto the continent by way of itinerant Breton *conteurs* who became acquainted with an oral form of the legend while travelling in Wales or Cornwall, then returned home to Brittany and composed songs based upon these oral tales. Finally, it is also possible that Chrétien may have established his acquaintance with Geoffrey's *Historia* and/or Wace's *Roman de Brut* by a more direct path. There is evidence to suggest that, while at the court in Champagne, Chrétien himself may have travelled to England and Wales.

[36] Only one *(Lancelot)* of Chrétien's five Arthurian romances failed to be transmitted into the German language.

[37] Other, more direct lines of dissemination of the legend into Germany are also conceivable. There were, for example, Germans frequently present at the court of Henry II of England. It is altogether possible that certain of these visitors might at some point have brought home with them to Germany the stories (in one form or another) of King Arthur. Hence, a general acquaintance with the Arthurian legend within Germany may well have preceded, and even planted the first seeds of interest for Hartmann's *Erec*.

[38] Not until after 1500 did the great verse romances of this age finally fall into disfavor, not to be "rediscovered" until the middle of the eighteenth century by early philologists and later by the poets of the Romantic school.

[39] Fragments of three *Erec* manuscripts, in addition to the Ambras Manuscript, have survived. Because they are considerably older (dating from the thirteenth and fourteenth centuries) than the Ambras Manuscript, these three fragments are enormously helpful in reconstructing the language of Hartmann's original text—despite the fact that they transmit *in toto* less than ten percent of the 10,135 verses.

[40] Arthur plays a secondary role, for instance, in Eilhart von Oberg's *Tristrant*, which dates from around 1170.

[41] The theory has also been recently put forth (see Eberhard Nellmann, "Ein zweiter Erec-Roman?") that Chrétien's *Erec et Enide* may have inspired a second Erec romance composed in German by a poet other than Hartmann. This hypothesis is based upon a newly discovered double-leaf from one of the fragmentary manuscripts of Hartmann's *Erec*. The verses transmitted on this one leaf (but not, curiously, the lines preserved on the previously known leaves of the same manuscript) betray, in certain regards, a closer affinity to Chrétien's version than to Hartmann's, and may suggest a redaction of the Erec story written by some heretofore unknown German poet. Just what role (if any) Hartmann's romance may have played is unclear. Intriguing as this argument is, it is nonetheless riddled with a great many points of conjectural uncertainty. It is best to assume, at least for now, that the only proven German Erec romance is that of Hartmann.

[42] "H.s Iwein erscheint neben Chr.s Werk wie ein sorgsam zurechtgestutzter und gepflegter Baum neben einem wild ins Kraut gewachsenen, der im Winde sich wiegt." Hendricus Sparnaay, *Hartmann von Aue. Studien zu einer Biographie*, vol. 2, p. 48.

[43] Chrétien de Troyes, *Erec et Enide*, trans. W. W. Comfort, p. 64.

[44] In this one regard, at least, Hartmann's usual propensity for innovation is not very much in evidence.

[45] Both in terms of narrated time (that is, the number of hours or days which Erec is

reported to have spent at the court) and in terms of time of narration (the number of lines which Hartmann devotes to his account of Erec's visit to the court).

[46] Michael Curschmann, "Hören—Lesen—Sehen," pp. 251f.

[47] Brian Stock, *The Implications of Literacy*, p. 16.

[48] Stock, p. 26.

[49] Stock, p. 6. Franz Bäuml ("Varieties and Consequences of Medieval Literacy and Illiteracy," p. 244) sees the rise of vernacular literature—a phenomenon which began in earnest during the last half of the twelfth century—as a significant factor in eventually breaking the link between literacy and Latin.

[50] Stock, p. 13.

[51] The most persuasive proof is that the poets on occasion speak explicitly of this in their works. Also, as Curchsmann (p. 249) points out, the scattered use of acrostics in various works testifies to the notion that at least some private reading of literature must have taken place during this age.

[52] Curschmann, p. 225.

[53] Bäuml, p. 245.

[54] Curschmann (p. 233) finds such fictionalizing of the audience to be particularly characteristic of the first generation of German chivalric romances. Because (especially in Germany) knights were writing for like-minded knightly audiences, Curschmann sees little ironic tension—and therefore relatively little "distance"—between the originators and the recipients of the literature. Hence the narrator could more readily draw his public into the actual process of narration.

[55] Curschmann, p. 252.

[56] With reference to medieval works which—unlike *Erec*—are divided (in most cases, presumably by the poets themselves) into sections or "chapters," Curschmann (p. 223) notes that this technique of summarizing briefly events which have just transpired in the preceding chapter is characteristic of oral composition. In the case of *Erec*, it might be more relevant, *mutatis mutandis*, to speak of predominantly written composition and oral performance.

[57] Chrétien de Troyes alternates with great frequency between the present and past tenses, without any apparent design. In Hartmann's various works, however, the past tense is the overwhelmingly predominant tense of narration.

[58] In a different context, Bäuml (p. 262) speaks of the "creation of the fiction that the fiction is not a fiction."

[59] Shulamith Shahar, *The Fourth Estate*, p. 162.

[60] Angela M. Lucas, *Women in the Middle Ages*, p. 181.

[61] Shahar, p. 6.

[62] Shahar, p. 130.

[63] Shahar, p. 149.

[64] Shahar, p. 151.

[65] Shahar, p. 171.

[66] Shahar, p. 158.

[67] Susan Mosher Stuard, *Women in Medieval Society*, p. 8. Stuard points out in her introduction (p. 8) that most of the great medieval churchwomen belonged to an earlier period, predating the Gregorian reforms.

[68] See Shahar, pp. 170f.

[69] Frances and Joseph Gies, *Women in the Middle Ages*, p. 27.

[70] Shahar, p. 152.

[71] The largely anonymous poets of heroic epics such as the *Nibelungenlied* (ca. 1200) frequently imbue their female characters with a more active and in some ways more nearly equal role than do the courtly poets of Arthurian romance.

[72] The most striking exception to this general rule within the German tradition is Wolfram von Eschenbach's *Parzival*, an Arthurian romance which is suffused with strong Christian undertones.

[73] Keen cites from three different tracts on knighthood: (1) the anonymous *Ordene de chevalerie*, probably composed prior to 1250 in Northern France; (2) the *Libre del ordre de cavayleria* written by the Majorcan mystic Ramon Hull, most likely during the 1260's or 1270's; and (3) the *Livre de chevalerie* by the fourteenth-century French knight Geoffrey de Charny.

[74] Such sweeping observations as these entail, perforce, generalizations which may lead, if applied incautiously, to oversimplification. Nonetheless, with the proper caveats in place, this distinction between dualism and gradualism is a useful and, in the broadest philosophical and historical sense, accurate tool for characterizing a significant shift in the medieval Weltanschauung.

[75] These figures did not improve appreciably until long after the close of the Middle Ages, with the advances in medicine and sanitation which began to take place during the nineteenth century.

[76] See above, pp. 3–5.

[77] Cited from Borst, *Lebensformen im Mittelalter*, pp. 87 and 90.

EREC

by
HARTMANN
VON AUE

⊠ I ⊠

THE CONTEST FOR THE
SPARROW-HAWK

The tale of Erec, fils du roi Lac, commences at Karadigan, where King Arthur is holding court on Easter Day. A good many fine knights are in attendance there, as are fair ladies and damsels in ample number. King Arthur's proposal that they all set out the next day in order to hunt the White Stag elicits a warning from Sir Gawein: great woe might come of this, for whoever succeeds in killing the White Stag must, in accordance with ancient custom, kiss the loveliest maiden present there at the court. Inasmuch as five hundred ladies of noble lineage are assembled here, Gawein admonishes, the choice of one of them as the fairest might well give rise to strife. He explains that each damsel has a bold knight who will surely contend that his lady is the most winsome of all those gathered there. Undaunted by such peril, the King announces that the hunt will be held the following morning in the forest of adventure.

At daybreak King Arthur sets out in the company of his knights. Queen Guinevere, together with one of her damsels, mounts her horse in order to follow after them. Erec, a young knight who belongs to the fellowship of the Round Table, approaches and asks permission to accompany the Queen. Of all the knights who have ever journeyed to King Arthur's court, none can surpass Erec's praise: he is handsome, valiant and courteous, and he rides up in splendid attire, armed only with his sword.

Guinevere is pleased to have Erec in her company, and they ride off into the forest. By now the hunting party has already put the stag to flight and is in swift pursuit. Queen Guinevere, Erec and the damsel are soon left far behind, out of earshot of even the horns and the dogs.[1]

(1–13) . . . with her and with her damsels. This was Erec, fils du roi Lac, whose hallmark was valor and good fortune, and on whose account this tale was undertaken. Now they had ridden alongside one another but a short time when they espied in the distance a knight with two companions approaching in great haste from across the heath. Ahead of this knight was a dwarf and in between was a winsome maiden lovely and finely garbed.

(14–43) The Queen now wondered who this knight might be. His armor was finely crafted, as befitted a valiant warrior. The youth Erec inquired of his lady whether he should go and ascertain the knight's identity. The lady, however, did not desire this, and bade him remain there in her company. Instead she chose a maiden to be dispatched to the stranger, saying: "Be off and determine who this knight may be, and also his travelling companion, the damsel." The maiden set out, as she was commanded, toward where she saw the dwarf riding. With gentility she addressed him: "God's greetings, my comrade. Hear what it is that I desire. My lady has dispatched me here, she is queen of this land. She in her courtesy bade me greet you in her name and tell you that she would fain know who the knight and this fair maiden be. If you can tell me this, you shall do so without incurring any harm, for my lady asks it with none but good intentions."

(44–58) The dwarf, however, would tell her nothing and commanded her to fall silent and to be gone, for he maintained that he did not know the purpose of her mission. This was not enough to stop the maiden from riding on ahead to ask the knight himself after his name. The dwarf, however, blocked her path. The Queen and Erec watched him strike her with a whip which he bore in his hand. He lashed her head and her hands—much to his misfortune!—such that she was left with welts.

(59–72) With this as her reply, she departed and returned to her lady and showed her how badly she had been beaten. Most bitterly did the Queen lament that this had happened so near that she had been forced to witness it with her own eyes. Erec now deemed this knight a less than valiant man for having stood by and permitted his dwarf to beat the damsel. "I wish to ride over to them," he spoke, "that I might investigate this matter for you." "Then be on your way," the lady replied.

(73–94) Erec set out anon and rode until he was close enough to them that the dwarf could hear his words. "Can you tell me, little man, why you have beaten this damsel? This is a grievous mistake that you have made. Good breeding ought to have cautioned you against such an act. Now tell me your lord's name. It was my lady's wish to know his name as well as that of the fair damsel." "Cease your chatter," replied the dwarf, "I shall tell you nothing other than that the same shall happen to you! Why should your lady wish to know my lord's identity? You are not very prudent people for asking so much of my lord this day, for it may well bring down harm upon you. If you wish me to spare you that, then be on your way—and may the Devil take you!"[2]

(95–108) Erec was likewise about to ride on ahead, save that the dwarf did not permit it: with his whip he struck Erec, just as he had done to the maiden. Erec would fain have avenged himself, but instead he wisely managed to control his wrath. The knight would indeed have slain him, for Erec was clad in no more armor than a woman wears. Never had Erec experienced a more wretched day than this, on account of the blow from the dwarf's whip. And never had he suffered such shame as from the fact that the Queen had viewed this dishonor along with her ladies.

(109–143) Lashed by the whip, Erec returned in deep disgrace. Thus did he lament his misfortune, his face flushed red with shame: "My lady, since you have witnessed it yourself, I cannot deny that an enormous disgrace has befallen me in your presence—so great a disgrace that no man of my standing has ever experienced any greater humiliation than this. That so little a man has dealt me so shameful a blow, and that I was forced to allow it to happen—this brings such shame down upon me that I shall never again dare to be seen before you or these maidens. Indeed, I know not what purpose I have in living, save to make amends for what has befallen me in your presence. Barring that I should die in the near future, I shall endeavor to set the matter straight. Grant, my lady, that I depart in your good graces. May the Heavenly King preserve your good name, my lady. Never again shall you set eyes upon me, unless I avenge myself on this man, whose dwarf has disgraced me with such welts as these. If God honors me by augmenting my happiness so that my venture meets with success—and this is my heartfelt hope—then I shall return in three days' time, provided I am still sound of body."

(144–149) The Queen was deeply grieved that Erec, a man so young in years, was embarking upon so great a peril. She bade him forego this journey. Yet Erec persisted in asking leave of her, until finally she granted his request.

(150–159) The noble youth reflected that there was too great a distance for him to return immediately to where his armor was. He knew that he could never fetch it soon enough, for no matter how quickly he returned, they would have ridden off and left him altogether. Hence he made haste to follow them, still bare of all his armor.

(160–180) As Erec began to pursue them in haste, he lighted upon the trail of those people who had inflicted harm upon him. Quite soon he caught sight of them and began watching them. He was in no hurry to ride up to this company; instead he followed at such a distance that he could observe them without their knowledge. Erec's actions were those of one who suffers wrong: such a man spares no pains to repay the injury in proper fashion. Not for a moment during all that long day did they escape the attention of Erec's eye as they rode along, until finally the hour of dusk approached. Erec now caught sight of a castle on the horizon—a castle called Tulmein, whose lord was Duke Imain. Erec watched as the knight rode forth into the castle, where he was well received, as one ought to be in the house of a friend, and as was well fitting for the host.

(181–209) I shall now tell you why the knight had journeyed there with his lady-love. Duke Imain had held a festival there the two previous years. If the adventure is truthful, then he was at this moment hosting the third such festival. Out in the midst of a meadow he had placed a sparrow-hawk[3] high up on a perch crafted of silver. Each year this custom was to be followed, much to the delight of the people of Imain's land. No one was excluded from this, and as soon as they heard news of it, all of them—rich and poor, young and old alike— came for the bountiful accommodations which Imain delighted in providing. Whichever knight's damsel should be adjudged the most beautiful at the Duke's festival, she was to take the sparrow-hawk. This one knight had taken this bird twice before and was come in order to win it a third time. And if it turned out so, then he would be allowed to keep it forever, without dispute and with full acclaim.

(210–217) Now it was said that many a lady had been present who was more lovely than this knight's lady-love. This had then caused the knight to display his valor: so fearsome was he that he had taken the bird by force. No man amongst them had dared challenge him, and he had not been called upon to do battle.[4]

(218–227) Erec knew nothing of this matter. He was merely pursuing the knight in search of adventure, on account of the wrong that he had incurred. The day began now to draw to a close. At the foot of the castle there was a marketplace, which Erec entered on horseback. The fortress itself he avoided, lest the knight whom he had followed there might perchance recognize him.

(228–249) As Erec was riding along in search of someone who in his goodness might offer him shelter for the night, he encountered a great crush of people all along the way. All the houses were full with lodgers. Nowhere could Erec find a man willing to take him in as a guest. Moreover, he had come there altogether empty-handed. He had failed to make any preparations, for, as I have already told you, the journey came upon him quite suddenly. Save for his horse and the clothes he was wearing, he had nothing with him: this caused him much concern. Furthermore, he was unknown in that realm, so that no

one spoke with him or looked kindly upon him—though the streets were bus-
tling with merriment, as is proper in the midst of a festival.

(250–291) Erec rode about aimlessly in this fashion until he spotted a time-
worn abode far off in the distance. Since he lacked all manner of accommodations, he took a road which brought him there, for he intended to stay the night
at that place, inasmuch as there was no lodging to be had elsewhere. He set
about looking over the house and was convinced that he would find no one inside, which lifted his spirits. "My quest is now faring well," he thought, "for I
shall stay here in some small niche until sunrise, as I can find no more comfortable lodging. Certainly no one will begrudge me as much, for I can see that the
place is abandoned." As Erec stepped into the house and began looking about for
a suitable corner in which to stay, he beheld a hoary old man seated there, his
hair snow-white with age. This man took great pains, though, to keep his locks
flawlessly groomed. Most beautifully combed, they fell down over his shoul-
ders. According to what the adventure reports, this same old man was wearing
a sheepskin cloak, as well as a hat of the same material. Both garments were
only as costly as his circumstances allowed: he was not given to extravagance.
Yet his bearing was most proud, in the fashion of a man of nobility. Moreover, a
crutch was the support of this man who was seated there in the dwelling.

(292–307) Erec was vexed at this, for he feared the customary treatment:
that the old man would drive him away, as had happened to him before. His
horse he tethered to the spot and laid his cloak across it. He held his hands out
before him, as does a well-bred man, and walked up to the old man. With uncertainty Erec addressed him: "My lord, I have need of lodging." This request
caused Erec to flush red with shame. But when the old man had heard his
words, he replied: "I bid you welcome to all that I now call my own." Erec, fils
du roi Lac, gave him thanks for this.

(308–322) Now the old man had no retinue save for his wife and a child,
who was one of the fairest maidens[5] of whom we have ever heard tell! That he
was rich in spirit was evident from the fact that despite all his poverty he had
offered hospitality to the stranger Erec. He summoned his child and spoke:
"Go, my daughter, and attend to the horse of this lord, who deigns to be our
guest; and minister to it at once with great care, such that I can find no fault
with your grooming." "My lord," she spoke, "I shall do this."

(323–341) This maiden's beauty was worthy of praise. Her dress was green
in color, yet full of holes and rips, and threadbare all over. Under that her
chemise was sallow and in tatters here and there. In such places, however, her
skin shone through white as the plumage of a swan. It is said that there was

never a young maiden so nearly perfect in appearance. And had she been rich, she would have been wanting in nothing requisite for a praiseworthy woman. Her body shone through her dingy garb just as does the lily that rises up white from amidst black thorns. God had taken great pains, I fancy, to endow her with beauty and grace.

(342–351) Erec was vexed by the inconvenience which he had caused her, and he said to her father: "Let us absolve the maiden of this task. I fancy she has seldom if ever performed such a chore: it is far more fitting a job for me than for her." "It is meet and right," replied the old man, "that a host be allowed to carry out his will. We are without retainers here, hence it is proper that she should do this."

(352–365) The maiden did not fail to do as her father had bidden her. With diligence did her radiantly white hands tend to Erec's horse. And should it come to pass that God Himself were to ride a horse here on earth, I fancy He would be content to have such a groom as that. Though she was wearing wretched garb, nonetheless I know that there never has lived a man or a woman who had a more comely page than did Erec, fils du roi Lac, while this maiden was caring for his horse. It was well fitting that the animal should be fed by such an attendant.

(366–395) The guest Erec was provided for here with all they had to offer. Fine carpets rolled out and covered with bedding so rich as to be unsurpassed in all the world, bedding sheathed in velvet and sewn with pure gold thread, so that no man could ever lift the bed by himself, but only with the help of three others; and quilts spread out over all of this, as would befit the splendor of great lords, quilts of light taffeta, luxurious and brightly embellished—such things as these were quite lacking that evening by the fire. Clean straw, however, they did procure. And on this they were content to make their bed with little ado, covering it with a white sheet. Moreover, there was food there for a knight: whatever noble thing a wise man could imagine, of that they had a full menu and an overabundance—yet none of this was placed upon the table. Their sustenance they drew in ample measure from unblemished character, which was to be found there in that house, for it is the guarantee of all goodness.

(396–413) Now you may hear tell of who this old man was—this old man, who despite poverty did not fail to welcome the stranger with such warmth. In earlier times he had been possessed of wealth and esteem in greater measure than now. He was a powerful count who had been divested (though without loss of his honor [6]) of his inheritance by those amongst his peers who had been more powerful. It was not his malevolence which had brought down this poverty upon him. Rather it was the result of warfare. The superior strength of his opponents had robbed him of all he had ever possessed. So little did that powerful man have left of his great splendor that he could not keep a single retainer in his household.

(414–439) Now in their old age he and his good wife bore their poverty adroitly, and whenever they were wanting in material goods, they gracefully concealed their deprivation in whatever way they could, so that no one might know of it. And scarcely anyone was aware that poverty had so wholly overcome them. Compared with what his sense of shame inflicted upon him, the hardship which Erec's host suffered from his great poverty was as sweet to him as a cup of mead. Koralus was the name of the aged host, his wife was called Karsinefite, and their daughter Enite. Any man who failed to feel pity for these noble, yet impoverished people, had a heart harder than a stone. The maiden's uncle was Duke Imain, whose festival was to be celebrated, and who was lord of the land. She was of untainted birth.

(440–455) Now we shall also tell why we have reported all of this. Once Erec's horse was tended to, the host said to his guest: "Let us pass the time in conversation." Erec was greatly troubled by the insult which he had previously suffered. He therefore spoke up and asked his host about the meaning of the din amongst the people, which he had witnessed in the market-place. The host then told him of all that was going on, as I have already recounted to you, both of the festival as well as of the competition for the sparrow-hawk.

(456–473) After the old man had related this to him, Erec then questioned him further about the knight. He asked whether Koralus knew who this man was, who, as I have told you earlier, had ridden into the castle while Erec watched; yet throughout this Erec concealed his vexation from Koralus. The old man answered him in this manner: "All the land knows this man. Iders son of Niut is his name," and he told Erec of why he had undertaken the journey there: that he had come with his lady-love in order to take the sparrow-hawk. As soon as Erec had heard this, he made yet further inquiries, until the host Koralus had revealed to Erec the circumstances of his own life.

(474–494) When Koralus had told him all there was to know, Erec stood up and said: "I beg of you, my lord and host, not to refuse the request I am about to make. Since your circumstances are such, I shall ask for help and advice. In the hope of gaining your good will, let me tell you that I have suffered injury from this man, such that I shall lament forever if I cannot make amends for it. His dwarf struck me most violently, a matter which necessity compelled me to tolerate. He was armed and I was not, wherefore in truth he came away unscathed. A great humiliation I was then forced to suffer. My heart shall grieve over this forever unless God bring about the day that I am able to avenge it. I have pursued this man in hopes of such adventure as I have now related.

(495–524) "I must ask your help. Both my aid and my salvation are wholly and entirely in your hands, my lord. I shall tell you what I have in mind: if you could offer me any manner of assistance with armor, then this man would not be able to avoid doing battle with me. I have journeyed on horseback in fine style. Hence you ought to permit me to ride with your daughter Enite to the festival of which you have spoken. I should make the claim[7] that she is more beautiful than this knight's lady-love, and I would take the sparrow-hawk. Now consider whether or not this might be possible, and do so with the understanding that, if I should manage to gain the victory, I shall take Enite as my wife. Do not be moved to deny my request for fear that with me she will be badly provided for, since our union can bring high esteem to her. I shall announce to you my father's name: King Lac he is called. Both my people and my land, myself, and all that is mine, shall be made subject to her, so that she may have dominion over all of it."

(525–531) At this, the old man's eyes secretly grew sombre with anguish. His heart was suddenly moved to tears by Erec's words, such that he scarcely brought forth the words which formed in his mind.

(532–559) "My lord," he spoke, "refrain from this mockery, for God's sake! Your words are most insolent. God has imposed His will upon me. My life has turned out differently than it ought to have. I am willing to accept my lot from God, for His power is so great that He can, whenever He wishes, make the rich man like unto the poor man, or bestow riches upon the man who lives in poverty. The magnitude of His power has been verified by what has happened to me. I prevail upon you, for God's sake, to renounce this affront. You can easily do without my daughter as your wife, for she is able to bring with her no dowry at all. Although I now suffer great need, you must nonetheless believe me when I say that I once knew the day when your father, King Lac, called me his comrade. Together we took up the sword of knighthood in his land. Unless I am deceived and deluded, it is only with mockery that you now ask for my daughter's hand."

(560–587) Erec blushed at these words and said: "My lord, what manner of distress deludes you into fancying that I have done this so as to mock you? You must banish this thought from your mind and take my words seriously. What reason have I now to scorn you? Indeed, I ask for God's help in body and in soul, just as truly as I wish to take your daughter in marriage. If your assistance is to be of any use to me in rectifying my affairs, I can grant you only until the festival begins, and no longer, to make an answer, so that my feud with Sir Iders might be settled once and for all. I have heard you lament your daughter's poverty. Now say nothing more of this matter. It brings no harm to you in my eyes, for I shall gladly do without her possessions. Moreover, I would be a foolish man if I were to let material goods outweigh the leanings of my will. Now consider this, and delay no longer, since the competition is to take place in the early morn. All my reputation lies in your hands. And know also with full certainty that what I have promised I shall also carry out."

(588–613) The old man was pleased by Erec's words. "Inasmuch as you do mean to do this," he spoke, "we have here at hand a splendid coat of armor, both finely made and suitable for you. Poverty has never managed to compel or delude me into such despair that I should give it up. Rather I have retained it, in the hope that some friend of mine might have need of it—for this very reason I was willing to lend it to any such man. As long as God granted me as much,[8] I was always of a mind to don this armor myself most willingly in defense of a friend, until such time as old age assailed me in this matter—old age which has sapped my strength so thoroughly. Now this armor has come to render us good service, by sparing us the shame of having to beg from strangers. What is more, I have still kept both shield and spear along with the armor." For this Erec thanked the old man.

(614–623) Erec then asked to be shown the armor, so that he could determine whether it fit him, whether it was too tight or too heavy. The armor turned out to be suitable and sturdy, which infused Erec, fils du roi Lac, with a heightened resolve. Soon came the dawn, heralding the day on which Erec and Enite were to ride off together to the festival.

(624–632) Once the day was in full splendor, they set out for Tulmein, where Duke Imain welcomed them most grandly. Their coming took him by surprise. They led him aside and revealed to him fully the purpose of their journey and why it was that Erec had come there, and they sought his help in this matter.

(633–661) "Let me tell you what I shall do," he said. "I shall place myself and my possessions at your disposal, my esteemed guest, along with all of my good will, both for the sake of your own valor and for the esteem of my niece. In addition, follow my counsel and let me dress her in finer garb." Erec, however, demurred, saying: "That must not be done! Any man who would judge a woman solely by her attire would have been altogether deluded by his eyes. One should measure a woman by whether her beauty is worthy of praise, and not by her apparel. Moreover, I shall demonstrate today to the knights and ladies that even if she were naked as the palm of my hand and blacker than soot, my lance and sword shall guarantee me that Enite receive full praise. Failing this, I shall have to lose my life." "May God send good fortune to stand at your side," replied Duke Imain, "and be certain that your intrepid spirit shall bestow all manner of good upon you."

(662–675) With these words they entered the church, where they heard a Mass of the Holy Spirit. Such is the custom of nearly all those whose minds are bent on knighthood and who love the tournament. Afterwards, the banquet awaited them; no pains were spared in the solicitude with which they were served. Once the feast was ended, each of them embarked upon whatever joyful pastime seemed good and struck his fancy. Their sport took place around the spot where the sparrow-hawk sat atop its perch.

(676–689) The people kept watching, one and all, for when Iders son of Niut would come up with his lady-love and take the sparrow-hawk, as he had done before. But they then spotted Erec approaching with Lady Enite. He ushered her up to where the sparrow-hawk was perched, and in full earshot of Iders he spoke: "Loosen the straps, my lady, and take the sparrow-hawk onto your hand. For it is true beyond all dispute that no one present here is fairer than you."

(690–699) The knight Iders was vexed by this, and he spoke up most scornfully: "Let the bird be! You shall not fare so well, you beggar-woman! What sort of notions have you put into your head? Leave the bird for the woman whom it better befits and who ought rightfully to take it. This woman is my beloved here. The bird should rightfully be hers."

(700–707) "My lord and good sir," said Erec, "you have wrongfully taken the sparrow-hawk these last two years. Now know this in truth: it cannot happen again, unless the assembled company grants you this honor. Knightly prowess must settle this matter between the two of us."

(708–723) "Foolish youth," he answered, "if your life were at all dear to you, then you would forsake your childish fight in good time, for very soon now you shall forsake it with far worse consequence: it shall cost you your life! Let me divine what your fate will be: I shall have no mercy on you. Once I conquer you—and of that I have no doubt!—my mind is such towards you that I would then refuse all ransom in exchange for your life. Whoever counselled you to undertake this contest—be it man or woman—is bent on seeing your misfortune!"

(724–731) "My lord," replied Erec, "in declaring my position in this matter I have now gone too far to revoke my stand at this point." With that they parted company there and armed themselves forthwith, the other knight in a fashion well befitting him, and Erec as best he could manage.

(732–745) Iders was resplendent in all his trappings, for he had held his armor in readiness before coming there, as is proper when knightly deeds are to be pursued. His lances were finely painted, and a plume bristled from atop his helmet. His mount was adorned with a richly embroidered blanket of velvet. (Such a blanket was hardly to be seen on Erec's horse!) His tunic was just as exquisite, of velvet green as grass and hemmed with costly trim. As the adventure tells us, his armor was praiseworthy, and he himself gave the appearance of an excellent knight.

(746–754) Erec also came riding up. His shield was old and heavy, and large both in length and in breadth; his lances were big and clumsy, and he and his horse were only half covered. All this was what his aged father-in-law had lent him.[9] Fortune, however, did not refuse him her hand, and amongst all those gathered there a unanimous wish was uttered: "May God grant you success this day!"

(755–781) They cleared a broad circle straightway for the two men. The youth Erec was well suited for knighthood; his boldness was a fountain of great strength for him. Both men were goaded on by fierce anger. They gave spur to their mounts, and at once the horses' shanks were seen flying.[10] Haughtiness began to deceive the other man, for he fancied himself going into battle with a mere child. The two men crashed together, and the other discovered that in truth Erec possessed the valor of a hero. With the force of this joust Erec dashed the man's shield back against his head. So stunned was he by this blow that he scarcely managed to stay seated on his horse. Seldom if ever had this happened to him! The joust became so frenzied that the horses reared back and fell onto their haunches. Up until that hour Sir Iders had never encountered such an attack in battle. Thereupon he came to know the full meaning of what an adversary was. The shafts flew from their hands, splintering against one another's shields.

(782–797) After the two men (each winning equal measures of high praise) had fought five jousts without either once missing the mark, but with their lances striking home and splintering against the other's shield—after a good five such jousts had been waged, Erec's store of lances was exhausted. This was a great hindrance to him, yet he had held aside the old lance belonging to his father-in-law for the final tilt. It was for this reason that he had saved it for that bout: its shaft was large and sturdy. Erec had likewise reserved a full and strapping measure of his stamina for that encounter.

(798–823) Taking up this lance (he held his shield in just the proper fashion before his chin), Erec rode a few paces aside, in the direction of Lady Enite, whom he saw weeping there. He spoke out over the top of his shield to her: "Be of good cheer, fine maiden. I am even now quite untouched by fear. Your worries shall soon be put to rest!" Erec spun his horse around to carry him towards the knight. His lance he locked firmly under his arm. The knight Iders, equally well girded for battle, came plunging headlong toward Erec. By calling upon all their skills, they crashed together with all the ferocity they could possibly enkindle in the horses. So fiercely did they collide that the other knight's saddle straps both ripped apart (such distress as this he had never before experienced!), as did the upper strap and the harness. Although that knight was not wanting in courage, Erec unhorsed him, much to the scorn of all the assembled people.

(824–833) After Erec had had the good fortune to unseat the knight, he refrained from pouncing upon him from his superior vantage point.[11] This he did lest anyone could accuse him of the disgrace of slaying Iders as he still lay on the ground. It was a higher reputation which Erec desired to pursue. He dismounted and bade the knight stand up, and they set upon one another.

(834–849) The courtiers watched as Erec and Iders fought in the manner of two fine knights. Fire flashed from each man's helmet. They struggled like men prevailed upon by dire distress, for they had placed high stakes indeed upon the victory! Both life and honor, no more and no less, hung in the balance there. It was quite in accordance with this fact that they geared their actions, and their combat was heroic. They carried on the fighting in great and ample measure, until Iders dealt such a blow to Erec's helmet that the impact brought him to his knees.

(850–863) At the sight of this, Lady Enite was beset by woe and began to lament her beloved. She fancied him slain and thought he would never stand up again in the wake of that blow. Yet up he jumped, and turning the shield around onto his back he brandished the sword fiercely with both hands, fighting as if in a frenzy. Erec stripped Iders bare of his shield by chopping it right off his hand. Little did Iders let this go unchallenged; he parried every blow with a thrust of his sword.

(864–890) Each time he borrowed a mark from his opponent, he paid it back, but in such a fashion that he took ten additional marks instead. Both were playing a game that can easily rob a man of all he owns—a game of chance in which bids are dealt out to each player's head as well as now and again to their torsos, both front and sides. It was with a fury that they each collected their winnings. Just as one player was to have claimed his earnings, he was quite likely to be paid back by the other with a yard-long gash. Many bets were placed, only to be matched by the other man. Neither wished to give in, for that man's honor as well as his life would have crumbled to dust. They continued to wage this game with many a fiery blow, from early morn on until after noontime, such that they had nothing more to wager; so furious was the battle that both men began to feel the weight of fatigue. They had neither the strength nor the power left to make their bids with any vigor, nor even to lift their arms as they had done up until then.[12]

(891–909) By now they had raged and fought so viciously that they could carry on no more. Their sword-thrusts were like those of women: they dropped to the ground with weakness. So feebly did their swords languish that neither of the two opponents was scathed at all. Iders then addressed Erec: "Hold off, noble and good sir knight! What we have been doing just now is a dishonor to the spirit of knighthood. It is beyond all praise and without any glory. Our lame fighting is unbecoming for valiant knights. We are not wielding our swords in a manly fashion, and our fighting is ignominious. It is my advice—if you are not inclined to see this as cowardice on my part—that we stop this feeble fighting and each go off to rest for a short time."

(910–950) Erec was pleased by these words. Both men unfastened their helmets and sat down to rest. And once they felt their strength return, they faced off and took up their former game, as I shall now relate to you. They kept up the bout with great adroitness, with renewed vigor and with mastery in equal measure. They had kept at it for a long time, so that none of those standing about watching—whether they were versed in the art of dueling or not[13]—could tell at any given moment which man had thrown a slightly higher number with the dice. For a long while this remained unchanged. There was no certainty amongst them as to which man would be the victor—until the youth Erec began to think back upon the disgrace and the injury that had befallen him on the meadow at the hands of this man's dwarf. And in addition he gleaned vast help in his battle from the sight of the fair Lady Enite,[14] for he found his strength easily redoubled by casting his eyes upon her. With an eager hand he collected his winnings by hacking away at Iders' helmet. Though Erec had as good a throw of the dice as any gambler needs, his opponent furthered his cause by never allowing Erec out of range of his sword. And for a time Iders' fervor won him the advantage, until finally he lost the match and lay vanquished at Erec's feet.[15] With this, Erec had avenged that blow from the whip.

(951–963) Having broken open the knight's helmet, Erec also loosened the helmet cap underneath it,[16] as if to slay him, save that Iders chose to seek mercy. "For God's sake, noble knight, have mercy upon me! Bestow honor upon all women through me by letting me live, and be mindful of the fact, o virtuous man, that I have not inflicted such heartache upon you. You can do well by sparing my life."

(964–985) Erec then replied, saying: "How can you speak in this fashion? You mock me needlessly. Indeed, you were bent on nothing short of my death. If I let you live, you would be receiving all too light a penalty for your intentions and for your haughty arrogance. In fact, you would have accepted no ransom for my life in this duel. But God has granted me the good fortune that things have been reversed. Behold, I can now easily dispense with the need to offer any ransom in exchange for my life. However God may protect my life in other ways, at least I am certainly safe from you. Had you but tempered your haughtiness towards me a bit more, behold, it would now be to your advantage. But now your arrogance has brought you to your knees here this day and has made calamity your companion."

(986–999) "How do you mean this?" asked the knight. "I have never done anything to merit your hatred, for I never set eyes upon you before this day." "It is my desire that you now feel a sense of disgrace," answered Erec, "just as I did yesterday, when, because of you, I was forced to endure a humiliation which afflicted my heart deeply. Furthermore, I vow to you on this very spot that your dwarf in all his strength and great vulgarity shall never render enough good service to you to outweigh the harm he heaps upon you this day."

(1000–1009) "I regret it," replied the knight, "if you have ever suffered any distress on my account. Furthermore, your valor has extracted full compensation from me here for this transgression. Now deign to let me live. And if I have done anything for which I ought rightfully to make amends, I shall absolve that debt most excellently through service to you."

(1010–1017) At this, Erec's heart was moved to compassion. He then said to the knight: "I shall now spare your life, though you would have done nothing of the sort for me." Iders then gave his oath of surrender, that, in exchange for his life, he would be prepared to do whatever Erec bade him.

(1018–1055) Once this oath had been sworn, Erec commanded him to rise. And as they both then removed their head gear, Erec spoke: "You must now carry out a wish of mine, which I shall not forego: my lady the Queen must be compensated for the insult she has suffered. You have caused her great anguish, in such measure as has never before befallen her. You have done much harm to her, and you must make amends to her for this, for she is lamenting it most wretchedly. Yesterday at this same hour your dwarf beat her maiden; and afterwards he struck me so violently that I received these welts. Behold, I am the selfsame man! What is more, I would have pursued you forever before letting you escape my revenge. I shall not tolerate such scratches on my face, whose presence you certainly cannot dispute! Nor shall I condone the fact that your dwarf was guilty of such churlishness as to have whipped this maiden. He shall by rights atone for this. And let me tell you why: he indeed took such delight in his discourtesy that he ought to be requited for it. I am willing to disregard myself, but the maiden he ought not to have treated in such a fashion. I shall extract an acceptable lien from this dog: he must forfeit no less than his hand, that he may for evermore display a greater measure of honor towards ladies."

(1056–1077) The good Erec, however, did not in fact intend to do this; instead he wished to serve warning to the dwarf by this threat, that he should never again behave in such a way. After but a brief entreaty Erec refrained from executing his threat. Yet just revenge he did still obtain: Erec ordered two retainers to spread the dwarf out on a table and to thrash him soundly with two stout switches, such that the lash marks were still visible on his back for a good twelve weeks. The dwarf's discourtesy was avenged in that the blood ran down over his body. All the people amongst them—both men and women alike—were of the common opinion that he was justly deserving of this punishment, since he had been guilty of such ill-bred behavior. Maliclisier was the name of this dwarf.

(1078–1098) Erec then addressed the knight, whose dawdling displeased him: "I know not wherefore you tarry here instead of riding off to my lady the Queen. You ought to have set out by now. You must surrender yourself into her dominion and conduct yourself in whatever way she commands. Apprise her of who you are and of our duel, and tell her who it was who sent you there to her. Thus am I called: Erec, fils du roi Lac. I shall be off on horseback as soon as my time permits it, and I shall arrive tomorrow if I am at all able. It is a distance of but seven miles to that place. Be mindful now of your oath of surrender." The knight Iders then rode forth, he and his lady-love and the little dwarf, toward King Arthur's court.

☗ II ☗
EREC'S ACCLAIM

(1099–1111) In the meantime King Arthur had left his castle, which was called Karadigan,[1] and had gone into the land where the stag was being hunted, as you have previously heard. Now it had come about that King Arthur had captured the stag by his own hand, and the privilege ensuing from this had fallen to him: that he should choose from amongst all the maidens the one whom he wished to kiss.

(1112–1149) After they had arrived back at Karadigan, the King was about to claim his prize, as was the custom. However, just as they had all affirmed his claim, the Queen requested of him that this matter be deferred until she had related what had occurred and told of the vexation which the knight had caused her out on the meadow. And she then reported to him precisely what had happened to her on that day, saying, "My consort, I wish to lament to you the following: both my maiden and Erec, fils du roi Lac, have been most severely[2] beaten. On account of this whipping Erec took leave of me out on the meadow in much distress. 'My lady,' he said, 'believe this of me: I shall never rejoin you in the land of Britain until such time as I avenge this disgrace of mine. And if I am able to gain full revenge for this, then I shall return in three days' time!' My lord, tomorrow is already the third day. I am hopeful, yet I feel concern for the fate of this youth. I tried, but was unable to dissuade him from leaving. May God send him back to us alive! I entreat you now, my consort, for his sake as well as for mine, to delay claiming the kiss which you have won, until you hear word of Erec's fate. Would that he now were with us! Wait here only until tomorrow morn. If he meets with success, he shall appear."

(1150–1195) It was at the castle of Karadigan that Guinevere made this request. Immediately before that, Walwan[3] and his friend the seneschal[4] Keii had joined hands and had just left the ladies in order to keep watch outside the castle. Both of them soon spotted the knight Iders riding along in haste from far out in the forest. Without delay they reported this to the Queen, who stood up at once, gathered her ladies about her, and went to a window to see who it was who was approaching on horseback. Guinevere stood there together with all the knights, uncertain as to who this knight might be. "Forsooth," spoke the Queen, "insofar as I can discern from this distance, and as my heart tells me, it is the same man whom Erec was pursuing. Look now, there are three of them! The dwarf and the knight's lady-love are riding along with him out there. It is none other than he! He appears in fact to be coming from battle. You can see this from his shield, which is very nearly hacked to shreds all the way down to where he holds it, and from his armor, which is red all over with blood. I tell you in truth, he has slain Erec and is come here to boast for having gained the victory. Or else, Erec had dispatched the vanquished knight into this land for the honor of our court. It is for this that I do dearly hope!" They all agreed with the Queen that one or the other might well be true.

(1196–1207) Before they were even finished speaking, Iders, already present now at Karadigan, rode across the courtyard, stopping at a flat rock which protruded a short distance before the stairway. This stone had been placed in the castle for King Arthur to mount and dismount his horse there. The knight saw no better place to alight than there, and so he climbed down from his steed at the rock.

(1208–1259) Once their horses had been taken off, Iders, accompanied by the dwarf and his lady, went with all good breeding before the Queen, who bade him a noble welcome. At this, he fell at her feet, saying: "Powerful lady, receive mercifully into your command a man upon whom God confers no honor. With these words I refer to myself. I have acted rashly towards you; I did this not under force of necessity, but at the bidding of my own knavery. I am to do penance to you for this, for I have followed the counsel of my foolish heart. Now that it is too late, I rue what I have done. Indeed, just as the hare who already lies entangled in the net, I am espousing caution at an inopportune moment. This has been the source of much regret for me. The saying is indeed true, that pride comes before a fall. Only after suffering great disgrace did I see the truth of this and realize the full consequences of my actions, for Erec has well nigh taken my life, along with all my honor. I wish to surrender myself as guilty, for I have wronged you. It was I who encountered you on horseback yesterday on the meadow. I have suffered for having permitted the discourtesy of my dwarf, who struck your maiden. Erec, fils du roi Lac, has forced me to make amends for the misconduct of that lashing; in doing so, he was guided by the knowledge of my true guilt. With his own hand he defeated me and sent me here, my lady, that I might, despite my guilt, gain your favor and stand wholly in your service. Moreover, I shall tell you this in addition: you must not be concerned for Erec's safety, for he shall come to you himself on the morrow, bringing with him a maiden so lovely that no man constrained by the dictates of truth will claim to have beheld a woman more beautiful."

(1260–1283) Arthur and his Queen were most heartily delighted at these tidings, and they gave praise to our Lord that Erec, in his still blossoming youth, had met with such success, and that his first knightly endeavor had, despite his years, resulted in so laudable a measure of good fortune. For Erec had never before undertaken such a mission. No one among them, unless he were altogether envious of Erec, bore him any malice. Never was a man more loved by a court, for Erec had, from his childhood on, earned their unanimous good will. To the knight Iders the Queen then spoke: "Your atonement shall be lighter than you in fact deserve. It is my wish that you remain here and become a member of our retinue." And Iders had no choice but to comply without objection.

(1284–1293) After all of this, the King addressed his knights: "Let us now prepare a splendid welcome as reward for Erec. We should rightfully grant all honor to a man who can show himself so well deserving of it. He has made a propitious start to what shall be a praiseworthy life of knighthood." In this they were all in agreement.

(1294–1333) After it had come about, as you have heard before, that Erec succeeded in defeating Iders (who was ever a true warrior!) at the castle of Tulmein, and after Lady Enite was confirmed through battle as the fairest maiden present, both rich and poor sensed heartfelt gladness at Erec's good fortune. And they all proclaimed with one voice that Erec was beyond a doubt the most excellent man who had ever come to that land. There was no one present who was displeased at Erec's victory. They praised his courage, and they began to expand their games and entertainment in his honor. In one area commenced a great tournament of knights jousting en masse, and elsewhere there was dancing to be seen. Duke Imain removed Erec's armor, and the young girl Lady Enite offered him her lap to rest his head in after that long duel. Her demeanor was quite modest, as is the way with maidens. She spoke scarcely a word to Erec, for this is the custom with them all, that they are at first bashful and timid as children. Afterwards they acquire the wisdom to know fully what is good for them, to understand that what now seems disagreeable may someday be welcome, and to prefer, whenever they might rightfully receive it, a sweet kiss over a beating and a good night over a bad day.

(1334–1363) Duke Imain then requested that Erec, along with his beloved Enite, deign to remain with him that night as a token of friendship; the Duke also directed this request to Erec's father-in-law.[5] Erec, however, declined his offer, answering him thus: "My lord, how would I be acting if I were to abandon my host,[6] who has been so kind to me? Not knowing me at all, he extended to me yesterday—he and your sister—so warm a welcome that I must requite him for it. He could not, I am certain, have offered any greater hospitality. What is more, he also granted me his daughter's hand. Therefore, desist from this invitation without animosity, for I shall not neglect my host by remaining here. Should I waver from him now, he might well think he was being made to suffer because of his poverty, which God knows he shall never do. It is with great pleasure that I shall be in his company; my steadfastness shall become evident to him. And if we are to have even half a year to live, I shall in truth restore him to wealth, provided I am not wanting in resources. There shall be no end to my determination to help him acquire riches such as he never had before."

(1364–1385) "Since you will not accept my offer of hospitality," answered Duke Imain, "we shall remain with you and accompany you to your lodgings."

Sir Erec thanked him most profusely for this, as did also his father-in-law.[7] They then arose and, joining hands, proceeded to their quarters, with Lady Enite walking along between them. Joy in ample measure accompanied Enite too, for on her arm she bore the sparrow-hawk, which she had won. A true source of gladness was this, for thus had the maiden in her good fortune acquired great honor and praise. Yet she rightly felt even greater bliss with her dear husband, whom she had gained that day.

(1386–1399) Any man not averse to merriment found ample entertainment at the Duke's festival. A great commotion filled the air in and among the lodgings. Such a man could not help but see guests beyond any count that evening, both knights and ladies. For all who came there were invited to that festival. Lady Enite's father could not have sustained this great expense; the Duke, instead, had to take this upon himself. Foodstuffs in suitably large quantities were borne there from his castle.

(1400–1425) As soon as the following day had dawned, Erec, fils du roi Lac, would tarry there no longer. He made known his restlessness and said he would have to be on his way, taking Lady Enite with him. At this, her uncle, the Duke of Tulmein, asked Erec's permission to secure finer clothing for Enite. Erec, however, demurred. Gold and silver the Duke then offered him, but Erec claimed to have no need of this. Likewise did he refuse the offer of a horse and clothing. All that he took was a suitable horse for Enite to ride, which he accepted from a young maiden, one of her cousins. As the story goes, this maiden was in the company of the Duke and was a close kinsman of his. She persisted most kindly in her offer to Erec, until finally he accepted the horse from her. And be well assured that never before in the world had any man obtained a more handsome horse.

(1426–1453) This animal was neither too large nor too small, it was the color of ermine all over, its mane thick and curly, its chest strong and broad, with perfectly grown bones which were neither too heavy nor too light. It bore its head at the proper height, and it was docile and high-spirited, with long flanks (a fine horse it was to ride!) and with a back and hooves that were splendid enough indeed. O, how very gently it carried its riders! With the grace of a ship it moved swiftly across the field at an ambling gait. In addition to its smooth stride, the horse never stumbled. The saddle was such as to be most suitable for this horse: the metal fittings were of red gold, as was quite becoming. Why should I make a long story of how these fittings were crafted? Much of this I must suppress from you, for it I were to recount it all to you, there would be too much prattle.[8] I shall finish my praise of that saddle quite briefly by telling you that the saddle straps were decorated with fine embroidery.

(1454–1483) Once the horse had been brought out to Erec, they delayed no longer in setting out. As Lady Enite took leave from her dear mother to depart for foreign lands, she wept hot tears, which was proper for a daughter. "Powerful and most benevolent God," said her mother, "deign to watch over my daughter." The blessing was prolonged by the bond of loyalty amongst them. Their parting brought forth many a tear in the eyes of mother and daughter, and of the father as well, who asked our Lord God to keep Enite in His care. Erec told the old man that when his messenger came to him, he should follow his instructions, for Erec was intent upon making amends for the old man's indigence. Elated at the hope of this, Koralus bowed deeply before Erec. They then took leave of all the courtiers there and parted company forthwith, riding off on horseback. Erec would allow no one to accompany him as they left. Instead he bade them remain there with all good fortune.

(1484–1497) When the two of them came out upon the meadow, Erec began to contemplate his maiden. She, too, repeatedly cast a shy gaze at her beloved. Again and again they exchanged loving glances. Their hearts were filled with love, and they both charmed each other ever more. Neither jealously nor hatred found a receptacle there in which to lodge. They were, instead, possessed of faithfulness and constancy.

(1498–1531) Erec and Enite now rode on with haste, for Erec had promised to arrive on that same day. From what the Queen had told the good knights, they all knew quite well the time when Erec was to arrive. They had also heard it from the knight who had appeared at court, and whom Erec had defeated. The knights' horses stood ready, and Erec soon reaped the benefits of his valor. For riding out from the court together with King Arthur were Gawein and Persevaus, as well as a lord named King Iels of Galoes; Estorz, son of King Ares, and the cupbearer Lucans were also to be seen in the crowd. There was, in fact, the whole multitude, so that they all rendered him a fine and hearty welcome with knightly fanfare, just as one should for a once-lost friend who has been found again. At the same time my lady the Queen had walked out across the green towards Erec in order to receive him. She bade him welcome, for she was pleased with the outcome of his adventure. She then took Lady Enite aside and said: "Lovely maiden, you shall receive new clothing to replace what you are wearing."

(1532–1578) The mighty Guinevere then led Enite into her private chambers, where a bath awaited her and where she was washed most splendidly after all her travail. The becrowned Guinevere clothed her dear guest, for they had rich vestments in reserve there. The Queen herself sewed the alterations with her own hand on a chemise of white silk, so that it fit the maiden Enite. In a fashion evoking much praise she covered the chemise with a gown finely tailored in the French style, neither too tight nor too loose. The gown in which the Queen laced her up was of green velvet with trim as wide as an open hand, and with gold thread both left and right (as was proper) along each edge. In addition, Lady Enite's waist was girded with a belt from Hibernia,[9] which the ladies like to wear. Before her bosom was placed a brooch a hand's breadth across, which held a sparkling ruby. Yet the maiden with her radiant complexion utterly outshined its brilliance. The gown was gathered in[10] and hung with a cloak every bit as exquisite as the gown. This cloak was lined with fur of ermine, and its outer shell was of a rich silk embroidered with gold. The sleeves of this royal garb were trimmed with sable. Enite's hair was bound together by a ribbon, which was of becoming width and was tied crosswise over her head. So lovely was the garland that no more beautiful ribbon could ever be found. Enite's garb was marked by costliness, she herself by goodness.

(1579–1610) Lady Poverty then covered her head with great shame, for she had been most wantonly robbed of her abode. She was forced to abscond, and she fled her home, in which Wealth now took up residence. So beautiful had the maiden Enite appeared in her ragged clothing that, as is told, she now attracts the very highest praise in such precious finery as this. I would fain laud her as I ought to, but I am not so artful a man as to escape failure in that venture. Such craft is not mine to know. After all, many a wise tongue has busied itself with the praise of women, such that I cannot imagine any words of praise which I might invent for her that have not already been better expressed for other women. Enite must remain unpraised by me or, at least, not praised to the extent she deserves, for I—dull-witted fellow that I am—am lacking in the necessary skills.[11] And yet I shall still tell it to the best of my ability. As I have heard it, there was no dispute: Lady Enite was the fairest of all maidens who had ever, as the story goes, come to King Arthur's court.

(1611–1629) The Queen took Enite courteously by the hand and went to where the King was sitting, as was his privilege, at the Round Table together with many a fine knight. Of all those who had a seat at the Round Table, either at that time or since then, there was one who had acquired—and this was beyond dispute—the highest measure of praise. All among them agreed in this, for that man, according to the legend, was never guilty of any villainy, but rather showed such manifold excellence that even today he is reckoned one of the finest men ever to have gained a seat there. Hence this man, the good knight Gawein, had every claim to his place at the Round Table.

(1630–1697) Seated along with him were Erec, fils du roi Lac, and Lancelot of Arlac, Gornemanz of Groharz, Coharz the Handsome, Lais the Bold, and Meljanz of Liz, Maldwiz the Wise, and Dodines the Wild, and Gandelus the Good. Next to him sat Esus, then Sir Brien and Iwein son of King Urien and Iwan of Lonel, who was eager to win all acclaim. Likewise seated there was Iwan of Lafultere, Onam of Galiot, and Gasosin of Strangot. Next to him at the Round Table was one called the Knight with the Golden Cross-bow, as well as Tristram and Garel, Bliobleherin and Titurel, Garedeas of Brebas, Gues of Strauz and Baulas, Gaueros of Rabedic and the Prince of Ganedic, Lis of the five Broadswords, Isdex of the Dolorous Mount, Ither of Gaheviez, Maunis and Galez the Bald, Grangodoans and Gareles and Estorz son of Ares, Galagaundris and Galoes, and the son of Duke Giloles, Lohut son of King Arthur, Segremors and Praueraus, Blerios and Garredoinechschin, Los and Troimar the Young, Brien the Nimble-Tongued, and Equinot son of Count Haterel, Lernfras son of Gain, and Henec the Adroit, son of Gawin, Le and Gahillet, Maneset of Hoch-turasch, and Batewain son of King Cabcaflir, [. . .][12] and forsooth Galopamur son of Isabon, and Schonebar, Lanfal and Brantrivier, Malivliot of Katelange and Barcinier, the faithful Gothardelen, Gangier of Neranden and his brother Scos, the bold Lespin and Machmerit Parcefal of Glois and Seckmur of Rois, Inpripalenot and Estravagaot, Pehpimerot and Lamendragot, Oruogodelet and Affibla the Merry, Arderoch Amander and Ganatulander, Lermebion of Jarbes son of Mur, who wore four coats of armor. With this I have recounted to you the names of the men of that excellent company. According to the correct count, they were, all in all, forty and one hundred in number.[13]

(1698–1707) The Queen now led Enite in towards the assemblage. Enite was endowed with perfect beauty: her skin appeared as though the hue of roses had poured out and mingled together with white lilies, and her lips were as though imbued with the pure tincture of roses.[14] Never had anyone set eyes on a woman more fitting for a knight.

(1708–1725) As Enite first passed through the door into where the knights were gathered, and saw them seated there, she was beset by modesty. Her rosy color vanished, and she repeatedly turned first red then pale at the sight of all the knights. Her blushing was in a like manner as I shall tell you: when on a bright day the sun gives off its full radiance and suddenly a thin and whispy cloud passes before it, its radiance is diminished a bit from its earlier glow. Thus did the maiden Enite for a fleeting moment suffer passing discomfort from her timidity.

(1726–1735) As she stepped on into the hall, however, her lovely counte-nance then recaptured its joyful hue and became yet more exquisite than before. O, how becoming to Enite was this blushing of hers! It was her great sense of modesty that had brought this all about, for never before had she beheld so many heroes seated together—men selected for their undiminished excellence.

(1736–1749) As Enite entered, those sitting at the Round Table were startled by her beauty, such that they forgot themselves and gaped at the maiden. Not a single man amongst them failed to concur that she was the fairest maiden he had ever beheld. King Arthur approached her, and taking Lady Enite by the hand, he seated her at his one side, with the excellent Queen Guinevere at his other hand.

(1750–1762) King Arthur thought it now time to conclude without further delay the contest amongst the knights. You know that Arthur, because he had been so fortunate as to capture the White Stag, was to have claimed his prize (of this you have already heard full well) by kissing the lips of the woman who by common acclaim was said to be the most beautiful there. At the Queen's request he had delayed taking his reward until this moment.

(1763–1796) There was now no dispute that Enite was the loveliest woman present there at Arthur's court, as well as anywhere else in the world. For I shall tell you in good sooth how it was that her beauty surpassed that of the others. It was just as on a dark night, when the stars are unbeclouded so as to be in full view, one could not rightly help but find their twinkling pleasant indeed, as long as nothing more beautiful came along. But once the proper hour calls forth the moon to make its nocturnal journey across the sky, the sparkling stars pale alongside that lunar orb. These same stars would be thought worthy of praise, provided the moon were never present nor were it to obscure them with its brilliant splendor. In the same fashion did Enite's radiance outshine the other ladies from first to last. King Arthur then went without delay to uphold the tradition which his father (who was called Uterpandragon [15]) had passed on to him, the tradition of claiming a kiss from the one lady—but from none other—whom his good knights prescribed to him. The King stood up and claimed his reward forthwith from his nephew's lady-love. It was possible for this to transpire in the absence of any animosity, for Erec was King Arthur's kin.

(1797–1805) Great joy now burst forth at the court in Karadigan, and all of it was in honor of Erec and his lady. Where else could there be greater merriment than that which was continually pursued at Arthur's court? All those who were present there vied, as if in competition, to comport themselves in a manner that bespoke their bliss.

(1806–1837) The excellent Erec, in his most chivalrous way, then turned his thoughts to the indigence of his father-in-law and dispatched fine goods to his house by messenger (it was King Arthur who conferred them upon him). Two heavily laden pack mules bore silver and gold (for Erec was most fond of this man's daughter), such that he might clothe himself splendidly and make full preparations to travel to the land of Erec's father, which was called Destregales. Through his messenger Erec asked his father, King Lac, to place at his aged father-in-law's disposal two castles—castles which he should appropriate to him in his land, such that they might become the property of his father-in-law. Erec designated them by name: Montrevel and Roadan. All of this was carried out. As soon as Erec had acquired these castles for him, the noble man was compensated for all that had ever troubled him. Koralus was relieved of all his want and was made so wealthy that he could, with these two fortresses, live in a splendid fashion, as befitted his noble birth.

III
THE WEDDING FESTIVAL

(1838–1886) Let us now return to the path upon which the story first embarked. After Erec had come to court, and after King Arthur had claimed his prize, Lady Enite—who sat there like an angel, possessing both beauty and goodness—awakened in Erec's heart the deepest yearning for her. Erec thought the days too lengthy for him to wait any longer than till the coming night to enjoy Enite's love. She, too, was of a similar, though secret will towards Erec, so that, if no one had been there to see it, the sweet pleasures of love would have likely been pursued. And I wish to report to you in truth that the fruits of love were in evidence there, for Love held dominion over them and caused them great suffering.[1] As each of them gazed upon the other, they felt no less wretched than the hawk which, beset by hunger, catches a chance glimpse of his meal. And once he is shown this, then whatever he cannot have of it must cause him to fare worse than if he had never seen it at all. To this same degree and yet even more did the waiting thus afflict Erec and Enite. Each was thinking: "Indeed, I shall never be happy unless I lie together with you for two nights or for three!" They desired a different kind of love (this is as it ought to be for them) than when an unattended child yearns for its mother, who has accustomed it to kindness by speaking lovingly and by reaching out to protect it from harm. It was no small desire which they felt for that which they later were to obtain.

(1887–1901) Now came the time for their marriage, which gladdened the hearts of Erec and Enite. The upright King Arthur would have it no other way but that Erec's wedding should take place at his court, for the delight of all his land. To all realms within his reach he immediately sent out letters and messages that the princes should come to his festival, as well as all who might hear word of it, from all far-off lands. The wedding was set for the week of Pentecost.[2]

(1902–1940) Now I shall name for you all the counts as well as the host of princes who attended the festival, at which Erec took Lady Enite in marriage. Powerful guests were they: Count Brandes of Doleceste (he brought along five hundred comrades in his party, and they were outfitted in a praiseworthy fashion, each attired just as was the Count), and Count Margon, born of Glufion, the lords of Mount Alte (which is in the vicinity of Britain), and Count Libers of Treverin with a hundred of his comrades, the mighty Count Gundregoas, and Sir Maheloas, called the one from the Glass Island. Such was this man's realm that in all truth it was never afflicted with stormy weather. Moreover, great tranquility held sway in that land, for never had a dragon[3] been spotted there. And we know for a fact that they had neither cold nor heat in that place. Gresmurs Fine Posterne was also a welcome guest, as was his brother who was called Gimoers and who held the island of Avalon[4] as his realm. Gimoers was blessed in no small degree by good fortune, for his beloved was a fay, whose name was Marguel. Davit of Luntaguel likewise came. And Duke Guelguezins arrived with a magnificent retinue; his realm was called the High Forest. The dukes and counts, each and every one, I have now enumerated for you.

(1941–1977) Hear now the catalogue of kings. There were ten of them in number, five youthful kings and five aged, each powerful and wealthy. They had in knightly fashion formed two companies, the young monarchs amongst themselves and the old kings together with the old. This division they continued to uphold.[5] As the story has it, the young kings were all equal as regarded their horses and their garb. Quite the same were the older kings, as very much befitted them. The apparel of those younger kings I shall now describe for you: velvet and gold-embroidered silk were sewn together in contrasting colors and decorated down the middle with spotted fur lining, all cut quite as they wished, neither too tightly nor too loosely. Black as ravens from top to bottom were the horses which the young kings rode; they were capable of maintaining nothing less than a trot. These kings rode on ahead into the land, and each of them bore on his arm a sparrow-hawk which had gone through four moultings.[6] Worthy of praise was this company, for each brought there in his retinue three hundred comrades most scrupulously attired. The first was

King Carniz (Schorces was the name of his land), then King Angwisiez of Scotland with his two sons (one was called Coin, and Goasilroet the other), and finally King Beals of Gomoret.

(1978–2028) This was the younger group of knights. Now the five powerful aged kings approached in grandeur. They too were equal both in horses and in attire. They had arrayed themselves in garments befitting their age: as was reported, it was the best of a fine, dark fabric to be found in all of England. Their raiment was trimmed in gray fur, such that none better could be had anywhere else, either in Russia or in Poland. Their attire was long and wide, with heavy spangles sewn on all sides, and properly crafted of finely wrought gold, all of it splendid, skillfully fashioned, and costly so as to evoke the highest praise. Their garb was trimmed at the bottom hem in broad pelts of sable. This sable was such that no man ever acquired any more excellent nor found any more costly sable in all of Conneland. This land is ruled over by the Sultan, for it is subject to his authority. Long and broad are the borders of Conne, and it is surrounded by two lands, one belonging to the Greeks and the other to the heathens.[7] The finest sable in all the world comes from there; such was the finery of those princes at the festival. Underneath they wore rich furs fully in keeping with their outer attire. Moreover, each man's hat was of most splendid sable. A fine sight they were on horseback, as I must tell you, for their steeds sparkled white as snow and showed all the attention of detail well befitting powerful patriarchs. Their bridles were likewise exquisite, glistening with fine gold. Wherever the blacksmith's art was needed, silver rivets were used to hold it fast, and the silver was then coated with lustrous gold. Their saddle straps were broad and richly embroidered belts.

(2029–2042) As this throng rode into the land of Britain, each of them had sitting on his arm a beautiful hawk six times moulted or even more. For a distance of three miles along the road good entertainment was to be had, for they found excellent falconing there. Both brook and swampy meadow were teeming with duck. In ample quantity they encountered everything that a hawk might make its prey. Moreover, never had they seen their gaming birds execute so many graceful flights.

(2043–2063) Duck and hen, heron and pheasant they watched rising before them in flight, the crane on the field and the wild goose. In addition, their squires had their saddles hung heavy with bustards that day,[8] for they caught as many of them as they stirred up from the nests. The fields were altogether plundered of game and fowl. Each time the hare was startled into flight, this was destined to be his final dash. As they rode on after the falconing and sparred with words in friendly fashion, there was a clear rivalry amongst them; each man claimed his hawk had flown better there, just as men would do even today.

(2064–2085) King Arthur now rode forth from his court together with all his host to meet them, and he welcomed that splendid company with a high measure of grandeur. Most pleased he was at their coming! The good knights were received in keeping with their title and were accorded hospitality even surpassing their standing. Now I shall tell you the names of the aged kings. There was King Jernis of Riel, upright and wise. Along with him he brought a praiseworthy legion, three hundred of his comrades. Listen as I recount their ages: their hair and their beards were quite the color of snow and had grown so long as to fall upon their belts. The very youngest of them, this is true, numbered forty and a hundred years.

(2086–2117) Hear now what others were present: Bilei, king of the dwarfs, and his brother, who was called Brians. Antipodes was their land. Never were two brothers born of one mother and yet more dissimilar than were these two, Brians and Bilei. The true story tells us that Brians was one and a half spans taller than anyone else alive at that time in all lands far and wide. We are told furthermore that there never was, nor is, a dwarf tinier than Bilei. Whatever he lacked in growth, that minute guest made up for altogether in courage. No man could be found, moreover, who was his equal in riches. In great splendor did he make the journey there, and his company was august. With him he had brought two of his peers, likewise lords over dwarf lands; they were called Grigoras and Glecidolan. With this I have recounted the names of all the kings. King Arthur now received these mighty guests in his court at Karadigan with all the grandeur at his command.

(2118–2141) The day had now arrived when Erec, fils du roi Lac, was to take Lady Enite's hand in wedlock. Wherefore should they tarry any further? For both were delighted at the thought. A bishop from Canterbury in England then bound them together in marriage, whereupon a festival began which merits all manner of praise. Indigence showed not its face at that gathering! So many fine knights were in attendance there that I care to tell you but little of their feasting, for they were more intent on other fame than for having indulged themselves in gluttony. Hence I wish to report to you only briefly of the feast. There were copious stores of everything from which both humans and horses are said to live. All this was offered to them in profusion, yet they accepted only as much as was fitting for men of valor.

(2142–2165) Jousting and dancing commenced there once the banquet was over, and it lasted until nightfall. Thus was all sorrow banished from sight there, and by the time they grew weary of their games, their joy had truly taken hold.[9] They then proceeded to the company of the ladies, who welcomed them most elegantly. The hospitality was excellent, and their spirits were further gladdened by the beautifully sweet music of stringed instruments, as well as by many other diversions: story-telling and singing and swift footraces.[10] An abundance of all skills was to be found there, as was mastery in all vocations. The very finest minstrels in all the world—men called masters in their trade—three thousand of them were in attendance there, and even more. Never did greater acclaim resound, ever before or ever since, than at that very festival.

(2166–2195) There was one trait of which they failed to rid those who came there in search of payment for their songs of praise:[11] for itinerant people always behave in such a manner that, when much is bestowed upon one of them, but nothing upon the next, this man becomes jealous and invokes curses on the festival. There was, however, no such quarreling at this festival, for they were all made rich in equal measure. Great was the generosity practiced there. Many a man who never before possessed half a pound's worth was given thirty marks of gold there. In such a manner were they all rewarded, with gifts in such quantity as will probably never occur again. Both horses and clothing they gave to the needy, to whom no one had ever before ministered. Thus it was well prevented that any man present should feel jealous of another man's possessions, for they all were favored with gifts in abundance. No one amongst them was demeaned; rather they were all indulged with gifts. Never did they once run short of hospitality, until the festival ended on the fourteenth day. Such was the marriage of Erec, fils du roi Lac.

(2196–2221) As the wedding festival drew to a close, a great many minstrels, much enriched and positive in their words of praise, departed there quite merrily. With one accord they all spoke well of that festival. They wished all manner of bliss upon Erec and Lady Enite, and such in fact now awaited them for many a long year. This wish was fulfilled on all accounts, for there never were two persons who loved one another more, until the very day when death disjoined them—death, which darkens all joy when it uncouples two lovers. The princes who had been in attendance there were likewise about to take their leave. But now the host extended that festival for an additional fourteen nights. It was for Erec's sake that King Arthur did this, for Erec was most dear to him, and on account of Lady Enite, too, did he continue the celebration. Their joy was just as abundant at this second festival as at the first; the merriment was not diminished, but rather heightened even more.

⊗ IV ⊗
THE TOURNAMENT

(2222–2247) Now a number of those present agreed that it would be ill fitting if so fine a man as Erec[1] should depart before a tournament took place, inasmuch as they had come to the land of Britain in search of entertainment. Gawein responded forthwith to this, saying that they ought indeed to find such pastime there. He arranged a tournament straightway against these four comrades whose names I shall relate to you: Entreferich and Tenebroc, Meliz and Meljadoc. The contest was set for three weeks from the following Monday. According to what the adventure tells us, the joust was to take place between Tarebron and Prurin; this was equidistant from both parties, half the distance for each. These four men then took their leave and departed in order to make preparations for the tournament, for it was none too early for them to do so.

(2248–2284) Erec, fils du roi Lac, pondered in his mind how he might arrive at that tournament in a manner befitting his name, for to that day he had never been engaged in jousting. Again and again he thought of how one often retains forever the reputation which one acquires in his early years as a young man. He feared a long period of being jeered, and he went to even greater lengths in settling upon the best way to acquit himself well at the tournament. A lack of wealth, however, stood in Erec's way and blocked him from fully carrying out his intentions with what material goods he had. Yet regardless of what he lacked (Erec's land was far away, which made him a guest and stranger[2] there), the lord King Arthur conferred upon him everything for which he asked. Erec was considerate, on the other hand, and careful that this did not become too burdensome for Arthur. Whenever possible, therefore, he bade the King to hold in check his generosity, as befitted Erec's sense of modesty. Marvelous deeds would Erec have performed if he could have had the full measure of what he desired! But Erec set his sights according to what was now his lot. His armor was not so excellent nor was his retinue so large as if he had been a man of wealth. He embarked upon his venture in keeping with his own capability.

(2285–2317) The youth Erec now arranged three similar shields and three matching bridles, each furnished with the same coat of arms. All three were alike save for their color. The first shield quite met his needs for head-on thrusts, with a sparkling mirror coating on the outside (its radiance gleamed from far, far away!), with a perfectly proportioned sleeve[3] of gold mounted on it, and crafted of gold on all the inside. The second was red in color. To it he ordered affixed a sleeve of sparkling silver, which was crafted with such skill that none finer could be fashioned on such short notice; the inside was similar to that of the first one. Quite fitting for a knight was this shield! The third one was the color of gold all over, both inside and out, and fastened to it was a sleeve of sable, which could not have been more exquisite; mounted over this shield in the middle was a raised metal fitting. The bands, which were of silver and which were cut neither too broad nor too narrow, were excellently positioned and ran the length and breadth of the shield. Fastened to that was the sleeve. On the inside surface was the likeness of a lady at the farthest point to the top. The shield strap was a belt not without embellishment, for it was studded with precious stones.

(2318–2357) On the inside the straps were all alike and were similarly crafted. As dexterously as he could, Erec now laid out three corresponding banners, each of which matched one of the shields. In addition, the youth Erec obtained—with the aid of Arthur, King of Britain—five horses from Spain, helmets from Poitiers, suits of armor from Schamliers, and leg armor from Glenis. That lord young and wise acquired for each horse ten lances from Lofanige (the shafts came from Etelburg) which were embellished for use by a knight. Beautifully adorned was Erec's helmet: an angel appeared from out of a crown crafted of gold. His tunic and the velvet blanket on his horse were alike and were both quite readily recognizable. They were of green velvet and costly silk sewn together alternately and beautifully adorned with trim. Fifteen squires he also acquired, all of them so adroit that no more excellent ones could be found in all the land of Britain. Each was wearing fine armor, with a coat of mail and a helmet of iron and a club bristling with spikes. A wagon bore Erec's lances to where the tournament was to take place, between Tarebron and Prurin, even before Erec himself was ready for the bout. As I have already told you, it was there[4] that they had decided to hold the tournament. A great host of excellent knights came to attend that joust.

(2358–2367) Just as Erec was about to ride off and take leave of Lady Enite, there occurred an exchange between those two lovers—an exchange which betokened their loyalty to one another. I shall tell you just what this was: Erec, that most faithful man, departed, taking with him Enite's heart, and his own heart remained behind sealed within the lady.

(2368–2377) On a Saturday night King Arthur arrived there in his full grandeur, bringing with him all his retinue. The finest amongst them were given lodging at the tournament site, as they were well accustomed. A knightly din soon filled the air. The lodgings were dotted everywhere with lanterns which, forsooth, burned throughout the night.

(2378–2390) Erec took up quarters at a spot far removed from all the others. No din at all did he raise, but instead he comported himself as an altogether miserly man, squandering nothing in revelry; he had no wish to appear like a fine knight, and with all good reason. A man with more experience than Erec in jousting might well have permitted himself some measure of celebrating, but Erec thought himself neither so perfect nor so famed for his valor that he ought to allow himself any carousal.

(2391–2403) Whichever of his comrades, in search of friendly company, chose to seek out Erec's lodgings, was greeted warmly there, better indeed than anywhere else. Though there were other things which Erec could not offer them, his disposition was such that all of them were pleased at every opportunity to praise him. All who saw him loved him. Erec's actions were those of a man indebted to Good Fortune. Otherwise he would not have been so highly extolled.

(2404–2412) This throng of knights conducted themselves with the usual measure of joy, as was the custom at tournaments. On the following day, a Sunday, they did what was fitting for them: they had their armor polished and provided with new laces. There was hardly a man amongst them who was not well qualified for the tournament.

(2413–2439) Just as the sun had barely reached its midpoint in the sky, Erec, fils du roi Lac, buckled on his armor ahead of all the others present, so that he might ride the initial joust and gain whatever prior start he could on the others. Now two comrades (fine knights they were!) had already arrived there at just that moment with the very same intention. And once they had spotted Erec, they galloped off towards him, most decisive in their resolve. The one launched into a joust against Erec, but he was thrust down from his horse. The second man, too, suffered this same fate. Erec cared not to take their horses, but rather continued to seek out more knightly endeavor. Victory fell to his lot (and this victory decorated him with high praise!), such that he fought five successive jousts as adroitly as any knight had ever fought. There were two qualities which had ordained Erec's success: good fortune and his own great excellence. Both of these were gifts from God.

(2440–2451) Erec had already fought this joust before anyone else had arrived on the field, for it was still early indeed. But now they began riding up from both sides onto the middle of the meadow. Much to Erec's advantage, they all noticed the horses still running about there—those horses whose riders Erec had unseated. "Indeed, my lord," they all exclaimed, "who could have set these horses free? Certainly it must have been Erec who did this!"

(2452–2475) Lavish praise was heaped upon Erec there. Now the preliminary jousts[5] started up straightway with great splendor in the middle of that meadow. Since each side was equally matched in strength, the knightly combat was most excellent. In quite a knightly fashion did they joust and attack and deal blows with their swords. For the whole duration of this tournament, Erec, fils du roi Lac, strained his every nerve. His attendants had not a moment to rest their eyes; Erec could be seen everywhere. Never did a knight perform more admirably in tournament, and all of them kept their gaze on him alone. He was ever the first knight at the tournament and ever the last to leave. Erec received the praise that evening on both sides, and in this they concurred without dissent.

(2476–2486) Erec continued to ride in joust until nightfall forced him to stop. As they returned to their lodgings, the only words anyone spoke were: "Erec, fils du roi Lac, is the most excellent man of his age ever to be seen in our land. He could not possibly acquit himself more admirably." On this they all agreed most emphatically, and what had happened to Erec that evening was the source of much praise for him.

(2487–2500) Erec roused himself at dawn the following day. His first venture was one fitting for a knight: he betook himself to church and gave himself over to the One Whose full measure of grace is never ending. Never was there a truly good man who took counsel from any other than from Him. For any man who is mindful of Him in all his doings can be certain of success. Erec entrusted to Him most fully his knightly fame, that He should deign to nourish it.

(2501–2515) Once the benediction was given, his shield and his horse were made ready. At this point Erec's boldness would seem to me praiseworthy and great, for he then rode out onto the field bare of armor and weapons and unaccompanied by any of his comrades, save that he took along five squires, each of whom bore three lances. These lances he used up in actual jousting, without wearing any armor and in such a way that no one from his party was aware of his deeds. After this beneficial maneuver, Erec stole back to his quarters, as though nothing had been afoot.

(2516–2537) Now early in the morning Lady Rumor had dispatched a page out onto the field to observe whatever honor and praise had fallen to Erec's lot. This page informed King Arthur eloquently of what had transpired. The King began to rebuke those whom he found still in bed and to chide them for their sleeping. "Why are you still lying about here?" he cried. "What man has ever achieved any fame through sleeping? Erec has already wielded his lance and sword with a passion this day. May God grant him good fortune as often as he desires it![6] I shall ever speak well of Erec, for I have seen in him manly deeds such as will always bring honor upon him." Thus did Erec win over more well-wishers, and thus was he held in yet higher esteem than before.

(2538–2559) Erec took but a brief respite. Yet as soon as he returned, they had all come outside, having just heard Mass, as should every man who would take part in a tournament. Very little did Erec take to eat or drink, for the thoughts which stayed fixed in his mind left him hardly any peace.[7] All of them then strapped on their armor with marvelous speed, and Erec followed suit. No sooner had they done so, than they saw the four comrades Entreferich, Tene-broc, Meliz, and Meljadoc all galloping across the field holding high their ban-ners. They were accompanied by a large retinue and by a host of bold knights, with many costly banners of various colors snapping in the air.

(2560–2588) Erec and Gawein and all the knights present there roused themselves at once. Loud battle cries could then be heard there in advance of the standards. Erec was the first to reach them, which was the proper endeavor for any knight. His tunic and his crown set him off exquisitely from all the others, such that no other knight present was recognizable from so far away. Sir Erec advanced far enough to the front so as to gain a position from which to begin the joust. A valiant man it was indeed who rode against him: the haughty Landro, who made all the others wait their turn to joust. In the past he had truly performed again and again with such excellence that he was acclaimed the finest knight in his land.[8] Erec, however, had the good fortune then of unseat-ing him from his horse. Erec taxed all his energies, for he used up twelve more lances amongst the crowds of knights. Hence he was forced to rely on his great proficiency to protect himself, such that he came away unharmed.

(2589–2629) Erec continued on until such time as they had hacked up his shield and broken it apart so badly with their sword-blows that it was worthless to him. With all possible caution he galloped off from the others at a firm gait and discarded his shield and horse. Then he mounted a fresh steed and armed himself with a better shield and a new banner. No sooner had he done this than he spotted his companions riding into the fracas. With the two crowds of knights now on the field, Erec could no longer engage in individual jousting. They were fiercely striking and lunging at one another there, and many a lance was being splintered, as the knights on both sides ran together headlong with such eager force! The roar of the splintering shafts there was unlike anything short of an entire forest being levelled by the power of the wind. Erec, fils du roi Lac, led them all, for he emptied many a man's saddle on that Monday. All of those horses he set free immediately, keeping not a one of them, for it was not for the sake of material gain that he had come there. All of his efforts he focused on winning praise. I wish to report to you in truth that Erec was hardly spared physical travail that day. Once the tournament had begun in earnest, Erec could be seen most often in the thick of all the fighting, where he had to dole out, as well as receive the blows. Valiantly was Erec seen to comport himself!

(2630–2662) After he had jousted in ample measure and wielded his sword so much that he began to tire, Erec slipped away from the others in order to rest. As soon as he had dismounted, a mercenary took his horse with a hearty word of thanks. For but a short time did Erec's respite last. Once he had unfastened his helmet, his squires were at hand and untied his helmet cap, that he might cool his brow. Erec had no opportunity for this, however, for he perceived his men retreating in flight, albeit only slowly. As it was, they were losing ground inch by inch, and they appeared to Erec on the brink of defeat. So hurriedly did he race to his horse that he left behind his helmet. Bareheaded he mounted the horse, grabbing at random both his shield and lance. Wasting not a moment more, he came riding back to them splendorously, blazoning forth his banner. Had he not come forthwith to the aid of his men, they would have had to endure calamity and defeat. This was quite evident from the retreat upon which they had all embarked.

(2663–2690) Of all the company none had held firm to defend himself, save for these three: Sir Gawein, that noble man who was never blackened by dishonor and who was possessed of all good qualities; the son of Duke Gilules stood alongside Gawein, as did Segremors. These three unflinchingly held their ground against the opponents. They did so that day—this you ought to know— in a fashion unsurpassed by any three knights ever before or since, for no one could move them from the spot, either by thrust or by dint of sword. Yet they would of needs have been captured, and this would have come about because they were badly outnumbered (this is the highest power in all things, a power against which no man can fight), save for the fact that Erec, fils du roi Lac, came riding majestically to their aid—as was fitting for friends in distress—and with a roar as if of the wind itself. So great was his valor that before long he had put all the opponents to flight. Nonetheless he had to subject his hands to a fiercely toilsome task, without which this never would have happened.

(2691–2704) Once his men had seen this, they now returned forthwith. Boidurant then took up the joust against Erec, who unhorsed that fine knight with his lance. High acclaim did Erec win that day! He vanquished the enemy then and there, advancing singlehandedly and in but a short time a good three parts of a mile.[9] His fellow knights came up in full force to assist him, and encountering no resistance, they pushed the opponents back all the way to their abatis.[10] Erec then relinquished his third horse.

(2705–2719) His knights had attained a most excellent victory, none of which would have been possible save for Erec. Many a man profitted and gained much from him there that day. Great indeed were their winnings! They then gave thanks to Erec for this, and it became all the more proper for them to herald his good name. His greatest feat, they thought, was that despite the vulnerability of his bare head, he had not flinched from riding into the fray with pomp nor from setting the enemy to flight with such boldness.

(2720–2751) Gawein had performed feats of excellence there that day, as he had done elsewhere and as was his wont. They say that his custom was to act so as never to be seen doing anything pertaining to the practice of knighthood without always gaining the reputation of having been the best. Hence his praise remains constant to this very day. His spirit was of a most knightly bent; nothing save goodness was to be seen in him. He was powerful and noble enough indeed, and his heart bore jealousy towards no one. Gawein was loyal and unregrettingly generous, steadfast and well bred, his words were spoken without deceit, and he was strong, handsome and valiant. He was blessed with the full measure of all virtues. A happy man he was, and of fine breeding. Perfection had wrought Gawein in such a way, as we have in truth heard tell, that never did another man so perfect come to King Arthur's court. How well deserving he was of his membership in Arthur's company! For he strove hard in pursuit of esteem. Valor in prodigious measure did he display that day. Save for Erec, fils du roi Lac, no man gained more there, for Gawein acquired both possessions and fame.

(2752–2763) Gawein captured two knights that day: the one was called Ginses, the other Gaudin of Montein. These men were Gawein's prisoners. Yet to Erec, fils du roi Lac, I shall concede the advantage for that one day (more than that I dare not venture!), for it is said that Gawein's equal was never seen in the land of Britain. If such a man ever did come there, then it was surely Erec himself. All his many virtues gave evidence of this.

(2764–2779) After their enemy had been driven back to the abatis, as I have reported, Erec made inquiries as to whether any man wished to come forth and continue to joust for the praise of his lady-love. A knight then spoke up anon—Roiderodes was his name—and said that he desired to do joust, provided it were done peacefully. Erec was most pleased at this and pledged to him a peaceful bout.[11] He then rode onto the field towards this knight, for he was most fearless in his valor. This he had proven again and again.

(2780–2807) Both men were burning to combat one another. Each of them used up twelve lances there without once missing the mark. Thereafter the virtuous Erec dismounted at once and relinquished his steed. He then clambered onto his fifth horse, which was being kept ready for him. His mind was occupied with one constant thought, which he proceeded to implement. Wishing to keep them waiting no longer, he bade them all move aside. The lance he locked in place under his arm. It was firm determination which brought the two men thundering together. Erec now buffeted the knight such that he felt it in the four nails near his hand.[12] So ferociously did Erec batter him that the man's harness tore apart. The saddle belt and the upper strap burst as though they were all a rotted nothing. Roiderodes was left with but a meager remnant: the reins, now ripped apart, still hung in his hands. Now defeated, he tumbled a good three shafts' lengths from his horse. Erec, on the other hand, remained in the saddle, and this brought him great praise, for the victory added to his fame. With this, there was nothing remaining to be done.

(2808–2825) The tournament was now finished. Untainted by shame, the company of knights departed. Erec, that virtuous man, was praised in the fullest measure. He had reaped the glory there, so fully that they likened his wisdom to that of Solomon and his beauty to that of Absalom, while likewise seeing in him an equal in strength to Samson. His munificence they thought so great as to place him on an equal footing with no lesser a man than the generous Alexander. So hacked apart was Erec's shield, so splintered by lances, that a man's fist would have fit through the holes. Thus did Erec earn his fame.

(2826–2851) When the word spread and Lady Enite heard tell of such great and heroic deeds by her consort Erec, she was filled with both joy and sorrow at his valor. It pleased her that they spoke so well of Erec, yet it distressed her to know that her husband was of such a mind that, without God's merciful protection, she feared she would not have him for long. For Erec was to risk his life often for the sake of glory, and he never flinched from danger, whereas a coward would be unconcerned about whether his reputation were good or bad. Yet once given the choice, Enite had been quick in her own mind to decide that she would prefer a hero as her husband rather than a worthless coward. Her lament was but scant, and she was both proud and happy at Erec's valor.

(2852–2869) After the conclusion of the tournament, King Arthur rode off to Karadigan with all his following. Each knight was then welcomed joyfully by his lady-love. Lady Enite likewise greeted Erec. The two of them remained there at the court but a short time, for Erec requested leave of King Arthur at once, in order to ride home to court in his father's land, which was called Destregales. With good reason Erec thought it high time for this, for he had not been there since he was a little child. What better time could there have been for his return?

⊕ V ⊕

HONOR LOST

(2870–2903) Once having set his mind upon returning home, Erec took aside sixty of his comrades and outfitted them in attire to match his own, making certain that they were all well equipped. That excellent man then took them along as comrades in his retinue. Thereupon Erec sent a messenger on ahead to his homeland to inform his father of his coming. The messenger ran off forthwith toward Karnant (this was the name of their capital city) and, finding the King there, delivered to him at once the message from his son. For this the messenger was richly rewarded,[1] for King Lac had never seen a more joyous day than this, when he heard the tidings that his dear son was coming to his court. King Lac was jubilant and pleased. Without delay he then sent for both his kinsmen and his vassals, five hundred of whom he assembled, and rode out ahead for three days to meet Erec. According to what the adventure says, all of them together received Erec and his wife in a most cordial fashion. No woman could ever be rendered a finer welcome than was Enite as they received her.

(2904–2923) The aged King Lac rejoiced greatly, for the two of them—Erec along with Lady Enite—were a fine sight for his eyes. Regardless of which direction his glance fell, he was gladdened, for both of them were well able to lift his spirits. His son he held most dear, as every father should with a child whose beauty has blossomed and who is so highly esteemed. And yet he was even more partial to Lady Enite. Then he gave them full proof of his favor: accompanying them to his home in Karnant, he turned over his land into both their hands, such that Erec was to be king, and Enite queen. He bade them both assume the reins of power.

(2924–2953) Erec was upright and good and, up until such time as he took a wife and returned to his homeland, his mind had been bent on knightly deeds. Now that he was come home, however, he turned all his arts towards his love of Lady Enite. He thought of nothing else save how he might avoid exertion in all that he did. Erec altered the way in which he lived: he spent his days as though he had never been a bold hero. Every morning he lay in bed to make love with his wife, until such time as the bells rang for Mass. Then they both hurriedly arose together and walked hand in hand to the chapel, where they tarried only as long as it took to sing the Mass. This was the extent of Erec's exertion. Their breakfast then awaited them; as soon as the tables were removed, Erec fled from the others to take his wife to bed. There began, once more, their love-making. Erec never left the bedchamber again before going to dine in the evening.

(2954–2965) Although Erec, fils du roi Lac, became neglectful of his knightly duties, he did nonetheless exercise the good custom (this he observed faultlessly, though he himself sought out no tournaments) of seeing to it that all his comrades were able to ride out on their own fully outfitted and equipped. He ordered that they be provided for just as though he himself were accompanying them. For this practice I offer Erec my praise.

(2966–2998) Because of his wife, Erec became accustomed to great complacency. He was so deeply in love with her that for the sake of her alone he neglected all pursuit of honor, until finally he lay about in such complete inactivity[2] that no one was able to hold him in high regard any longer. Thus the knights and men at the court began—and with good reason—to languish with boredom. Those people who had previously been filled with gladness were now drooped with deep gloom there, and by and by they abandoned the court. For not a one of them doubted that Erec had met with his downfall. This was the sort of praise which Erec had acquired. A change came over him. The kind words which they had once spoken of him now turned to disgrace in the eyes of those who knew him. All the world reviled him, and his court became devoid of all joy and stood in disrepute. No longer could men come from foreign lands seeking joy at Erec's court. Hence those who numbered among his followers and who had wished him all happiness began to invoke curses, saying with one tongue: "Woe be to the hour when we set eyes upon my lady the Queen! It is for this that our lord is going to ruin."

(2999–3012) Such talk became so prevalent that it finally reached the lady's ears. Hearing these bitter words of condemnation, Enite was overcome with heartache, for she was upright and good of character. She pondered all sorts of means whereby she could reverse such widespread disaffection. She did not fail to recognize that the fault lay with her, yet this distress she bore in a fashion most befitting a woman. She dared not reveal her sorrow to Erec, for she feared she might thereby lose him.

(3013–3033) Now it came about one day at noontime that Erec lay in her arms, as was their wont. As was meet and right, the sunshine was to minister to them, for it shone through a window pane onto the two lovers and had filled the chamber with enough light that they were able to see one another. Enite's thoughts turned to the curses which had been heaped upon her. Quite hastily she moved away from Erec's embrace. Thinking him asleep, she sighed deeply and set her glance keenly upon him. "Woe to you, most wretched man!" she spoke, "and woe to me, miserable woman that I am, for that I should hear such manifold aspersions cast upon me!" Erec heard these words quite clearly.

(3034–3049) As soon as she had fallen silent, Erec spoke: "Tell me, Lady Enite, what are the sorrows which you secretly lament here?" Enite then tried to deny it all. "Cease this talk," said Erec, "and take full note of my desire to have an answer. In truth, you have no choice but to tell me of what I heard you lamenting just now, and which you have been keeping from me in this manner." Enite feared that he would accuse her of other misdeeds, and she told him all, in the hope[3] that he would promise to relinquish the matter without ill-feelings.

(3050–3092) As soon as Erec had heard the full story, he said: "Enough of this." He instructed her straightway to get up, that she might dress herself well and put on the very finest clothes she had. Explaining that he wished to go riding for diversion, he told his squires to have his steed made ready, as well as Lady Enite's horse. At this they all hastened to do his bidding. Erec then secretly armed himself, concealing his armor beneath his clothing. The helmet he strapped on over his bare head. He took great pains to keep secret his intentions, and he employed the cunning of a clever man. "My helmet is not quite right," he said, "it is good that I have noticed this, for had I had need of it, I would have been quite entirely lost. I shall tell you what is wrong with it: it needs to be outfitted with better straps." Now there was not a man amongst them, however, who was able to understand what Erec really had in mind. Taking down both shield and spear from the wall, he let out a battle cry, as though preparing to ride off into the joust. All the host of knights and men wished to accompany their lord, but he bade them remain there. Erec sent word at once to the kitchen that the cooks be instructed to have food awaiting them as soon as they should return.

⚅ VI ⚅
FOREST ROBBERS

(3093–3105) After giving these instructions, Erec set out and commanded his wife, the lovely Lady Enite, to ride on ahead of him at the risk of nothing less than her very life. He forbade her then and there to open her mouth and speak at all during the journey, regardless of what she might hear or see. Enite had no choice but to promise to follow this strange and dismal regimen, for she was fearful of Erec's threats.

(3106–3124) They now both rode out across a broad moorland devoid of all woods,[1] until the daylight faded. As night began to fall, the moon shone majestically. The good knight Erec had ridden out in the hope of finding adventure. The trail now led them into a mighty forest, which was under the rule of three bandits. In truth, any man riding in their direction in those days—any man with whom they could have done battle—would have found the road barricaded by these robbers, who for the sake of that man's possessions would then strip him of his honor and his life. The woman Enite was the first to espy these men, for she was riding far out ahead of Erec.

(3125–3144) This was the first ordeal which befell Enite during that journey, for she could see from their appearance that they were robbers. She tried to signal this to Erec with gestures, but he failed to understand, and moreover he had not yet seen the men himself. For this Erec well nigh came to suffer harm. Enite was overcome by both sadness and misery at this, since she saw danger approaching, such that she feared losing the very dearest man a woman ever had. For Erec was in great peril. What could ever approach the devastating woe which Enite, faithful woman that she was, suffered in order to please her husband?

(3145–3166) Riding along uncertain as to whether she dared tell Erec or whether she ought to remain silent, Enite said to herself: "Almighty and benevolent God, of your mercy I seek counsel. You alone know of my dilemma. Manifold are my cares, for I am faced so soon with a brutal choice, which must be made all too hastily. I cannot tell what is most advantageous for me to do. What shall become of me, wretched woman that I am? For regardless which course of action I choose, I stand only to lose. If I warn my dear husband, I shall suffer harm, for he shall take my life. On the other hand, if I fail to alert him, it will mean death for my beloved. Indeed, a woman's heart is too weak in such a crisis."

(3167–3179) At this moment, however, her thoughts were buoyed by courage. "It is better that my life be lost—I am a woman so unworthy of any lament—than the life of so eminent a man, for many others would incur loss by his death. Noble and powerful is Erec; I, however, am not as worthy as he. I am sooner willing to die for him than to see him perish. Let my fate be determined in accordance with God's will. My beloved shall not lose his life this way, not as long as I am able to prevent it."

(3180–3189) With trepidation she turned around to face Erec, and spoke: "Look up, my dear lord! With your permission, I wish in all faithfulness to tell you this, for I cannot keep silent about something which might injure you: there are knights closeby who will, if they can, bring harm to you unless our Lord protects you." At this Erec prepared to defend himself.

(3190–3215) One of the robbers, who had been the first to descry Erec and Enite, then said: "I have good news to tell you, which can be a boon to us. I see a man riding yonder accompanied, insofar as I can tell at this distance, by a woman. From their demeanor it is easy to see that they are wealthy, for their attire is splendid. This marks the end of our poverty! I fancy they have great riches with them. Let me remind you, my lords, to show your faithfulness to the covenant which we have made amongst ourselves: you must leave me the choice of the booty here, and you must both agree to permit me the first joust against this knight, before either of you. For I was the first to espy these two. If I shall slay him, then I wish to take nothing save his wife. Of his possessions there is nothing else which I desire." The others then granted him this honor."

(3216–3234) With that, the bandit lifted his shield up to his chin and put the spurs to his horse as Erec approached. "My lord," he cried, "you have lost both your life and all you own!" With fierce resolve Erec offered him no reply, but felled him from his horse, killing him. The man's comrade attempted to avenge him, and was dealt a similar fate. Unprotected were this man's legs and arms, a fact which helped Erec to the victory. As is the way with robbers, both these men were crudely armed—this was much to Erec's advantage—for each of them had only iron headgear with a coat of mail. In but a short time thereafter, Erec had thrust them all to the ground alongside one another.

(3235–3258) After Erec's excellence had earned him so just a victory, he then addressed Lady Enite: "What have you to say for yourself, strange woman? Indeed, I have forbidden you, at risk of your life, to utter a single word. Who bade you break that oath? Everything that I have heard tell about women I have, in truth, seen fully confirmed here: to this day they have always been so attracted to precisely that thing which is emphatically forbidden to them, that they could not help but try it. It is utterly useless to enjoin you to avoid a thing, for it then entices you such that you cannot abstain from it. For this you shall suffer shame. Of all the unforbidden things that a woman would never do, there is not a one that she will leave undone as soon as it is prohibited. At this point she can no longer resist it."

(3259–3290) "My lord," she replied, "I would never have spoken up save to safeguard your life. It was only out of faithfulness that I called out. If you now wish me to rue this,[2] then for the sake of your honor forgive me. It shall never happen again." "My lady," he answered, "so be it. I am willing to leave the matter unavenged. If ever it happens again, however, I shall not tolerate it. And yet, you shall still not benefit from your exploits. I shall have some measure of revenge for myself. For you shall not extricate yourself from the task of giving the horses full and proper care. I will not do without your services as my squire on this journey." "My lord, this shall all be done," spoke the most excellent Enite, for such was no burden to her. Quite in a womanly fashion she then endured both this labor, in which she had never been trained, as well as all the heartache which beset her. She set about caring for the horses and, taking the reins into her hand, she rode out ahead onto the trail—all of this at Erec's command. From then on she tended the horses as well as any lady can. There was no more that she could do than that.

(3291–3309) They both had then ridden but a short while, no more than three miles, when once again Enite was beset with worry, for she espied five robbers lying in wait ahead. It is said that these men belonged to a band, and that they shared their booty with the others, whom Erec had slain. Both groups maintained contact with one another. These five men, together with the three of whom I have already told you, held sway in that forest and lurked along the path to ambush anyone who eluded the first group.

(3310–3347) As you have already heard tell, Erec had made his way past the first three robbers in an honorable fashion. The one bandit, who was keeping watch at some distance from the others, was pleased to see Erec approach, once he came into view. "Rejoice!" he cried to his cohorts. "We shall all be made rich! I descry people on horseback against whom we can easily hold our own. As far as I can see, there is only one man. He has in his company a noble woman, who appears to be in a state of woe. She is leading three horses by their reins and unless I am mistaken, she was not born for this vocation. I am curious as to where he obtained so unusual a squire. She ought to be taken from him; that would be just. So far as I can discern at this distance, she is fairer than any other woman I have ever seen. My lords, you must allow me to have her, for I was the first to spot her." They all then agreed that he had a rightful claim to Enite. "Listen," spoke his comrade, "to what I wish to have of this plunder: the knight's suit of armor, nothing more and nothing less." The others then divided the five horses amongst themselves. This was churlish of them however, for the armor was rightfully in the service of Erec, that fine knight, who knew how to make good use of it. What is more, these men were never to obtain what they had divided up.

(3348–3385) Erec still knew nothing of what was transpiring. Once having espied Erec, one of the robbers now readied himself for the attack. Lady Enite was again beset with most distressing gloom. "If I warn my husband," she thought, "then I shall be breaking his commandment anew. Neither his sense of honor nor God Himself will deter him from killing me. O woe, a wretched woman am I! I should prefer to die than to face this dilemma, and I would be far better off if I were dead! I shall be plunged into grief if I am to witness the slaying of this man, who has lifted me out of great poverty and made me mistress over vast wealth. All of this has brought me high esteem, and I now bear the title of a powerful queen. For if he perishes, my soul shall perforce be blighted by faithlessness and shall rightfully die along with my body. God counsel me—poor woman that I am—as to what I ought to do in order to avoid going astray! I fancy I ought to hold my tongue. No, in truth, I must tell him! Regardless of what tribulation it may bring down upon me, I shall venture it, just as before." Enite looked back at once and called to Erec with trepidation: "Listen to me, my lord, for God's sake: be on guard or else you shall be killed! I have spotted five men who would slay you." No sooner had she spoken these words than Erec prepared to defend himself.

(3386–3399) One of the robbers had left the others and had ridden on ahead in order to engage in joust against Erec; but much to his detriment, for Erec, fils du roi Lac, dashed him to the ground, such that he lay dead beneath his horse. Still, there were four of them left. With dispatch Erec thrust another of them down dead from his horse, while splintering his own lance in the process. Then he put his sword to work. The battle lasted for but a short time, for Erec went on to slay the three remaining thieves alongside their companions.

(3400-3424) Once Erec had singlehandedly won his fifth victory and was about to ride on, he spoke to Lady Enite: "Tell me, most ill-bred woman, why have you once again broken your oath? Because I tolerated this the first time, you felt dissatisfied not doing it once more. And if a man could gain any esteem by doing battle with a woman, then you should not be spared my taking your life here and now." "Please, my lord," the woman replied, "absolve me of punishment, for I have acted only out of loyalty. Regardless of what you may do to me now, I can more readily suffer your anger than can I watch you lose your life. And had I hesitated at all, my lord, you would have been slain. I am gladly willing to keep silent from this moment on. Grant me your forgiveness now, for God's sake. If ever again I breach your commandment, then take your revenge at once."

(3425-3439) "My lady," said Erec, "let me assure you that you shall gain nothing but hardship from all your disobedience. You shall not remain free of my revenge. You shall have to endure what I impose upon you: I wish to keep you as my servant for the duration of this journey. Now take the horses into your care and tend them carefully so as not to bring down my punishment upon you. And if one of them is lost, then you must bear my anger, which, if you had your wits about you, you would certainly wish to forgo!"

(3440-3471) Lady Enite then took the horses. There had been three of them before; now there were eight in all. She led them as best she could, but she was hardly adept at this. Though such a task was quite at odds with a woman's usual practice, as well as with Enite's own birthright, she endured it serenely and without discontent. Such was the teaching of Enite's goodness. Great woe did the lady suffer, but in her heart she turned her sorrow into gladness, as her humility instructed her to do. If anyone wishes to have things put into perspective, four servants would have their hands quite full if they were to lead and care for eight horses properly, whereas Enite had to make the journey single-handedly with just as many horses in her care. Her journey would have been distressing, save that Fortuna[3] attended my lady and God's courtliness hovered over her and prevented her suffering any great burden from the horses. Against any such hardship the lady was well protected. For the sake of such an attendant as Enite, moreover, the horses willingly and rightfully had to abandon their boisterous tugging and fidgeting, and march along gently.

⊕ VII ⊕
THE TREACHEROUS COUNT

(3472-3489) Soon thereafter they began riding out of the forest at a fast clip. The sun lifted its orb most radiantly into the sky, and as the night slipped away, Erec directed his glance straight ahead to where the path pointed him to a nearby castle, in which resided the lord of this land, a powerful count. Now Erec and Enite had ridden all night without food and were both beset with gloom. The sight of this castle raised their spirits, for they had in mind to spend the day resting there in a marketplace which stood at the foot of the castle. They now quickened their pace toward this market.

(3490-3498) Along the road Erec and Enite encountered a squire, who had in his care boiled hams and bread wrapped and carefully preserved, as he had been instructed, in a cloth of white linen. In his hand he held a tankard of wine. I was not told to whom all of this was being sent.

(3499—3514) As this squire approached, he began to look closely at the care-worn Lady Enite. Greatly amazed was he at her circumstances. Enite greeted him most excellently as he rode up to her, and he bowed in return. His path took him onward, where Erec, unrecognizable beneath his helmet, greeted the man and wished him a good morning. The page could easily discern that Erec, who was riding in full battle gear, had suffered great affliction that night, and he was moved by their distress.

(3515–3540) "My lord," he spoke, "if you should not object, I would inquire of you as to your intentions. In all modesty do tell me this, for my question is only meant in good will. I perceive in you a stranger to these parts. I, however, have always dwelt in this land, and am presently in the service of the Count. It appears to me meet and right, and it is my earnest request, that you honor my lord by making your way to his castle and resting there in the wake of your ordeal. They all stand ready to attend to you there. Furthermore, I ask this of you, for the sake of God: in the event that you are beset at all by hunger (for you seem to have suffered great tribulation while on your journey), I have with me here hams and bread as well as excellent wine. Now find it in your grace to bid the lady stop and turn back, and both of you deign to take some food and drink at this place."

(3541–3555) Erec did just as the squire bade him. This gladdened the squire, and he rode on at a gallop toward Lady Enite to relieve her of the horses. Thereupon Enite returned to her husband's side. The squire hitched the horses together and doffed his cloak and left it there. Then, taking his hat in his hand, he went to find water. He brought Erec and Enite enough with which to wash their hands. He then spread out the linen cloths on the grass and placed onto them the food which he had with him: meat, bread and wine, all of which was in more than abundant supply.

(3556–3579) After they had both eaten in sufficient measure and were mounted once more upon their horses, Erec addressed the squire: "You shall rightfully receive some manner of reward, sir squire, for what you have done for us. You have indeed earned my affection. However, I have neither silver nor gold with which to reward you. Do what I bid you, my friend, and choose from amongst these horses the one which pleases you best. And be assured of this as well: if ever the day comes when I can accord you better treatment, you shall not find me lacking. Honor our request now, and choose a horse." This the squire then did most gladly. Erec would have given him all the horses, save that this would have softened Lady Enite's lot. It was only to cause her distress that he failed to do so.

(3580–3603) After taking the horse which suited him best of all, the squire thanked Erec profusely, saying: "Grant me, dear sir, this request, which, if fulfilled, will ensure that you have treated me well indeed. The burden of caring for these horses is inflicting a great ordeal upon the lady. Permit me to lead them. Such service I shall gladly perform." "You must refrain from this, sir squire," replied Erec. "Indeed, the lady is certainly not enduring this without good reason. She shall have to live with discomfort for now." "In that case," replied the squire, "I shall be on my way." "God reward you for your kindness and for what you have given us. May He guard over your honor, that you may live in happiness. Place yourself in God's hands, sir squire, and be off." The squire was pleased with his gift and spun the horse around to depart, his joy spurring him on to a gallop. Erec followed in the same direction, but at a sluggish pace.

(3604–3625) Now the lord of the land espied this same man, the squire, and recognized him from afar, for he had gone out and sat down before the castle gates. He was most amazed to see his squire returning so quickly, and he inquired as to whose horse it was that he was leading along in tow. The squire then informed him forthwith and in detail of all that had just transpired. "Look, my lord," he cried, "there they are, riding this way. I do not understand why you hesitate now and are not going out to the road to meet them. It is a mistake not to do so. Indeed, you can behold in this lady the most beautiful woman either of us has ever set eyes upon. You ought to offer her a cordial welcome." With that, the lord made his way to the road to receive Erec with a friendly greeting.

(3626–3643) As he saw them riding up, he walked forth to meet them, saying: "Welcome, my lord and my lady." He entreated them most earnestly to honor him by coming to his castle and staying there. "My lord, absolve us of this request," said Sir Erec, "our long journey has rendered us unfit for the court, and we are heavy with fatigue. Permit us to bow in thanks for your graciousness and to refuse this in all faithfulness. Allow us now to be on our way, so that we may find a place to rest." Thereupon they persisted in asking leave of him, until finally he had to grant their request.

(3644–3667) Erec then had a squire show him the way to the finest inn nearby.[1] Once there, he proceeded to remove his armor. Lady Enite was greatly pleased to have a respite from tending the horses, which were then taken from her. Her feelings were not unlike those of a soul just freed by the Archangel Michael from the fires of hell after many long years of dwelling there.[2] Erec had a bath prepared, for he had become sweaty and grimy with rust from the burden of wearing armor during his journey. He then cleansed himself of this, and after he and his wife had bathed, a meal awaited them. Hearing word of this, Erec ordered the table made ready. He did not permit Lady Enite to dine together with him, for he was seated separately at this end, and she yonder at the far end of the table from Erec.

(3668–3693) Now treachery was beginning to get the upper hand in the mind of the Count, and he came to rue the fact that he had left Lady Enite and had not ordered her taken away from Erec. In his mind, smitten by the lady's beauty, he devised numerous ways of obtaining her. Deceit whispered into his ear and told him to go so far as to snatch her away from Erec. It was unjust indeed that he wished to seize the wife of the good knight Erec, who, as a stranger in the Count's land, was supposed to enjoy his protection against all harm. It was love which had planted these thoughts in the Count's mind. For we have heard tell of this Count that he was in fact both upright and good, and, up until that moment, well confirmed in his integrity. But love revealed perfidy to him and robbed him of his good senses.

(3694–3721) For even a man so clever that no one can capture him in any other way is quite often ensnared with the noose of love. The world is full of men who would never set foot on the ground of misdeed, if only love would not constrain them. And if love did not so ennoble the spirit, then we could all render ourselves no greater or wiser a service than by renouncing her altogether. No one, once seized by her power, has the strength to elude her grip.[3] Love, however, would never neglect to reward any man who knew how to nurture her properly and reliably, nor would she let him regret his travails—provided he kept better watch over his integrity than did the Count. Infidelity consorted with that man, for Lady Love had led him onto the path of falsehood, such that he became resolved to abduct the wife of the most upright Erec.

(3722–3751) Taking along four knights in his company, he arrived at the inn and found Erec and Enite at the table. The Count shed his cloak and, with a word of greeting, went and stood before them. Erec had no inkling that this man intended him any harm, as indeed he did. The Count was much astonished that they sat so far apart at the table and were not eating together. "If you would not object, my lord," he spoke deceitfully, "you ought to tell me what this all means. Is this lady your wife? She is winsome in appearance and is charming enough that it would be more fitting for her to sit together with you, rather than all the way over there. Why have you had her take a seat apart from you?" Erec's reply was this: "My lord, it is my desire that it be so." Whereupon the Count requested Erec's permission to sit with Enite during the remainder of the meal. "If that is what you wish," answered Erec, "I am happy to grant it."

(3752–3796) "I shall tell you, my lady," said the Count as he joined her, "why it is that I have come here to you: in part to turn things to your advantage and certainly to enhance your esteem. Never have I felt such pity for any man or any woman as I do for you in all your loveliness. Ever since I saw you this day suffering unbecoming woe, such as never was proper for any lady, my heart has been deeply touched and indeed is even now troubled more and more. It is not with ill design that I take issue with your great poverty; rather, it awakens pity in my heart. In truth, you ought well to be mistress over the Empire.[4] Who has handed you over, poor woman, to such a man, who is incapable and unable to extend rightful honor to you? He has you in his service as a squire! This man, your companion (may God strike him down!), is making every effort to inflict hardship upon you. Had God granted you to me, however, you would be in a position to enjoy esteem of a higher order. If you so wish, then all good things shall still fall to your lot. I shall tell you, my lady, what I have in mind, and if you are wise enough, then you will offer no resistance. For I wish to free you from all cares. I shall tell you of my situation: I am lord of this land, but I have still not found—never, so help me!—the proper woman to take as wife, though I have searched both far and wide. You, however, please me so greatly that I shall gladly make you mistress over this land. By accepting my offer you shall have changed your lot in life much to your advantage, and without a trace of shame."

(3797–3825) "May God grant you a wife," spoke the noble woman Enite, "who will more properly adorn both you and your land than would I. For it would not be long at all before you would of rights have to regret this scheme. Moreover, it would run counter to my own sense of loyalty. Once it became known and all the world heard of it, it would mean nothing short of scorn for you. Therefore, drop this matter, for God's sake, for you are deserving of better. I am not fit to be a countess, for I have neither the birthright nor the wealth.[5] Regardless of what my husband inflicts upon me, I shall rightfully tolerate it. I am at his command as his wife, his squire, or for whatever else he wishes me. My lord, what further words can I speak? For I would sooner choose to be burned alive here and now and have my ashes scattered to the winds than ever to do what you propose. My husband and I are from like circumstances: neither of us is wealthy and we are well suited for one another. May God grant him a long life for my sake!"

(3826–3837) Once the Count had heard this reply and had noted her resolve as well, he then spoke: "I shall tell you what I have in mind. Let your actions be guided by this. If you are unwilling to yield graciously to my request, then it shall be done against your will. Whatever resistance you might offer me here is insufficient. Let your husband go wherever he wishes. But you must remain here with me. Let nothing more be said."

(3838–3895) When Enite saw that he meant this in earnest and was speaking from his heart, she looked most kindly at him—deceitful man that he was!—and laughed with well-executed cunning. "I believe now that you are serious," she said. "My lord, be not angry, for there is no need of such. In truth, I was deluded into thinking that your words were only meant to mock me. For you men are both accustomed and ever willing to deceive us wretched women (I dare not say to lie to us!) by making many fine promises to us which you never intend to fulfill. Full many a time have I seen women incur great sorrow as a consequence of this. Had I not feared this, I would have responded more favorably. For I am indeed not so wholly devoid of my senses, my lord, that I would not act to change my disgrace into esteem and to lighten my heavy burden, if I were once given the opportunity. For my life is so terribly harsh, as you yourself have seen. Let me tell you just how it was that my husband first acquired me as his wife. He is not my equal. He stole me from my father, who is truly of noble and wealthy lineage. Often did he visit my father's court. In the usual manner of a child I used to run about here and there. One day he was playing with us children, and it became well apparent to him that children are easily deceived. With great cunning he lured me out through the castle gates. There he grabbed me suddenly and carried me off, and has held me thus ever since. He subjects me to many grievous conditions, for because of this he must avoid ever returning even to his own land. I, wretched woman, am accustomed to constant hardship and disgrace. I would gladly follow a better man, one who would free me from this with my honor still intact. Moreover, God would reward such a man for his aid.[6] I had thought that this scheme was merely mockery on your part. If you demonstrate to me with some degree of certainty that you are earnest, then I am ready to accede to your request."

(3896–3905) The Count was delighted at Enite's words. "You shall not be able to find any excuse to extract yourself from this," he replied laughingly, "for I am willing to swear my steadfastness to you." He raised his fingers, and the lady phrased an oath for him to repeat. Then, with both their hands raised, she likewise pledged her faithfulness to the Count, thus giving him a vague and dubious token of her obedience.[7]

(3906–3925) Once this vow was given, Enite said with cunning: "My lord, I shall now offer you some sound advice—from one friend to another, for there is no man of whom I think more highly than you—and I ask that you follow my counsel. Indeed, it shall cause you very little distress. Since you are resolved to carry me off, I advise you to wait until tomorrow morn. By doing so, you can take me and yet avoid a fight, as well as any danger. Come here while my husband is still in bed. For in this way he cannot harm you, and you will be spared any tribulation in carrying out your wish to possess me, since I shall steal his sword during the night.

(3926–3947) "I harbor a fondness for you now," she continued, "for you have thoroughly earned my affection, and I shall be vexed if you should suffer harm on my account. And indeed, this is precisely what shall have to happen, should you fail to do as I have spoken. For if you seize me on the spot, things are such between us that my husband will not willingly let me go. He has his sword with him, and I know full well that he can use it to inflict much harm." "Your advice is prudent," he replied, "and it pleases me such that I shall gladly follow it." By resorting to her shrewd womanly cunning, Enite set about defending both her honor and her husband's life. Lady Enite was a faithful wife. In this fashion she persuaded the Count to take his leave and depart from there, hoping for an uncertain reward, such as I have told you.

(3948–3953) After they had finished dining, Erec ordered beds brought into a chamber for both of them, but he had them placed at a distance from one another. He would not permit Enite to lie together with him, and with that, they went to bed.

(3954–3971) Erec and Enite lay there, apart from one another. It was indeed amazing that any grudge could have planted in Erec's mind the notion of avoiding so lovely a woman. Because of her faithfulness and her goodness, the lady's mind was greatly clouded by worry as to how she might inform Erec of the matter at hand. For he had forbidden her to open her mouth and speak (as I have already told you), regardless of what things she might hear. Yet Enite had not neglected to speak up, for by doing so she would have lost him. As a consequence he was renouncing her company out of anger, for he ate and slept apart from her.

(3972–3997) The good woman now thought to herself: "I have come to the point of certainly losing the very dearest man whom any woman ever had, if I fail to warn him. Furthermore, I know that I shall suffer for it if I break his commandment once more. Give me counsel now, o Lord and almighty God! Never have I had such need of this. I know full well that it means my death, for he has indulged me twice now. Yet what of it if I am slain and he takes my life? There shall still be many an excellent woman in this world. I, moreover, am not so terribly worthy of any lamentation. On the other hand, he, my dear lord, is noble and powerful. I am sooner willing to choose death than allow him to suffer harm." At the command of her loyalty Enite then went to Erec's bed and, kneeling before him, revealed to him this matter in its entirety. Fear drained all color from her complexion.

(3998–4027) After this was made known to him, Erec stood up at once and asked that the innkeeper be awakened. Erec then began making preparations to depart: he told the innkeeper's servants to have the horses made ready. This was quickly done. Thereupon Erec bade the innkeeper come to his chamber, addressing the man as he approached: "You have shown us fine and excellent hospitality here in your house, and I owe you payment for this. Listen and I shall tell you what you will receive. I have with me neither silver nor gold with which to pay you. Do as I bid you and take the seven horses as recompense from me." The innkeeper bowed deeply before Erec and was heartily pleased, quite in the manner of a man who stands only to reap advantage. To ensure Erec's good fortune, the innkeeper brought him straightway a dram to be quaffed in memory of St. Gertrude.[8] Thus did the stranger Erec ride off in the night and leave that land at once, together with his wife, who had deceived the Count and had hatched an untruth, though without incurring any sin.

(4028–4043) Before Erec had embarked upon his journey, the Count, that most faithless man, pondered the possibility that Erec might already have tried to take Enite off[9] by the time he was to come to her. He started out of his sleep as he lay there in bed, for he feared that this had happened, and in his delusion he fancied that he had missed the appointed time. "To arms!" he cried out in a thunderous voice, "we have overslept. Get up, my comrades, those who wish to aid me!" There were nineteen of them all in all, and he himself made them twenty in number.

(4044–4057) After he had assembled his men and arrived there at the inn, he kicked down the door after giving a discourteous greeting. This vexed the innkeeper, who was about to issue a cry for help. "Come now, you can clearly see that it is only my men and I," spoke the faithless Count. "Be not afraid, but tell me, what is the meaning of all these lights burning here?" These were lanterns that the excellent Erec had left behind upon departing.

(4058–4083) Of Erec's departure the Count still knew nothing. "Where are your guests sleeping?" "My lord, they have left." "No they have not!" replied the Count, shaking with anger. "I would be a fool to lie to you, my lord." "Forsooth, you are mocking me." "No, my lord, so help me God!" "Indeed, you are! Now show me to where they are." "Then order the house searched yourself from top to bottom." "In truth, I shall do just that." "And I shall gladly grant you permission to do so." "How much longer shall I have to interrogate you?" "See for yourself where they slept. Why should I disclaim them to you?" The Count then replied, ready to strike the man dead: "You are, I suspect, a decoy, set to lead me onto the wrong track." "My lord, they have ridden off, Christ knows it!" "Then it was your doing." "No, with your mercy, it was not." "Otherwise they would have waited till daybreak." "My lord, they just now left." "Then tell me, are they at all far from here?" "No, in truth they are not, my lord. They departed this very hour." "Whither have they gone?" "This I do not know."

(4084–4109) The Count's treachery sowed the seeds of great gloom in his heart. Furiously he cursed his having slept. "Honor was not intended to be my lot," he cried, "for I have let slip away the most beautiful woman I ever set eyes on, including all women I have ever known or not known—and all because I was intent upon my own comfort. Cursed be the hour that I fell asleep this night!" He then called for the horses. "Any man who arranges his affairs with nothing but his own contentment in mind, as I have done tonight," he said, "shall forfeit his esteem and find disgrace awaiting him. What man has ever attained anything worthwhile without enduring some discomfort? What has happened to me I have justly earned." The squires now came riding up with the horses, and they tarried there no longer. "Let us be off, you lords!" cried the Count. Because of their haste they had armed themselves with shields and lances, and nothing more.

(4110–4132) Daylight then began to break upon the landscape, enabling them to discern clearly the hoofprints and the trail, which they pursued with great dispatch. In the meantime Erec had already ridden a good three miles. It was only fear for his wife, and not at all alarm for his own safety, that made him race to depart that land. He knew full well that they were in pursuit of him. Once he had managed by his headlong dash to put enough distance between them such that there was occasion for words, he said: "Lady Enite, you have assumed too subborn a stance of defiance towards me. I am greatly vexed that you continue—and all the more persistently!—to do precisely that which I asked you to forgo, and which indeed I forbade you at the risk of your very life. Let me now tell you my resolve: I shall not tolerate this of you, and if you are not prepared to renounce such behavior, it shall in truth cost you your life!"

(4133–4138) "Forgive me, my lord," the woman replied, "you ought not to punish me for this. Indeed, had I not done so, you would have lost your life. For this reason it would have been wrong for me to refrain from what I did. From this moment on, however, I shall always guard against it."

(4139–4149) At this moment Enite heard them riding closer in their wrathful temper. Although the good woman had just then promised not to warn him, her vow remained irresolute, for she broke it right then and there, compelled to do so by the bond of loyalty. Their pursuers were at that moment still far distant. "My dear lord," she cried out, "a great company of men is fast upon your heels. They are pressing on in such haste, it is clear they intend to do you harm!"

(4150–4165) Now let no one pose the question: "How was it that the lady was better able both to hear and to see than was Erec?" I shall tell you why this was so: the lady was riding unarmed, whereas Erec was fully suited in armor, as is meet and right for any good knight. Hence his hearing and his vision were not as sharp from underneath his coat of iron as they would have been with less covering. Thus did he have need of warning, which was a boon to him more than once in fending off death. Though this was a source of anger for Erec, he would have lost his life on several occasions for lack of vigilance, save that the woman warned him.

(4166–4196) Enite had not yet finished telling him of this, when the Count rode up. And once he spotted Erec, his voice bellowed with hostility and with unbecoming anger—all of this in a most unchivalrous fashion: "Turn about, you common thief! What man should be content to see you drag about a noble and lovely woman in these lands in such a manner as to bring down disgrace upon us all? And be well assured that you shall even now give up your life to me. I would order you hanged on the spot, save that your knighthood exempts you from such punishment. You have this lady in your custody against the wishes of her loved ones. Forsooth, your riding off in the night was an evil ruse. From this it is quite evident that you stole her away from her father. How else would you have gotten your hands on her? Even a fool could readily tell by looking at this lady that you do not deserve her. If you wish me to spare your life, you good-for-nothing scoundrel, then let the woman go. I wish to return her to her loved ones. No longer shall she live in such degradation. Now let her go, and be off on your way at once!"

(4197–4204) "Your conduct towards me is a vile transgression against all courtliness," spoke Erec. "Who was it who instructed you to disparage any man bearing the title of knight? A vulgar court it was indeed at which you were schooled! And now you have reason for shame, for you have concocted a lie. I am more noble a man than you."

(4205–4214) The battle now commenced. Wasting no more time, they crashed together with fierceness. From this collision the faithless Count was rewarded for his deceitfulness: he was dealt a jab in his side which many times afterwards caused him pain, for beneath his shield he was bare of armor. What is more, one of his arms was also broken.[10]

(4215–4231) At the sight of Erec thrusting him from his horse, the Count's faithful men began to feel most severely troubled by his plight. They went and fell down over their lord, so that nothing more could harm him. Quite a number of them were present who wished to avenge him at once with their swords. Yet they endured but a short time, for Erec slew six of them—six who received their fill of dueling! All the rest were cowards and fled, unpursued by Erec.

With this, the battle was ended. Untouched by misfortune, Sir Erec embarked swiftly upon his way.

(4232–4242) "Benevolent Lord God," he prayed, "keep me in your protection and aid me in leaving this land without incurring any shame. If the inhabitants of the land hear word of what has happened, they shall all set out after me at once and shall slaughter me. Nor will it take long for that to happen." This notion of Erec's, however, was unfounded, for no one heard tell of what had transpired until after Erec had made his way out of the forest altogether. Such was a great salvation for him.

(4243–4257) This is why that tale remained untold: the knights who had escaped with their lives, and who remained there with their lord, not a one of them would leave him, and it was from them that the people would have heard the story. (The cowardly ones, who had fled and were ashamed of this, dared tell nothing until such time as Sir Erec was far gone from the land.) The knights then dressed the Count's wounds and transported him home on a litter with great lament, carrying with them all the dead as well. Thus was that man rewarded for his treachery.

(4258–4267) As soon as Erec had ridden off to a safe place where he no longer feared the Count, he reproached Lady Enite for disobeying his command so often. His ire grew vast and furious, and harsher than before. Thereupon Enite promised never to do this again, from that moment on. Yet she failed to fulfill her vow steadfastly.

⬙ VIII ⬙
GUIVREIZ LE PETIT

(4268–4279) Whatever dangers Erec had endured till now were but a minor bother—indeed mere child's play—alongside the distress of which I now wish to tell you, and which was yet to befall him. Both peril and tribulation fell to Erec's lot, nor was he spared suffering in great and sufficient measure. His path soon led him into an alien land, whose lord was unknown to Erec.

(4280–4298) Marvelous tales are told us of this man's valor. He was a very short man and—unless I have been told untruths concerning this—well nigh the equivalent of a dwarf, save that his arms and legs were immense in size. Moreover, he appeared powerful and stout enough indeed in his chest, wherein he bore a heart which beat with undivided courage. It was his heart which gave the little man his strength, for the heart determines everything. Take good note of this: if a man were to grow twelve fathoms tall,[1] yet if his heart were weak and born to cowardice, then that big oaf would be lost. Such was not the case, however, with the lord of that land.

(4299–4317) A large part of his tale we must pass over in silence. Much could be told of it, save that this story would then become too wordy. For that reason I wish to abridge his tale for you. This fine lord had good fortune and a noble disposition and had fearlessly acquired fame from his knightly enounters with many and many a man. Wherefore it is still said of him that, up until that day, his valor had never failed him. Whoever crossed his path with ill design, be he strong or weak, the little man always took the victory. Never was he caught napping when knightly deeds were being performed (nor was anyone better at it than he!), and he always sought out such pursuits in his day, as far and wide as his horse could carry him. [. . .][2]

(4318–4347) As Erec once more found himself faced with doing battle, he was again shown proof of Enite's loyalty. No sooner had she warned him than they saw the man approaching swiftly on horseback. He greeted Lady Enite, and upon coming into earshot of Erec, he then said: "Welcome, my lord! Whether you have come from near or far into these lands, it seems to me indisputable that you are a great warrior. This is clear to me on two counts: you have in your company, upon my word, the very fairest woman of whom I have ever heard tell. What father would ever give such a woman to a common man? In addition, you are wearing fine armor, quite in the proper manner of a good knight who wishes never to be caught defenseless, and who is out in search of adventure. If God wills it, then you shall find a good measure of adventure here. And if good fortune falls to your lot—this I wish to tell you in truth— then you can acquire fame here which will cause your name to be highly praised. Now defend yourself, sir knight, the time has come!"

(4348–4365) Wishing to make light of the little man's words, Erec answered him thus: "God forbid, o fine and upright knight, that you should ever violate your integrity so gravely. You would of needs come to rue this later. Forsooth, you have offered me your greeting. How would you ever rid yourself of the disgrace of turning right around and attacking me? You would be acting rashly, and you would fail to gain any praise for doing so. Leave me in peace, for God's sake, for I have done you no harm. I have journeyed here from distant lands and have endured such woe that every nerve in my heart counsels me to forgo doing battle."

(4366–4377) "He is a coward," thought the noble man, "for he complains of having to exert himself." Then he said to Erec: "It is superfluous to defend yourself by citing the fact that I offered my respects to you. This I have done for no other reason than in hopes of pursuing knightly exploits. Regardless of whatever else now happens to you at my hand, you may not question my integrity on that account, for my integrity I shall never breach. If you value your life, then defend yourself, for the sake of your lovely lady!"

(4378–4403) Once Erec had seen that a fight was imminent, he spun his horse around, as his courage instructed him to do. Two men, neither of whom ever had a drop of cowardice running in his veins, then bore down on one another. Strength and good fortune were the judges which had to decide the victory between those two. Their lances they thrust so hard at each other's shields that they shattered to bits. So violent did that joust become that the horses fell back on their haunches onto the ground. With this, they had no choice but to drop the reins and find another way to assail one another. Both men together dismounted in a frenzy and unsheathed their swords. Each of them was granted here in ample measure that which he had long requested of God: that He send him an opponent against whom he might truly test his strength.

(4404–4420) They now commenced to do battle in the manner of two fine knights. It was around mid-day that this bout began. Erec, fils du roi Lac, fearing both disgrace and death, held forth his shield and began defending himself through cunning and without dealing out blows with his own sword. This notion was alien to the other man, and he dashed Erec's shield right out of his hand, leaving behind only the strap. Because there was no one present out on the meadow to separate them, the man then struck Erec in his side and opened up a wound. At that, he fancied the stranger Erec to be a coward.

(4421–4431) The fair Lady Enite, moreover, was stricken with deep despair at the sight of blood pouring from Erec's side. "O woe, my dear lord!" the good Enite cried at the top of her voice, "if only it should be I instead of you! In truth, I fear I have lost you." "My lady, you are mistaken," spoke the undaunted Erec, "for I should lose even more by that than you!"

(4432–4459) Most excellently did Erec then confirm for her his words. No longer did he indulge his opponent: stepping forward slightly, he brought down such a blow onto his helmet that the little man fell wounded at Erec's feet. Erec, fils du roi Lac, well nigh committed a wrong, for he was about to slay the man. "No, good knight!" cried the little man, "for the sake of your goodness and for the sake of your beautiful wife, let me live, and do honor unto God by sparing my life. I shall gladly swear an oath of surrender to you. Accept me now as your vassal, in the knowledge that I have never before served any master. Save for the fact that your valor has earned you acclaim, I would sooner be prepared to die than to subject myself to anyone. But no man of nobility would ever find fault with you.³ Thus it makes no difference to me: regardless of who your father may be, your courage ennobles you such that I shall gladly take you as my master."

(4460–4477) Now this battle had lasted all that long summer day till three o'clock in the afternoon.⁴ Having thus emerged the victor, Erec was gracious enough to spare the dwarf's life. He then took him by the hand and pulled him up. Unfastening his helmet, Erec spoke: "I desire no further deference from you than that you tell me straightway your name, and without any sense of shame. At this time I wish nothing save to know who you are." "My lord," he answered, "that shall be done! I am willing to tell you that I am King of Ireland, and am called Guivreiz le Petit."

(4478–4505) Erec refused to take the dwarf as his vassal. Each of them began to lament the other's injury. Erec tore off a piece of his tunic at once to serve as a bandage. Where else could the little man have found at that time a bandage more indicative of Erec's friendly intentions? Guivreiz le Petit likewise took a bandage from his own tunic. They both then wrapped each other's wounds, which they had meted out with their own hands. This was indeed a gesture of friendship! Lady Enite helped with this in a manner befitting her customary kindness. The two men then joined hands—each was pleased with the other— and sat down on the grass, for they had great need of rest. The battle had made them very hot, and they were drenched with both blood and sweat. Lady Enite then went to join them. She was filled with joy intermingled with sorrow, just as I shall explain to you: on the one hand she was pleased at her husband's victory, but on the other hand she wept for his wound.

(4506–4534) The good Enite now wiped them clean of sweat and of blood with the hem of her sleeve. After exchanging words of friendship, the two lords sat on the meadow and refreshed themselves by cooling their brows. "Listen, my lord, to what I now wish to say," spoke the King to the stranger Erec. "Take it as harmless talk, and let it not be grievous to you. You have overcome me with your valor, such that I was willing to become your vassal; in that you have indeed succeeded. Your own excellence is now apparent, so that I would even more gladly be your subject if I could know—and if you would tell me— whether your lineage too is of equal lustre. If so, my own honor would be so much the greater. Despite what has happened to me at your hand (something to which I was never, up until this very day, forced to submit), nonetheless I have fared well and am willing to forgo all lament, as long as it was a noble man who has done it. If such is the case, then I am willing to be forever contented with my fate."

(4535–4579) This was Erec's reply: "I shall tell you the name of my family, which can be said, I think, to be of most noble birthright. My father is King Lac, and I am called Erec." At this the King was pleased. Once he had heard who the stranger was, he remained sitting but very briefly. Instead he jumped up with joy and fell at Erec's feet. "How gladly I shall remain faithful to you forever as your vassal," he spoke, "in whatever ways I am able to serve you. Your father is well known to me. Both I and all my land shall be at your command. Moreover, you must permit me the pleasure of rendering you constant faithfulness, unmarred by any regret, for as long as I shall live.[5] And grant me one favor, for which I exhort you most earnestly. Where else was greater loyalty ever beheld than between two friends who both have a firm trust in one another? In the name of such loyalty I beseech you, as a favor to me, to ride together with me to my castle and remain there until such time as you are rested. Let this transpire in the absence of any objections, for you shall be treating me well thereby, such that I can always repay you for it by my service." "I am willing to grant you this," answered Erec. "But you must not ask that I remain for so long a time. This you must concede without resentment: I cannot tarry here any longer than tomorrow morn. And I shall tell you the reason for this: it is not in search of comfort that I have embarked upon this journey. I pay little heed to whatever comfort comes my way, for this is not what I wish to pursue."

(4580–4613) Pleased to have Erec as his guest, the King walked to where the horses were standing and said: "Let us be off!" He helped Lady Enite onto her horse, doing so with fine manners. With Erec riding behind them, he led Enite along the way. And once they came into view of the castle, the young noblemen in his court wasted no more time, but ran out before the gates to meet their lord. In front of the castle gates they welcomed him with a merry din, for they were all buoyed up by the delusion that their king had, as was his wont, taken the knight captive. "Things have not turned out as you fancy they have," he said, and he told them straightway exactly what had taken place. "All of you who hold me dear," he said, "turn all your efforts, such that I shall forever reward you for it, towards preparing an exquisite welcome for the very most excellent man of whom I have ever heard tell." And they gladly did just this. Never was Erec offered finer hospitality anywhere else than he was there that night.

(4614–4627) In the evening after they had dined and were then sitting about, the host spoke: "My lord, it is my advice that you permit us to summon a physician to see after our wounds. It seems to me hazardous for you to depart at this time before you have been healed. You are, alas! severely wounded. Moreover, you are unfamiliar with this land and might very well encounter some misfortune." "Let us now have done with this matter," replied Erec, "for I cannot remain here save till daybreak."

(4628–4629 [17]) All acclaim and honor now awaited Erec that night,[6] for Guivreiz le Petit spared no pains in showing him lavish hospitality till the following day . [. . .] [7] According to what the adventure tells us of the virtuous Erec, after taking leave in the morning, he entered a magnificent forest, into which King Arthur had ridden from his castle Tintajol to go hunting together with an exquisite assemblage, as Chrétien informs us.[8] Arthur and his company were encamped by the roadside for a quarter mile's stretch.[9]

⊛ IX ⊛
KING ARTHUR'S ENCAMPMENT

(4629 [18]–4629 [43]) During this time Sir Walwan[1] had come riding up and had tethered his horse Wintwaliten to a tent, where Keii found it. Sir Walwan had no objection when Keii then mounted the horse to romp about on it. Both the shield and the lance of Sir Walwan Keii found leaning against the tent and, picking them up, he rode out alone onto the path. Sir Erec then came trotting along in his direction. Keii espied him from afar. Once he had had a good look at Erec, Keii could see that he had endured tribulation while on his journey, and that he had ridden a great distance and was covered with blood. At this, Keii resolved to attack him, and he spoke up with treachery: "Welcome to this land, my lord." Then Keii grabbed the reins of Erec's horse. Daring not to attack him in any other way, he intended to capture Erec like this. He asked Erec after his name. [. . .] [2]

(4629 [44]–4629 [55]) "Your anger is unfounded. I merely wished you to ride with me now to where you can be comfortable. I can readily see that you are badly wounded. My lord King Arthur is encamped not far from here. In the name of Arthur and Queen Guinevere I request that you now ride there with me and rest in their company after all your suffering. They shall both be pleased to see you."

(4629 [56]–4664) Keii's plan was this: once having brought Erec to the court, he would claim that he was the one who had dealt Erec this wound, and that Erec was his prisoner. This was clear proof that the world has never seen a stranger man than Keii. His heart was divided up into four parts:[3] at times it was endowed with immense integrity, so that Keii rued all the wrongs that he had ever before committed and that he guarded against all indecorum in thought and in deed—so much so that he was as unclouded by falsehood as is a mirror. In this, however, Keii was inconstant, for sooner or later came the day when he neglected all integrity. At such times he could not get his fill of pursuing wickedness with all his energy—wickedness both in what he did and in what he said. Such was the counsel of every urge within him. In addition, Keii was courageous on one day, and a notorious coward on the next. These two temperaments stood at odds with one another. In this way Keii brought dishonor down upon himself, so that all were forced to dislike him and no one held him in esteem. Because of his deceitfulness he was called Keii the Maligner.

(4665–4703) Now Erec recognized quite clearly what Keii had in mind, as he then proceeded to show him. "My lord," he said, "I have too far to journey and I cannot at this time stray from my path. Had I the time to do so, I would travel a thousand miles for the sake of the King's greeting. And now, permit me to be on my way. May God protect you." The false Keii then replied: "Drop this notion, my lord! You must not depart in such a manner; it would be unfitting for both of us. In truth, if it is at all within my power, I shall bring you to King Arthur's court." Erec, fils du roi Lac, was irritated somewhat by Keii's words. "You are, I fancy, incapable of doing any such thing," he spoke. "Hence it is just as well for you if you have little appetite for such exploits. For if you wish to take me there, you shall have to do so by force. Yet if you are equal to this task, you will indeed conduct me there, for I am quite a prize for you if you can vanquish me."[4] "I have no doubt," retorted Keii, "that I am certainly capable of this. Long before you will ever convince me to allow you to ride off like this without beholding my lord (for this cannot do you any harm), I shall first force you to do so through friendly means. Therefore, you must yield and go to face my lord. Forsooth, this must be done!"

(4704–4733) Only now did Erec begin to bristle with anger. He put the spurs to his horse and bellowed: "Get your hand away!" Then he flung aside his cloak and drew his sword. Because Keii would have well deserved it, Erec lunged to cut off that vile coward's hand. But Keii pulled it back in time and fled without offering any resistance. Although he was riding Wintwaliten, the finest horse any knight ever owned, he was so slow in turning it about to ride back to camp that Erec overtook him. But as soon as Erec had noticed (a stroke of good fortune was this for Keii!) that he was unarmed, how greatly did Sir Keii benefit from Erec's goodness! With most astonishing quickness Erec reversed his lance so that it did not harm him. He turned the shaft around toward Keii and struck

him with such force that he came to rest beneath his horse quite like a sack—
much in keeping with what he deserved, but hardly in the fashion of a fine
knight!

(4734–4755) Erec led the horse away, and Keii, that scoundrel, chased full
speed after him, crying out loudly at Erec: "No, most excellent sir knight! I ask
in the name of your valor that the horse remain here with me! Otherwise I
shall for evermore be subjected to disgrace and scorn for this. In truth, this
horse is, God knows, not mine." At this, the good knight Erec spun about with
a laugh and hearkened to Keii's lament. Then he spoke: "Now tell me, sir
knight, what is your name? And apprise me also of this horse's master. I wish to
know your name, no harm can come to you from that.[5] You need not hide your
face so in shame. This has been the lot of many a man who indeed never once
flinched with cowardice."

(4756–4776) "No, my lord!" cried Keii. "I beg of you: if you are to show
me favor, then be kind to me in all regards, and absolve me of answering your
query as to my name. My timidity has brought down such shame upon me
here that I must indeed reap heartfelt woe from this if I shall reveal to you my
name, for I have fully earned your scorn. For the sake of God forgo this now."
"Sir knight," said Erec, "out with it! In truth, there is no one here save you and
me. I cannot renounce my wish; otherwise you have lost the horse." And Erec
then urged on his own horse with the spurs as though he were about to ride off.

(4777–4815) Keii begged him to remain there, saying: "I wish to lament to
God that I myself must announce my own disgrace. Now I shall tell you who I
am: my name is Keii, and King Arthur deigns to keep me as seneschal at his
court. One of his nephews, the noble Sir Gawein, lent me this horse. I regret
that he did not refuse me it, for I would be spared the disgrace that I must now
endure. As my lord was dining this day, my ill fate counselled me to ask to
borrow his horse. I have not the devil's notion of why I was unable to conduct
myself in a peaceful way! I have striven after dishonor, of which I have attained
a goodly portion. Gawein then loaned me the horse right then and there. Had
he not done so, I would be absolved of the shame which has befallen me, as
events have transpired—though no man, to be sure, can escape his fate. Noble
knight, be so kind and return the horse to me for the sake of God, else I am the
scorn of all who see me returning to camp on foot." Erec replied: "So be it. I
shall give you the horse on one condition: you must return it to Sir Walwan for
me. This you must promise me upon your word of honor." Keii answered: "I
shall do this," and indeed he carried out his promise, for he was pleased with the
outcome of this matter.

(4816–4832) Once Keii had won back the horse, he said: "I now bid you, virtuous sir, since you have been kind to me, to show a full measure of kindness, so that I might recognize you: deign to tell me your name. It will do you no harm and will be of benefit to me. Because of your valor I would fain know your name. It shall forever vex me if I must depart without discovering your name or how I should call you whenever I should wish to think back kindly of you. For the sake of God, do tell me who you are." Erec replied: "No, not at this time. Perhaps it will be revealed to you in the future."

(4833–4845) They then parted company forthwith. Each of them, Keii and Erec, rode off on his way. Keii returned to the court and was compelled by his pledged word to conceal nothing. Rather, he told in full the shameful tale of how he had fared. And he did such justice to the description of his debasement that they took his shame as scorn enough, and they refrained from holding him up to reprobation.

(4846–4859) As soon as they had heard tell of such valor on the part of the other knight, they all, each and every one of them, became greatly curious as to who that knight might be. Keii then spoke: "I was unable to recognize him, and he refused to reveal his name. But I heard his voice, for he spoke with me quite at length. Insofar as I can tell from his voice, it is Erec, fils du roi Lac." Hearing this, they all then believed that it was truly Erec.

(4860–4879) King Arthur then spoke up: "I would be most heartily pleased and would reward benevolently whatever man could find Erec for me. Gawein, this I shall direct at Keii and at you. You have shown me such honor thus far that I can only speak well of you. If you do this for me now, I am inclined to hold it above all the favors you have ever done me. Gawein, be now reminded of our relationship, that you are my closest friend, and tarry no longer, as a favor to me! Render us—Queen Guinevere and me—your assistance in welcoming Erec here. No greater favor can fall to my lot."

(4880–4888) "My lord," replied Gawein, "you need not take such pains to persuade me, for I am eager to undertake this journey. Forsooth, there is no man alive whom I would rather see at this time than Erec. And if God favors me by ever allowing me to encounter him, let me tell you, my lord, what I shall do: if I can convince him to come, I shall bring him back here."

(4889–4920) With this, they rode off at once. Keii led Gawein straight to where he had left the knight. With most astonishing speed they both galloped after him, already on his trail. And as soon as they had caught up with him on his journey, the excellent Gawein greeted him courteously, with a friendly voice, and not with animosity. With that he proved to Erec that his intentions towards the two of them were peaceful. Gawein wished him a good day. As soon as Erec, fils du roi Lac, spoke up to thank him, Gawein recognized him from his voice; and once he had identified Erec, he spoke his name. Compelled by the joy of seeing Erec strong and fit, Gawein embraced him tightly. He bade him welcome and his lady-love as well, and he offered Erec most hearty thanks for the courteous regard which he had shown Gawein by returning his horse. It was Erec's good character which had obliged him to hand over the creature.

(4921–4958) As soon as Gawein had spoken Erec's name, he addressed the warrior: "We have followed you with great alacrity through the forest. If you ask why we are in such haste or what it is that I desire, my lord and former comrade, then I shall not conceal this from you. I ask you now to prove whether you hold dear my lord King Arthur, and I shall tell you just how you can do this. When our friend Keii returned my horse to me at the court and spoke of you as possessing such great valor, once he had told me his tale, we all, each and every one, wondered who might have done this. Following a guess, however, we unanimously surmised that it was you. The Queen and my lord King Arthur then immediately prevailed upon us with such urgency to hurry after you (hence our haste!) and bring you back to Arthur's court. If ever you bore a liking for King Arthur or deemed him a worthy man, then see to it that he be not rebuffed, and deign to pay him a visit. If this can now be done, then no man has ever received a greater favor than he from this. Do not object to discharging this request if you are willing to serve King Arthur. We shall all, moreover, be pleased by your coming."

(4959–4983) Erec answered him thus: "The King has certainly earned my never-ending obedience to him. And whenever I refuse him that obedience, such that his command is not fulfilled, then it is not my own willfulness which prevents me from doing what he orders. Yet this request I must refuse him. I shall clearly demonstrate to him my favor if ever I have occasion (as indeed I very well may) to risk my life and all I have for his sake. Then there shall be no doubt, for I shall prove to him unequivocally what he means to me. For now, however, he must permit me to depart with his good graces. I have renounced all comforts at this time. Wherever I shall journey, deign to let me be your servant. Inform my lord and the Queen of my desire to serve them, and deliver me from their displeasure."

(4984–5017) Sir Gawein was quite unhappy to see that Erec was resisting all entreaties. He then signalled to his comrade Keii and whispered to him, saying: "Noble knight, you must now perform a task with the same virtue and excellence with which my lord and I shall reward you. It is my counsel that you do the following: Be on your way at once and tell them that Erec does not wish to return. Therefore, my comrade, I have concocted a ruse for us with regard to Erec—a ruse which shall yield us the greatest advantage for now. Tell King

Arthur that, if he wishes to see Erec, then it must be done in accordance with this plan, which I can readily explain to you. Direct the King to leave the spot where he is encamped in the forest and to advance along the road in haste to where, on the other side of the forest, Sir Erec shall ride out. In the meantime I can easily detain him along the way with cunning and prevent his arriving there first." "And if this turns out to be of benefit to us," said Sir Keii, "then it shall all have been done in good faith."⁶ He rode off straightway and discharged everything in accordance with Gawein's request.

(5018–5025) As soon as King Arthur had heard Keii's report, the Round Table was removed. With a great sense of urgency they hastened to proceed in accordance with the advice of the King's nephew, and they pitched camp right alongside the roadway, so that Sir Erec could not come anywhere near there without riding directly into their midst.

(5026–5036) Gawein, that excellent man, began to detain Erec with craftiness in every possible way, until he had consumed enough time with diversion for the King to have gained a good headstart. Each time that Erec asked once more to be off, Gawein would say: "In but a moment now"—until with exquisite trickery he finally rode out of the forest together with Erec at the very place where the King had pitched camp along the road.

(5037–5067) And when Erec, fils du roi Lac, discerned all the tents, it was not a pleasing sight to him, for the whole field was dotted with them! What is more, he recognized them readily, for he had seen them often. "What has happened to me?" he asked. "I fancy I have lost my way. You have not done well by me, Sir Gawein, this is all your plan! Seldom have I heard tell of your committing such a wrong. Coming here was the very farthest thought from my mind. You have lured me here by wicked means. Any man who comes to the court with as little to gain from it as I do now, might just as well remain at home. All who are to be present at the court ought rightfully to be of a joyous disposition and should do credit to it. I am now incapable of such, and as a man limited in where I can go, I must wait before appearing there. You clearly see that I am at present fatigued and wounded, and so unfit for the court that I would certainly have forgone appearing there if you had spared me this. You have not done well by me!"

(5068–5080) Gawein requited this outburst of anger with kindness, pulling Erec toward him in an embrace and saying: "My lord, calm your anger. To be sure, it is better to lose a friend properly and rightly than to retain his friendship in a less than fitting way. And if that friend is a bit hasty with his ire, he will recognize afterwards what is proper and will hold the other one dearer than before. What more can I now say? For if I am said to have aggrieved you, then certainly I have done so with none but good intentions. You must pass judgment on me yourself."

(5081–5099) Thus did Gawein most gallantly bring about a reconciliation with him, so that Erec's ill-humor and anguish began to subside. Never was a man accorded, moreover, greater glory or fuller honor than was extended to Erec there at the court. Arthur and the Queen, together with all the assemblage of knights, demonstrated quite clearly that they were glad to see him there. Erec and Enite, who had on many occasions encountered affliction along the unfamiliar paths of their journey, were both welcome there and were received with equal acclaim.

(5100–5128) Queen Guinevere then displayed her kindness as Lady Enite approached her. She took Enite into her care and led her off apart from her husband into her inner chambers, where much in the manner of women they both lamented and asked many questions and talked of the unusual woes which Lady Enite had endured. For as long as was possible, that most noble Queen lavished comforts upon Enite to ease the burden of these vexing matters. Sir Erec, too, was led off from the knights to where, wounded as he was, he found respite from his fatigue. The knights went to him and removed his armor straightway. Erec had many noble squires attending him there, each of whom competed to prove himself superior to all the others. They strove with an equal purpose to discharge whatever service Erec could have wanted.

(5129–5152) In good time the Queen arrived with all her damsels to lament Erec's trouble and to visit with him. With her she brought a bandage, which had great powers in healing wounds, as I shall now recount to you. Because of it many a mortally wounded man lived to regain his health. Whenever a man had his wound wrapped with this bandage, the wound caused no further pain and was healed no less than fully. Never was there any further bad effect, and it drove out all harmful things. Whatever it came upon that was beneficial remained, and all who were made better by it watched it rid them of scars, so that their skin appeared smooth, as though there had never been a wound. Using this bandage Queen Guinevere wrapped the knight's side with her own hands. Never at any time has the world beheld a more excellent bandage.

(5153–5164) If there is any man who is curious and would like to hear whence this bandage came, it was left there long ago by Famurgan, the King's sister, when she died. What powerful sorcery and strange arts perished along with her! Famurgan was a goddess. It is impossible to recount all the marvelous things about her; the greater portion of the arts in which this lady was engaged must remain untold.

(5165–5189) And yet I shall tell you as much as I can of her powers. Each time she commenced to demonstrate her sorcery, she travelled around the world in a trice and returned again instantly. Who taught her this I do not know. Sooner than I could turn my hand or blink my eye, she took off and reappeared again in a flash. She lived a splendid life, for she could just as easily seek out repose by hovering in the air as by lying on firm ground, and she was able to live both upon the surface of the waters as well as beneath the waves. Moreover, she dwelt just as comfortably engulfed in fire as on a bed of dew, it made no difference to her. All of this the lady had in her power. And whenever she wished, she could turn a man into a bird or a beast, soon afterwards giving him back his human form. The power of magic was truly at her call.

(5190–5215) Famurgan lived very much at cross purposes with God, for the birds along with the wild animals heeded her command in forest and in meadow; and what seems most extraordinary to me is that all the evil spirits which are called demons there were under her control. She could work marvelous feats, for the dragons were forced to come from the skies to assist her in her ventures, as did the fish from the waters. Furthermore, she had kinsmen deep down in hell. The devil was her comrade, and he sent her as much aid as she wanted from out of the hell-fires. And whatever Famurgan needed from the earthly realm she took herself without trepidation and in ample measure. The earth bore no herb whose power she did not know, just as thoroughly as I know the features of my own hand.

(5216–5242) Ever since the death of the Sibyl and since the demise of Erichtho (of whom Lucan reports that her magic powers commanded the dead— anyone she chose, including those long since deceased—to rise again fully whole . . . but of her I wish to tell you no more at this point, for my story would become too long),[7] the world has never seen (be certain of the truthfulness of this!) a greater master of the art of magic than Famurgan, of whom I have told you. Hence only a fool would claim to have incurred great dishonor from any bandage which she had prepared for him. Forsooth, no matter how unceasingly one wished to research this power in books of medicine, one would never find anywhere, I fancy, such potent sorcery as that which Famurgan practiced at will and in contempt of Christ.

(5243–5269) This same bandage wherewith the Queen wrapped Erec's wound, Famurgan had carefully fabricated with all her art. Erec readily felt the beneficial powers of the bandage, for as soon as he was enveloped in it, his thoughts turned to taking up his journey once more. He thought himself wholly recovered, and he desired to tarry there no longer, regardless of how much they entreated and harangued him, those knights and ladies who came to visit him. But that night they entertained the noble guests to the full measure of their ability and as best they could, and indeed they would fain have done so for a long time had Erec but been willing to allow it. Such, however, he would not permit. Despite whatever wiles were attempted, neither King Arthur's appeal nor that of the Queen was of any avail to them in delaying Erec any longer than till the very early morn. Indeed, no entreaty of theirs was equal to that task.

(5270–5287) As the dawn then came and Erec still would let no one dissuade him from embarking upon his journey, they all thought this unbecoming. For Erec's sake, however, the King took an early breakfast, after which the horses were brought up. Erec then took leave of the knights and ladies, as befitted his good breeding. Only now could it be seen from the bearing of all those present that they held Erec and Enite dear, for they wept with sorrow—both women as well as men—as the two of them departed. So distressed was the King that he wished to tarry no longer in the forest; instead, he set out on the journey toward Karadigan.

☖ X ☖
SIR CADOC AND THE GIANTS

(5288–5311) The good knight Erec now rode forth, not knowing himself whither he was bound, but following the path wherever it led him. His sole design was to pursue adventure, wherever it was to be found. For a short time he rode on, covering scarcely but a mile, when he heard a voice calling out, at some distance from the path, in most wretched distress and anguish: a woman's voice it was, crying out pitifully for help, for she was much afflicted. Upon hearing this cry, Erec was eager to discover what might be amiss. This was indeed proof of his valor. He bade Lady Enite await him there and had her dismount alongside the path. As Erec rode off from her, Enite, following the precepts of her heart, placed her sorrow in the hands of God.

(5312–5334) Setting out through overgrown forest unmarked by any trail, Erec followed an unhewn path, with the woman's voice as his only compass[1], until he came upon the spot in that forest thicket where with loud lament she was in the throes of misery. Her hands, seized by spasms of anguish, had most undecorously torn off her wimple. In her loathing of life this woman had so grimly scratched and tousled herself that her garments as well as her body were covered with blood. She was afflicted by such woe that (since it is my duty to report the truth) there is forsooth no man alive who is so hard of heart that, once having witnessed her anguish on that day, he could fail to take pity on her.

(5335–5353) At the sight of this wretched woman in such disarray, Erec, that most laudable man, fought back tears[2] as he said: "Speak, my lady, and tell me, for the sake of God, why it is that you weep. How is it that you are so alone in these woods? Tell me forthwith, for God's sake, whether I can be of aid to you." The bitter rage of grief had well nigh robbed the lady of her voice,[3] and the sighing of her heart rent asunder her words such that it was with great pains that she commenced to speak: "I have much cause for weeping. My lord, I have lost unto death the most beloved man with whom a woman has ever been blest."

(5354–5377) Then spoke Erec: "How has this come about, my lady?" "Two giants abducted him from me, my lord, they dragged him off the trail away from me. They shall not spare his life, my lord, for they have been bitter foes of his for many a day. O woe, how well indeed may I weep for sorrow!" "My lady, are they perchance far off?" "No, that they are not, dear sir." "Then direct me to where I might find them." "My lord, they rode off yonder," and she pointed Erec in the direction in which he had been abducted. Then said Erec: "Be temperate in your demeanor, my lady, for in truth I shall help him from his distress or else perish along with him." Thereupon the good lady entrusted him, both with words and in her thoughts, to the protection of our Lord. Most abundant was her prayer, and faithfully spoken was the blessing which she bestowed upon the hero.

(5378–5428) In a short time Erec had come upon their trail, and with haste he approached closely until he had caught sight of them. These two[4] towering men had, unlike Erec, neither shield, nor lance, nor sword. This was rightly to Erec's advantage: they were without any manner of knightly armament. What, then, was their means of defense?[5] Two heavy clubs, long and stout, the shafts of which were plated with iron. Forsooth, a coward might well lose all courage to do battle with them. Moreover, these churlish fellows both bore whips with strands each as thick as a man's finger. In a ghastly fashion they prodded onward with their whips that man whom they had taken captive there. Bare of all garb and naked as the day he was born, he rode along on horseback. His hands were bound behind his back with rope and his feet were lashed together under the horse's belly.[6] Many a stroke did he suffer from the whips as he rode along before them. They beat him mercilessly, so much that the wretched man's skin hung down in shreds from his head all the way to his knees. They transgressed against the code of chivalry and mistreated this honorable knight; even were he caught red-handed as a thief, such punishment would be excessive. He had been beaten to the point that there was no more blood to seep from his wounds, and he was benumbed into such silence that he had no will left to cry out. Blood dripped like rain down the flanks of his horse, which was matted all over with the red sap. Dire torment did this knight suffer, such unheard of pain that never could a man endure greater affliction—save death itself[7]—than befell him.

(5429–5445) Once having beheld this, Erec's heart was so moved by the knight's agony that he would sooner have been slain along with him than not to intercede: the very sight made him turn pale with horror.[8] Addressing the two giants, Erec spoke: "My lords, I mean not to affront you, but can you tell me, for the sake of God, what it is that this man whom you have taken captive has done to you? Tell me, what manner of wrong has he committed? A truthful answer to my query can do you no harm and would please me greatly.[9] Is he a murderer or a thief? Or how is it that he merits such severe punishment from you as he is now enduring?"

(5446–5497) One of the giants made reply (little regard did he show for Erec's question): "Fool, what business have you to ask what this man has done to us? We shall tell you nothing. See here, you babbling ape, you dishonor yourself by asking so many questions—questions to which you shall receive no answer. Now why is it that you are stalking me?" Erec replied: "My lord, that is not my intention." Yet with cunning he persisted in his talk, in the hope of thereby saving[10] the knight: "I heard his cries from afar. Believe me, my lord, it was not with ill design that I have followed you here. I merely wish to know what is astir here. It is my hope that this should not vex you. Yet I must say to you in truth—about this I cannot remain silent—if this man bears the title of knight, then you ought to feel everlasting shame that he enjoys no advantage from his knightliness and that this fails to deter you from such remarkable misconduct. He has surely been dealt punishment enough, whatever it be that he has done. Will you, for God's sake, set him free?" The immense giant responded thus: "Your prattle is loathsome to me: put an end to your questioning, for you are gravely endangering your life. I should snap you like a twig, were there any esteem or any fame to be gained from it. Of what benefit to this man are all your queries? Help him by fighting for him as you would for your own kinsman; of that he has ample need!"[11] Before Erec's very eyes he then flogged the knight once more and ordered Erec to be off. Even so, Erec would fain have won him over by friendly means such that he should set free the knight. Yet this request was quite in vain, and only served to fan the giant's ire. Wishing to affront Erec, they began to torture the knight even more cruelly than before, for they did not fancy, nor did they fear, that he would dare to challenge them.

(5498–5517) And as that adroit hero Erec saw that the knight was suffering on his account, this vexed him most grievously. No longer did he then tarry, but he boldly locked his lance into place beneath his arm [12] and gave spur to his horse. It was anger which thrust him headlong toward the giants. Of little concern was this, however, to them, save that one of the giants, to show his disdain, lingered there, until a thrust of Erec's lance, bearing down upon his head, robbed him of one eye. With such force was this lunge executed that the shaft stood out a full arm's length from the giant's eye. Though the giant little wished such a thing to transpire in open view,[13] Erec dashed him to the ground in death, as God in His courtliness willed it.

(5518–5569) Once the other giant saw his burly comrade take this thundering fall, he whirled around in anger and began to swing his club about, grasping it with both his hands. Erec then dismounted, which pleased the giant, for he now fancied a speedy victory in his reach. False hope buoyed him up, as was God's will. Like a mad man he clubbed away at Erec. Save for the fact that Erec was on his guard and was able to defend himself most deftly, he would have been cut down by the very first blow. His quickness was ample to bring him beyond reach of the giant. His shield he held forth [14] in self-defense, and little was it spared the buffeting blows of the giant's club. Wherever he struck the shield, the hard wood became brittle, such that it finally broke apart into three pieces and all the metal fittings flew high into the air. So massive was the club that each time the giant swung it, it dragged him down along with it, so that he could not readily hoist it up again. Before he ever had a chance to lift it for the next blow, Erec in his swiftness was able to lunge at the giant and then recoil again. In this fashion he had meted out a good four blows to the giant's leg. The giant paid little heed to this, until finally Erec lopped off his leg. Once the enormous fellow began to sink to his knees, Erec pounced upon him. Even now, however, this fiendish creature fought on without a trace of fear. So many a dreadful blow did he yet deal out that we may well marvel at the fact that Erec came away from him alive. Fighting alongside Erec, however, was He who gave David the strength such that he was victorious over the giant Goliath. In like manner He helped Erec to victory that day,[15] so that he felled the giant with brute force and chopped off his head. Therewith ended the fight.

(5570–5599) By the time Erec had won his victory, the horse had borne that captive knight off into the forest, so that no one knew where he was to be found. And yet this is what brought Erec onto his trail: everywhere the knight had ridden, the trees and the grass had become quite red with the blood from his body; this blood was to be seen on every leaf and blade which he had brushed past as the horse carried him away, for he was tied up such that he was unable at any point along the way to steer clear of the trees and avoid dashing against them. The good knight Erec tracked him following the trail of blood, which led all the way to where he finally found him. Erec then untied the fetters from his feet and his hands and guided back to his lady this wretched man, who, though not unharmed, was nonetheless alive, albeit severely flogged by the whips, as Erec had found him. Yet little cause would he ever have for lament, for he had remained alive and was in course healed of this pain.

(5600–5627) As the lady espied him, both joy and sorrow welled up in the shrine of her heart, ill paired as those feelings are with one another. When the good lady caught sight of him covered with blood, the flame of hope within her heart flickered and died, for she was most unaccustomed to seeing him in such anguish. Never before had she beheld him so brutally castigated. At the same time, however, joy overcame her and won out over her sorrow. The source of her gladness was that he had come back to her still alive. The gloom in the lady's heart was then transformed, not unlike a fine glass fashioned of crystal which, wholly encrusted in black grime, is painstakingly scraped clean: as the stain comes off, that which once was dingy now turns lovely and radiant. In the same fashion the lady's heart became a glass of sparkling crystal, washed clean of previous cares and lifted up to the light with guileless bliss as though never before blackened by woe.

(5628–5633) The two lovers were happy, and they thanked Erec most profusely, saying: "My lord, we shall give ourselves over into your command as serfs. It is from you that we have our lives."

(5634–5661) Erec replied thus to the knight: "My lord, I would be forever pleased at this had I served you in any useful way, and this shall yet happen, God willing, to the extent it has not yet come about, for I have every good intention of so doing. For now I ask as recompense no other kind of fealty than that you reveal to me your name." The knight gave his name as Cadoc, from the land of Tafriol, and he told Erec how it had come about that the two devilish creatures had captured him. He had wished to leave his own realm and travel to the land of Britain, so that he and his lady-love might make themselves known there to the King's knightly company. Now his journey had taken him onto a path through the forest, and the giants had been alerted to this. For quite a long time indeed they had been enemies of his. What score they had to settle with this man is unknown to me, save that they had then lain in wait for him, completely encircling his trail with an ambush, and had captured him there as he rode up.

(5662–5698) After Erec had heard the story of this knight's ordeal, he spoke with gracious diplomacy, so as to relieve Cadoc of his distress: "My lord, be not chagrined by this affair with the giants. Forsooth, no man desiring to perform such deeds of valor is spared the occasion when he must perhaps suffer some shame. Then, at a later date he will make amends for it. How many a time have I been subjected to worse treatment!" With these words Erec consoled him. "This is my advice," he continued, "that you let no one prevent you from completing your journey to the land of Britain, just as you had planned. In Britain things are such (this I wish to tell you in all good sooth) that no knight can acquire greater fame elsewhere, in any other land than there. Whoever can further his cause in Britain will soon become a happy man. I now desire of you one act of homage, and nothing more: when you enter the land, take your lady-love by the hand and go before the Queen and tell her of my devoted service. Reveal to her the particulars of your business there, and tell her that I have sent you there to her retinue. Erec is my name; she is quite well acquainted with me."

(5699–5709) This Cadoc vowed to do, and they then parted company. Cadoc journeyed to the court and discharged all that Erec had bidden him. He offered the Queen his fealty, in accordance with the instructions which Erec had given him earlier. Cadoc placed himself at Guinevere's command. The most noble Queen, she who bore the crown atop her head, then wished aloud that Erec might be rewarded by the hand of good fortune.

⊛ XI ⊛
COUNT ORINGLES

(5710–5729) The excellent Erec then rode back out of the forest forthwith and sought the trail where he had directed Lady Enite to await him. In the meantime Erec had so exerted himself in battle that his wounds were unable to remain intact; instead, they had opened up once more. Erec was utterly drained of blood, and the sword-blows had so weakened him that his complexion was altogether pale; and his strength was so nearly sapped that he rode back with great effort to where the lady had been awaiting him. Had he needed to ride on any farther, he would certainly have met his death. This was proven by what then happened.

(5730–5745) As the half-dead man leaned forward to dismount (for now he was to have some rest), so stupified was he that he came down head over heels off the horse. He took such a tumble that he lay there as though dead. At the sight of this fall, bitter woe and the gall of all tribulation welled up in Enite's heart. Compelled by misery, the good lady raised a lament most pitifully, a lament which welled up from within her broken heart.

(5746–5773) Her cry gave off such a din that the forest echoed it back to her ears. No one else was at hand to help Enite lament her sorrow—no one save for the echo which the forest issued forth with undiminished loudness all the way out onto the fields. Only that echo helped her to bewail her wretchedness, for no one else was there. She now fell over him, that good woman, and kissed him. Then she beat her breasts and, kissing him again, cried out; her every other word was: "Woe, o woe!" With a fury she tore at her hair and took vengeance on her body, much in the manner of women, for it is in this way that they wreak their revenge. Those fine creatures undertake nothing against the source of their suffering; instead, they are wont to put their eyes and their hands to work, with tears and with beating, for there is nothing else that they can do. Therefore, may ill fortune bring down its curse upon any man (this I wish upon him!) who inflicts suffering upon women, for such is neither valiant nor good.

(5774–5832) Lady Enite opened the vials of her anger towards God, exclaiming: "Lord, if this is your command, that so fine a knight has lost his life because of his noble spirit, then it is an extraordinary sort of anger indeed which has snatched away all compassion from your mercy. How shabby an example you give in me, most wretched woman! of the compassion which I have heard ascribed to you! If you are able to have mercy on me now, behold! it is high time to do so! Look now at my husband lying here half-dead, or perhaps entirely dead and gone. Have mercy now! There is great need for such, for my heart is bereft of life. Behold how I stand here in grief. Have mercy on me, o Lord, for it is pitiable that I, bereaved woman, should live on any longer in such sorrow. Save for the fact that all your works are without blemish, Lord, I would accuse[1] you of a misdeed in allowing me to live on, since you have taken from me the one man for whom I was to live my life. If you can demonstrate, Lord, that the innermost chambers of all mens' hearts are open to your sight (for nothing is able to remain concealed from you), then show this by having mercy. And if in the time that he has been my husband I have in any way brought about his misfortune, either intentionally or by chance,[2] and such that it is ill-becoming, and if you in your power then take him from me, then I shall welcome this judgment, for in that case I am justly deprived of him. If I have not done so, however, you must absolve me of punishment. For the sake of your kindness, Lord, have mercy upon me and bring him back to life for me. Yet if it is not your will to return him to me, then be reminded, Lord God, that all the world is familiar with the words which you have spoken (and I beg you to confirm them!): that a man and his wife shall be one body. And do not render us asunder, for otherwise I shall endure a tremendous wrong at your hands. If your mercy be manifold, then help me that I too might die here.

(5833–5841) "Come out, you hungry beasts—both wolf and bear and lion—one of you come hither and devour us both, that our one body may not separate in this way and embark upon two different paths! And may God deign to watch over our souls! In truth, they shall not be wrenched asunder, regardless of what befalls our bodies."

(5842–5856) Seeing none of them coming, Enite cried out once more to them, saying: "You most stupid beasts, you have killed and devoured many a sheep and swine, little animals belonging to poor people, who begrudged you what you took and who were altogether disheartened by their loss. If you had any sense, you would fetch your nourishment right here with a voracious bite, for I would readily deliver myself to you. For that very reason I ought to be well fitting for you. Come forth, you may gladly take me. Where are you now? Forsooth, I am waiting!"

(5857–5869) Enite's summoning failed to reach them such that any beast heard it or came to that place. Yet even if some creature had come and fully beheld her sorrowful demeanor, I know forsooth that, no matter how hungry it might be, in the end it would perforce have helped her bewail her grief and proven outright that she was deserving of pity. Enite survived against her will.

(5870–5907) Only when she most certainly perceived that she was not to die, did she begin to lament in earnest, and she well nigh struck herself dead. Never has greater misery been observed. "My dear lord," she cried, "since I must lose you, I shall now renounce all men for evermore, save for one, whom I love passionately in my heart and with all my mind. Towards him I have suddenly become well-disposed. If I could earn his fondness, I would be willing to be a faithful wife to him. Sweetest Death, it is you of whom I speak! Because of my love of you do I reverse the usual custom, such that I, as a woman, am suing for a man. I have so great a need for your love! Deign now to have me, purest Death! Alas, how well suited I am, wretched woman, to lie in your arms! You are indeed well provided for, wedded to me. Why do you not take me forthwith? Since you must one day take me, I advise you to do it now. I am well suited to be your wife, for I am still possessed of both beauty and youth, and I am in my best years. You cannot be too hasty to fetch me. On the other hand, what use am I to you later on, once both age and sorrow have gutted me of beauty and youth? What am I to do for you then? Now, however, a good husband would still find me suitable as his wife."

(5908–5938) After Enite had poured forth many words without managing to persuade Death with her entreaty or to see her wish fulfilled that he take her into his dominion, she then chastised Death in a most womanly fashion, as she was inclined to do. "Woe to you, most pernicious Death!" she exclaimed. "And cursed be you! How often you parade about in your recklessness! Indeed, all the world speaks truthfully of you in saying that you are infested with treachery. You thirst to bring down harm upon many men whom suffering ought never to befall. I have witnessed much of this from you. You are advised by a coterie of villainous counsellors, for you rashly take the life of a man whom no one in all the world can surpass. And yet another man, upon whom everyone has long since wished death, you set free and suffer to grow old! It is with impropriety that you show your might. You have cut down an excellent man here, and you have brought me together with him in a fashion which is unseemly and which shall deter me from ever speaking kindly of you.

(5939–5973) "Now I know not where I ought to turn, poor woman that I am. I was born of misfortune, for I have now lost both body and soul, as is the just fate of any woman who has committed so great a misdeed as to betray her husband, as have I with my lord. He would have been spared death here had I not brought it down upon him. Indeed, he would never have invented this loathsome journey had I but held back that deep sigh of lament when, lying beside him that day, I fancied him asleep. Cursed be the day that I broached the matter! For I have squandered away my happiness, along with great honor and comfort. O woe! how wretchedly have things turned out for me! What did I intend to gain, foolish woman that I am, by speaking as I did? Regardless of what I felt in my heart, God had certainly provided that my life was blessed with all good things. I acted in the manner of a fool, who stupidly begrudges himself esteem and wealth and cannot bear to see things going smoothly for himself, and who at the counsel of the devil manages to destroy his happiness, for the devil gladly sees such a man stripped of his acclaim.

(5974–6007) "O woe, dear mother and good father! At this moment you are unaware of my great distress. You had both hoped to improve my circumstances greatly; and such was quite likely too, since you had married me to a powerful king. For me that hope has been contorted into adversity. Any man deceives himself who fancies he can alter or prevent from being fulfilled that which God has set in motion. No manner of cunning serves to thwart God in executing His will, which likewise must now be discharged against me. Ill fortune must perforce be my lot. This much has been demonstrated to me by the terrible anguish which I have suffered thus far. God has marked me, poor woman, for a life of woe; this I have come to see quite clearly. What thoughts He has concerning my soul, that I cannot know. Yet whatever now happens to my body shall evoke but a scant outcry from me, as long as my soul can still be saved. I have now seen confirmed those words which I often heard spoken: that regardless of what one does for an ill-fated man, his fortune will, in truth, never improve.

(6008–6041) "If a man were to take a lime-tree from alongside the road where it was poorly tended, and if he then planted it in his garden and by cultivating it atoned for the fact that it had until then stood neglected in parched soil, and if he then went on to think he could expect from it a good fruit-tree for his orchard, such a man could not be more thoroughly deluded even by a dream. For no matter how zealously one tended to it, it could not be made to bear any better fruit than its species had previously allowed, before it was dug up from the scrubby earth along the roadside where it stood so poorly nourished. Regardless how beautiful and noble a tree it is, a great deal of digging and fertilizing can be squandered on it. From this, one ought to draw a parallel with me (most God-forsaken woman that I am!), and the world might take pity at my vast misfortune. Even if all the world crowned me mistress over all women, God has still inflicted such ill fortune upon me that I must endure heartache for as long as I shall live, unless it be God Himself who ends it for me.

(6042–6061) "Since things have come to the point that God has taken from me the very dearest man a woman ever had, and since Death does not want me, let Death now take full note of this: the steadfastness between the two of us shall not simply vanish. Indeed, I shall discover a ruse whereby Death, against his will, must accept me into his retinue. Why should I so eagerly beg at his feet if he rejects me? Right here and now I can quite readily accord to myself that for which I have so urgently entreated Death. What is more, I will not see it postponed any longer. In truth, I have now made a wise decision."

(6062–6083) Enite's hand then sank toward the ground. She grasped her husband's sword and drew it from the scabbard, ready to stab herself with it for grief and to take foolish vengeance on herself for her husband's death. But God forbade her this and saved her life through His merciful wisdom, such that she cursed the sword as soon as she set eyes upon it. It was a wonder that Enite's heart did not crack open with grief. Her voice broke quite in two—into high and low—with the fury of her lamentation. Frightfully did the forest reverberate with her cry; again and again it resounded with "o woe! o woe!"

(6084–6109) Her eyes fixed upon the sword, Enite cried out with an ear-splitting wail and with plaintive lips: "O woe, cursed be the hour that the blacksmith ever set about forging you! You have killed my husband. It is your fault that he has lost his life. In truth, he would never have gone into battle against any dreadful adversary, here or anywhere else, except at your encouragement. Thus, you have bereaved me of him. At risk of life and limb my dear lord rode full many a time into battle, which he would have forgone had he not been bolstered by his profound trust in you. On many an occasion did he proclaim your excellence. Now you have failed to keep watch over him, and I know not whether you even rue it. You have thoroughly violated your loyalty towards him, and this shall be avenged on you. You shall not escape so easily: you must commit still more murder!"

(6110–6137) Enite then gave full proof that she meant these words: in her eagerness for death, she turned the point of the sword around toward her breast, as though about to cast herself down upon it. At this very moment a man came riding up—a man who thwarted Enite in her resolve, and whom God had dispatched there. A noble lord this man was, a count, whose domain was not at all distant from there. Oringles was the name of this powerful man, and he was born of Limors. God had chosen this man to protect Enite, for he came travelling from his castle, riding through the forest to save her. Wherefore he had set out, this was not explained to me, but my heart tells me that it was Enite's good fortune that had occasioned his riding forth that day. Along with him he had a goodly number of knights. By chance the same path where Sir Erec lay in such great distress and where Lady Enite cared for him led Oringles into the forest.

(6138–6177) While this lord was still quite far from Erec and Enite, he heard the woman tormenting herself with loud wailing. And as soon as he heard her voice, he proceeded out of curiosity in that same direction, that he might see for himself what strange things were happening there. Oringles arrived at the very moment when Enite had placed the sword at her noble breast to kill herself. He came riding up to that spot, and upon seeing her gesture—that she was about to plunge the sword into her own body—he was quick to jump down from his horse, for he was well nigh too late and unable to prevent her thrust. In a flash he pulled her toward him and turned aside the blade. He wrested the sword from her hand and hurled it away with these words: "Tell me, strange woman, why is it that you were intent upon taking your life and destroying in yourself the fairest creature, wild or tame, upon which any man has ever set eyes?" With effort Lady Enite replied: "See for yourself, my dear sir, what it is that troubles me." "Was it your wish to take your own life?" "My lord, I had every reason to do so." "Was he your lover or your husband?" "He was both, my lord." "Tell me now, who was it who slew him?" At this Lady Enite began to recount the full story of what had happened to Erec.

(6178–6211) The Count now began to reflect and think to himself that in all his days he had never beheld, near or far, a more lovely woman. The knights too told him the same. He then dismissed the lady and went for a short consultation. "One thing is quite evident," he said to his comrades, "and can be readily seen from the lady. Wherever this knight acquired her or however she came to this place, she is most certainly a noble woman, as is proven by her delightful beauty. Speak up now, what is your advice? You know full well my circumstances, that I am without a wife. Moreover, all the reflections of my mind counsel me urgently to take her as my wife. Methinks she would be well suited to be mistress over my land, for I recognized at once from her appearance that she is of sufficiently high birth for me. Likewise have the dictates of my heart elected her as my wife. Now I ask your willing acquiescence—I shall ever be most glad to reward you for this, for as long as I shall live, and I urge that all of you be equally well satisfied in approving this counsel without opposition." Hearing his words, they all recommended this course of action to him.

(6212–6240) The Count was well pleased with their advice. He then offered Lady Enite zealous and friendly consolation, as one should to a friend in distress. "Delightful woman," he said, "why do you torment yourself so fiercely? For the glory of God, as well as for me, my lady, do what I say and carry your head a little higher than your fate might actually warrant. I must rightfully say to you that your behavior is in accordance with the custom of women, and that from the bottom of my heart I find it good that you are lamenting your husband, for thereby do you prove your loyalty. Yet you have now done enough of this, for it can be of no avail to you. The finest device, and the one most effective in the face of injury, I believe, is this: that one console himself for such harm in due time, for protracted grieving yields nothing save a person steeped in misery. Think about this, lovely woman. And if you could bring him back to life with your weeping, we would all help you to lament and likewise to bear your grief. Unfortunately, however, this cannot be.

(6241–6281) "And as I have seen it, if I am able to discern things correctly, your husband was neither so noble nor so powerful, so strong nor so handsome, nor was he so highly esteemed that you cannot be fully compensated for your sorrow. You can easily see him replaced if you are obedient to me. God has sent me here to you, I believe, at an opportune moment. Most beneficial relief is about to come your way. Events which repeatedly cause a person great harm can quite easily reverse themselves and yield more welcome circumstances, just as has happened here this day, my lady, with your sentiments: they cannot help but be transformed into great honor. Forsooth, your poverty shall grow into great wealth here. I bear the title of count and am in truth lord over a powerful land, over which you shall be mistress. Behold, you shall now see quite clearly that your husband's death is to your advantage and will sow the seeds of all happiness for you, for only now are things beginning to go favorably for you. I have no wife, and I wish to marry you. This way of life is better able to suit you than that you should journey unprotected from land to land[3] together with some man, in a manner inappropriate to your true merits. Knights and squires, ladies and wealthy vassals, all in such numbers that no count has ever had more of them in his service—all of these I shall place at your command if you will now cease your weeping."

(6282–6301) Beset by great sorrow and heartache, the good Enite could say nothing more to him in reply. She then spoke, however, as her heart compelled her to speak: "My lord, spare me your many words. For the sake of God, my lord, leave off your mockery of me, poor woman that I am. And if you are indeed rich and powerful, that is to your advantage. But take note of my resolve, my lord, which I shall explain to you succinctly: it can never transpire that I should become your wife, or the wife of any man on earth, tomorrow or in a thousand tomorrows. I would never willingly let that happen, unless God should give me back my husband. The first man I ever had shall also be the last man for me. Believe this, my lord, for it shall certainly be proven true."

(6302–6307) The Count then addressed his knights with these words: "Women will talk this way. She ought not to be reproached for it, for she will readily abandon her unhappiness. I shall yet marshal things to my advantage."

(6308–6323) The Count was most delighted by Lady Enite. Thereupon he directed his squires, as many of them as were present, to fashion a litter. In a short time it was finished, and on it Erec was then placed, in the manner of a dead man. At this, they bore him off to Limors, and the Count assembled as many people as he could for the wake. He also ordered tapers brought, to burn over Erec until his burial. Lady Enite could not but feel bitter gloom, for she thought him dead.

(6324–6341) It now came about, once the host had beheld the full dimensions of Enite's beauty, that he could not wait until such time as her husband was buried. Rather, he wished her to be elevated that very night as mistress of his land. Though all his vassals thought this disreputable indeed, he dispatched his messengers into the land in all directions to fetch at once those lords whose office is to interpret God's law, so that Enite might be given to him in marriage. For he fancied himself unable to live any longer without her. This is how great the power of love is: the Count desired to lie together with Enite that very night!

(6342–6351) Bishops and abbots journeyed there, and all the clergy that could be reached in a day's ride on horseback. However loathsome and grievous it was to the lady, she was wedded to the Count against her will.[4] All her recalcitrance was of no avail to her either, for he was resolved to have her as his wife. Only God had the power to bring this about, yet the Count had the determination to see it done.

(6352–6377) And now came time for the banquet. The host raised no objections to this, for he welcomed the advent of nightfall. In his mind he fancied a most splendid night together with Enite, a thing which certainly failed to come about. I myself care but little if this man was deluded by false hope! The host betook himself to the banquet hall, and once he was seated, he sent two chaplains and three of his vassals to fetch the lady (as she kept watch over her husband, who lay upon the bier) that she might come to the table. Yet it was of little avail, I fancy, for Enite did not even look up at them while the one man addressed her. This they now reported back to the host, who then sent a great many more lords for her the second time. This he did in order to honor her, that she might be more willing to come, upon hearing word that food was waiting on the table. Yet overcome by heartache, she failed to notice any of the messengers. Having heard this, the host exclaimed: "I must go to her myself."

(6378–6387) When he came to where Enite was, he took her by the hand and ordered her to go with him to the banquet. The lady asked to be spared this, saying: "It would be a meal unbecoming to any woman if I were now to eat and to forget so quickly the very dearest husband a woman has ever had. Alas! How would such a thing befit me?"

(6388–6423) "What is it that you are saying?" he retorted. "There is no cause for you to continue so furious a lament. You have lost a man whom I shall quite easily replace, God willing. Most gladly shall I atone for your loss, both with myself and with all that is mine. Such would be my inclination, save that you thwart me in this through behaviour unbecoming to you, so that no one is able to console you this whole day long. This resistance, at which you are indeed so tenacious, is without merit. Your loss is not so great, for I am quite easily his superior, or certainly just as excellent as he. Do as I say now, my lady. I wish to bestow upon you my person and my land as well as such powerful riches that you can well forget your poverty and your suffering. Now leave here and go with me to the meal." "God forbid," she replied, "that I should have to forsake my husband in this manner." And then she swore this most solemn oath: "I shall sooner choose to be given over to the earth along with him. Since God has taken him from me, I shall renounce all men forever." "Drop this matter now once and for all, for my sake," he spoke, "and accompany me to the banquet, for in truth I shall not be deprived of this."

(6424–6445) Yet however much he entreated her, Enite refused to move from the spot, until finally he resorted to force by pulling her off against her will, for she was unable to hold her ground against him. The Count did not then seat her at his side; instead, at his command she was given a portable chair across the table from him, in order that he could better see the lady. Again and again he bade her eat. But Enite could not put her dear spouse out of her mind. She began shedding tears, and the whole side of the table where she sat became wet from her weeping. She wrung her hands in grief, that most wretched woman, and her lament was most persistent. Despite all the host's entreaties that she restrain herself, she could not put a stop to her wailing.

(6446–6494) Again he spoke to her: "My lady, you are making your grief all too unrelenting for yourself and for me, as well as for my cherished guests, who have come here to pursue merriment. Were you not so childish, moreover, you could stop your lamenting and open your eyes wide to how very splendidly things have improved for you in but a short time—though in fact you had but little cause for distress.[5] Never have I witnessed anything so extraordinary as your inability to fall silent and to accept the fact that your affairs are now in most excellent order and indeed have been changed such that you are accorded this fine treatment. Anyone enjoying such success as must now fall to you here, might better strike up a song than weep and lament. Yet I cannot but tell the truth: your grief is all too persistent. Your affairs are indeed in a different state today than yesterday. Before, you were poor, now you are rich; then you were distinguished in no man's eyes, now God has bestowed honor upon you; then you were quite unknown, now you wield power over an entire realm; before, you were held in low regard, now you are a rich lady; then you were forced to be without title; now you are a powerful countess; then you wandered about aimlessly, until your good fortune elected me; then you were devoid of all comfort, now you are possessed of full grandeur; then you suffered great distress, from which God has led you away; before, you led a lowly life, now God has granted you all you could wish; then you were forced to endure much affliction, now you must praise the Lord for delivering you from that tribulation, and you must cease your foolish lamenting; then you lived without esteem, now you enjoy more acclaim than any other woman in the land.

(6495–6506) "You are tormenting yourself, if you wish to know it, without cause. You have lost unto death a man of no consequence, and I am here to compensate you for that. Such an exchange you ought gladly to accept at any time. I advise this course to all women, for it could never harm them to take a powerful lord instead of such a man as your husband. I forbid this foolishness of yours. Now do as I wish, and eat!"

(6507–6524) The noble Queen then answered: "My lord, you have said enough to me. Indeed, it would have been just as well left unspoken. You may well waste a great deal of talk, but I wish to make my answer to you quite brief. Believe this, upon my oath: never again shall food pass my lips until my dead husband has eaten first." No longer could the Count now control himself, nor refrain from exhibiting his churlishness. His anger led him onto the path of great foolishness and great impropriety, such that he then struck Enite with his hand so brutally that the good lady bled quite profusely. "Eat, you lowly wench!" he cried out.

(6525–6549) All of them alike, rich and poor, whether they kept silent or cried out loud and clear, thought this a great outrage. Moreover, a good many of them reproached him to his very face for what he had done, while the others spoke secretly of it, saying it was a foolish deed, and one which he could easily have forgone. Much rebuke did the Count incur for this: they remonstrated with him to the point that this churlish man began to grow quite furious with rage. Their chiding was vexatious to him, and he spoke out most harshly: "Your behaviour is extraordinary, you lords, for denouncing me for what I do to my wife. It is indeed no one's privilege to speak either ill or well of what a man does to his wife. She is mine and I am hers. How is it that you would prevent me from doing with her what I please?" With that he silenced them all.

(6550–6586) We shall not leave you uninformed about Lady Enite's demeanor once she had been struck: the blow made her happy—happier indeed than at any other moment that day. Whence did she manage to cull this joy? This you might well wish to know, for seldom does a beating make anyone happy. Enite's joy came about in this manner: she would have preferred a thousand times over to die rather than to come away alive. And as she sustained that blow, she nourished the hope and the comfort (since it was dealt with the full strength of a man) that she would be delivered from this life, and that whatever further words she uttered the Count would likewise avenge by striking her, until he finally struck her dead. Hence her lament grew most excessive, and she cried out in an uncourtly fashion, hoping thereby to earn death. Enite then stepped back a good distance from the Count and exclaimed: "Believe me, my lord, I pay no heed to your blows or to whatever befalls me at your hand, and even if you take my life, I shall, in all truth, never become your wife! Take full note of that!" At such length did she rant on that he finally struck her again brutally on the mouth. Enite did not shun his blow, rather she most willingly left herself open to it, that she might be dealt yet more. She fancied her will was being implemented.[6] "Woe to me, most miserable woman!" she cried. "Were my husband but alive, this beating would assuredly not be tolerated!"

(6587–6612) As the lady was raising her lament so loud, Erec, fils du roi Lac, lay still unconscious in apparent death, and yet still untouched by death. He had rested a bit, though little more than before. Lying there in a stupor, he was suddenly startled by Enite's scream, just as a man awakens when frightened by a sinister dream. With a peculiar look, he sat up from the bier and opened his eyes. He wondered what had stricken him, and he had no notion of how he had come to be there. Once more he heard Enite, for she cried out again and again: "O woe, my dear lord, o woe! It is futile for me to desire your help, for you are dead, as ill fate would have it." When she then called out his name, Erec recognized her at once and could readily tell that she was in some manner of distress, though he knew not how or where.

(6613–6662) No longer did he lie there, but once he recognized her voice, he jumped up in a fury and stormed fiercely into the hall where they were all gathered. A great many swords were hanging nearby on a wall. Erec seized one of them. Anger in ample measure welled up inside him. With the very first lunge he slew the host along with two others, who were sitting on either side of him. The rest then took to flight. No one present heeded the dictates of good breeding, for not a one of them there could be seen stepping aside and saying: "After you, my lord." For whoever found the way out took to flight (such were their likes!), the laymen pushing ahead of the priests. Despite all claims to high standing in the Church,[7] none was accorded special treatment, be he abbot or bishop. All the court was fleeing this hall. At the doors it was becoming quite crowded from all the great crush. Squires pushed ahead of their lords. It seemed to them a long way indeed before they could get through the doors. Such a wedding[8] as this I have never attended! One single step was to them as a mile. They began beating a retreat and running about in mad confusion. Many a fine warrior cowered underneath the benches, contrary to all the knightly code. There is one thing which is quite common, and which I fail to find at all surprising: that any man fearing for his life oft-times flees from great turmoil to ensure his safety, retreating from the valley for the security of the fortress. These men, however, were fleeing *from* the castle and were slipping off into holes like mice. The wide castle gates were for them too small and narrow, both inside and outside the portals, so that they dropped over the wall in a throng thick as hail, for they were driven on by frantic fear.

(6663–6687) Limors was left abandoned by all the people. Most compelling was their urge to flee, for they had fear of death. Yet their flight was without disgrace, and anyone who saw shame in what they did would be speaking rashly in this matter. For tell me now, if ever a dead man—with bloody wounds, already laid out for burial, head and hands wrapped in cloth, and feet in a bandage—were to rush in headlong and without warning upon an assembled throng like Erec, brandishing a drawn sword, and if this man were then to threaten them with a call to arms, then anyone who cherished his life at all would take off in flight. And had I been present there myself, I too would have fled, however courageous a man I may be. No one amongst them, save for Lady

Enite, dared to wait about for Erec. Enite was most delighted to see the dead man; all her grief melted into happiness and her joy was multiplied.

(6688–6701) Erec grabbed Enite's hand. He rushed about searching until he finally found his armor as well as his shield and lance, and he donned the armor just as before, as though never beset by any woe. His horses, however, he could not find: "O woe that this should happen! Shall we now go off on foot? Few are the occasions when we have ever done that before!" May God now send this stranded pair, Erec and Enite, horses upon which to ride!

(6702–6731) Failing to find the horses anywhere, Erec acted as the circumstances demanded: he grabbed his shield and with his left hand picked up the lance and, leading Lady Enite on his right side, he dashed out through the castle gates. Here his horse was brought to him, though this had never entered his mind—nor that of the man who was riding it! But in this way Erec's good fortune became fully evident. One of the host's squires had taken the horse to water, and was now riding it. He was singing a rotruenge,[9] and his thoughts were altogether untroubled, for he knew nothing of this whole matter. At that moment he rode onto the path leading up to the fortress. Erec recognized the horse as soon as he first saw it off in the distance. This was a source of great joy to Erec, and it was God's will that had ordained it. Erec then stood there, not making a sound until the horse came close enough that he could seize it by the bridle and return it to his own keeping. And with this he was off on his way.

(6732–6749) The Queen, Lady Enite, he seated in front of him (better accommodations were then out of the question), and his plan was to ride on straight ahead through the land. But the trail was unfamiliar to him. Furthermore, the journey was rendered aimless by the darkness of the night. What is more, Erec had fear of incurring injury and dishonor from the people of that land once they heard tell of what he had done. Following Lady Enite's counsel (for she instructed him as to the path), he turned onto the road along which he had come to Limors on the litter. This he did to ensure their safety.

(6750–6759) The land in which Erec slew the Count, the domain belonging to the little man who had dealt Erec his wound, and King Arthur's realm were all adjacent to one another and quite close together. These three lands were separated only by a forest, in the midst of which Erec was now riding in the wake of this perilous encounter.

⊗ XII ⊗
RECONCILIATION AND HEALING

(6760–6791) And as they entered the forest, leaving the grip of tribulation and returning to their familiar path, King Erec inquired of Lady Enite how he had come into the hands of the Count, whose slaying I have recounted to you. Enite then revealed to him what had happened, much to the discomfort of her eyes, which shed tears throughout her story. Erec put an end then and there to the feigned cruelty and the strange dissimulation to which he had until that day subjected her without good cause (namely that he had refused to speak with her since departing from his castle with her). By now Erec had resolved all the questions which had led him to assume this strange behavior, and he understood things quite without illusion. He had done this in order to test whether or not Enite was a fitting wife for him. Now he had examined her full well, just as gold ought to be purified in the forge, so that he knew with certainty that Enite was possessed of loyalty and constancy, and that she was an unswerving wife.

(6792–6813) Erec pressed her to his breast, kissed her again and again with a full measure of love, and asked the virtuous lady full forgiveness for the hostile regimen and the manifold hardships which she had suffered while on that journey. He promised her better things, and indeed he fulfilled his promise. Enite then forgave him on the spot, for his entreaties were delivered in a most friendly fashion. "My dear lord," she said, "there was in truth no other burden which weighed as heavily on me as the fact that I was forced to shun your company. There were countless other burdens, yet all else seemed insignificant to me. Had I been forced to suffer this deprivation any longer, it would certainly have cost me my life in good time."

(6814–6851) Whilst this strange event was taking place at Limors, behold: a squire managed to slip away! Off through the forest he sprinted, in order to report it anon to the little king who was so courageous. I have already told you of him: his name was Guivreiz, the same one who had with his own hand dealt the wound to Erec. The trail was quite familiar indeed to this squire, and he set out with much haste. Furthermore, he had not far to go at all: nothing save the forest stood between their two realms. The squire then knocked on the fortress doors. He waited but a short time outside the portal, and was let in forthwith.

He now went before the King and set about recounting to him how Count Oringles had been slain, and that it was a dead man who had done this feat. Only as the story neared its end did Guivreiz begin to grasp that it was Erec. Still, he was hardly guilty of sloth:[1] with a very loud voice he cried out: "To arms! What a loss it will be, if the finest knight on earth is to lose his life! Unless God grants him His favor, the people of that land shall murder him at once if they hear word of this. O woe, if only I could defend my friend, I would prove to him my willingness to do so! Yet I shall make the attempt, if God wills it."

(6852–6861) Guivreiz now armed himself straightway, as did all the knights in his company. All in all they were a good thirty knights in number. Their horses were then brought up. Full of uncertainty and infelicity, the King set out in good time toward the forest, that he might aid the stranded Erec in escaping that land.

(6862–6891) Now they had both set out on the very same road, on the one end Erec and on the other Guivreiz, the one travelling in this direction, the other in that direction, so that they could not help but encounter one another. Thus did fate ordain it. Neither of them knew of the other's journey, which led to peril for Erec. While they were still far apart, Erec, the foreigner, discerned quite clearly the armed throng, for their shields were clattering and clanging loudly. To Lady Enite he spoke: "My lady, I hear a great army riding in our direction. I do not wish to withdraw from the road in so cowardly a fashion without defending myself. My strength is very meager, yet I shall show them some measure of my knightly prowess. Now dismount and wait on the trail until you see how things are resolved." Never before, I fancy, had the lady suffered greater distress, for she saw that Erec was feeble.

(6892–6909) Erec stopped on the same path upon which the others were riding. The moon, suddenly unveiled by scattering clouds, revealed to them the loveliness of the night. King Guivreiz, who was riding at the head of the company, now spotted Erec and saw him holding firm in the road. Erec then made preparations to defend himself right in the middle of that trail. Let it now be in God's hands to protect him! And what would you have King Guivreiz do, other than likewise make ready to do joust—unless he were to allow himself to become a coward? And this I shall say of him with all assurance: a coward he was certainly not! This he proved well time and again, both there and elsewhere.

(6910–6925) They commenced to lower their lances and give a show of their strength. The bore down on one another and performed a mighty joust. Those most excellent knights both hit right on the mark. It was only his strength which helped the better-rested man to come away with the praise and to fare so well. Erec he struck down from the saddle and onto the turf, a full lance's length behind his horse. Thereupon he dismounted over where Erec lay. At this, Lady Enite ached with consternation.

(6926–6956) Never before had this happened to Erec. Nor could any man bound by the precepts of truthfulness ever claim to have unhorsed Erec. What is more, that esteemed knight would most certainly have been spared such a fate that night, had he only been healthy. His strength had been so sapped that he was forced to endure subjugation at the hand of King Guivreiz. The little King then unfastened Erec's helmet and was about to slay him once and for all. This the lady could not bear to watch. She tarried no longer where she had been standing hidden from view and beset with great tribulation; out from behind the hedge she sprang and threw herself down on top of her spouse. "No, good knight," she cried, "if ever you possessed the knightly spirit, do not slay my husband! Bear this in mind as well: he is gravely wounded, and you shall gain no honor at all from whatever more you do to him now, for it can only bring down sin upon you. King Guivreiz, if I recall his name, has wounded him in the side."

(6957–6984) Guivreiz recognized Lady Enite by her voice and was also aided by her mention of his name. He jumped back quite hastily, saying: "My lady, tell me who this knight is, and tell me also how it is that you know me. I am the one whose name you have mentioned. Evil circumstances, I fancy, have overtaken me. Tell me, my lady, about yourself: is this lord called Erec, and you Lady Enite? Tell me this, that I might not linger here too long, for I have ridden forth for the sake of Erec. And let me tell you that I have heard reports of him which are grievous to me, that he is in peril not far from here at Limors. Judging by what I was told, I fear you may lose him unto death if I am not off at once on my journey—I and my comrades, who are ready to come to his aid. I am wasting time in this forest; I ought to ride to him at once. It is a loss if he is slain."

(6985–7002) At this Enite began to entreat him once again with words and with gestures: this is what saved Erec's life. She untied Erec's helmet cap, and then Guivreiz recognized him straightway. He was most happy to see Erec, and he spoke in good faith: "Welcome, my lord! Tell me whether anything is ailing you and if so, what it is." "Nothing ails me," replied Erec. "Aside from where you wounded me, I am otherwise quite well." Guivreiz was most pleased at this. He doffed his helmet, and these two men bounded toward each other out of joy and kissed one another in loyalty.

(7003–7030) Guivreiz was haunted by regret at Erec's discomfort, which stemmed from the joust with him. As he began lamenting this, Erec interrupted: "Speak not of this and disregard it. You have committed no wrong towards me. Whenever a man acts foolishly, it is just that he be requited for it. You have accorded me just treatment, inasmuch as I—fool that I was!—in my folly first became inclined to such great immoderation that I desired to hold forth alone on unfamiliar paths and to challenge so many fine knights. My punishment was too light, since I, all by myself, coveted all your acclaim. I ought to have incurred a harsher penalty." After they had spoken these words, Guivreiz bowed to Lady Enite and bade her welcome. The Queen thanked him for his greeting. Once they had ascertained fully that Erec had no mortal wounds, they were with one mind happy.

(7031–7045) At this they mounted their horses and rode off, though for but a short distance. Taking them joyfully into his care, Sir Guivreiz led them off the road onto an open meadow. For Sir Erec's sake they spent the night there, so that he might find rest in the wake of his exhaustion. As circumstances had it, they were provided with a most warming fire here. At this spot such a blaze was not at all hard for them to enkindle, for there was ample timber here for anyone willing to carry it over to the fire.

(7046–7078) After they had sat there by the bonfire and forgotten some measure of their dismal ordeal, and after Erec had recounted the distress he had suffered since his departure from Guivreiz (this was after they had both simultaneously dealt each other wounds; this same story I did not hold back without telling you all that I knew of it)—after all of this they began to lament most fervently the hardships endured by these esteemed guests, Erec and Enite, and to give great thanks to God that Erec was still alive. For time and again his life had swayed in the balance, just like that of a shipwrecked man who, clinging to a plank of wood, escapes the ocean's swell and comes running out onto the shore. Many a time had Erec's fate been very much akin to this and in doubt. Now, however, God together with Erec's adroitness had delivered him from out of the choppy waters of distress onto the sands of felicity, so that he had overcome all his suffering and sat there now in full happiness. May God now aid him in his further endeavors! Thus far—this is beyond dispute—he has met with success.

(7079–7111) It was now time for them to sleep. The knights set out together to look for the right place for beds to be prepared for them. In the course of their search they espied three beech trees standing off to one side of the campfire. These trees were wide and finely shaped, each grown equally tall, with luxuriant foliage and branches of stately breadth. Bedding was fashioned under these trees for the most esteemed guests. Beneath one of them and off away from the others were Erec and Lady Enite, who had on many an occasion lain apart from one another, and had not kept company in sleeping or in eating. Now they put an end to this intemperate animosity, and they chose a better life for themselves. The host was given a bed under the tree next to them (this one stood in the middle of the three), and the knights were bedded down beneath the third tree. "Now tell us, of what did their bed-linen consist?" In truth, it was just what is found in the woods: delicate foliage and clean grass, the finest in all the forest. What use is there of lengthy questions, save to say that they then lay down to sleep?

(7112–7123) The night ended pleasantly, and at daybreak they set out from there. That most tiny man, Guivreiz their host, took them to a place nearby where greater comfort awaited them: to a fortress of his where he knew they would be provided with full luxury. This castle was replete with everything good, just as I shall now tell you.

(7124–7157) It was situated in the middle of a lake, which supplied Guivreiz with enough and still more of all the finest fishes ever placed before any king, all the species one could imagine. Furthermore, they had there the most excellent hunting whereof we have ever heard tell. The King had enclosed a good two miles or more of forest around the lake, and had surrounded it with a wall. There was no other opening in this wall except onto the lake. This same area was, as I can describe to you, divided by walls into three equal parts. One of the first two parts contained red deer in ample quantity; wild boars inhabited the second. If you are asking what is in the third area, next to the others, only small animals were there, separated from the rest: foxes, hares and such. Quite amply stocked was this game preserve, so much so that no man who truly enjoyed the hunt could ever complain of not finding any game there. The host had also excellently supplied the hunting lodge with dogs trained to obey a man's command.

(7158–7187) Whenever Guivreiz watched from atop that castle as a squad of men hunted with the dogs—no matter where he sat along the turrets—even those who were down there participating in the hunt did not have a much better view of things. And who would wish to spoil his pleasure, when from up on the castle and in the company of the ladies, he could look down and watch the dogs running? For each time the red deer were put to flight, their final[2] tack was always in the direction of the water and into the lake; and what is more, they were never apprehended anywhere else but right there at the foot of the castle. And any man taken with an urge to hunt for swine or bear found very sturdy and stout javelins at his disposal; and if he wished to hunt the hare, as you have already heard tell, he could find the very most excellent harriers.[3] Hunt whatever you yourself prefer. There are dogs and game here, and everything needed for the hunt, nets and fine weapons for shooting, and whatever else your heart desires. Fine indeed was the entertainment here.

(7188–7206) Penefrec was the name of this castle, where nothing was found lacking and where there were full supplies of everything: fish and venison, and both white breads and wine. Nor was there a shortage there of anything else which was needed. For this reason the host had brought his most esteemed guest Erec here for a rest, for he had every good intention of seeing to it that Erec, together with his wife, regained his vitality there. They also had at this place fine provisions of rich bed-linen. As a reward for his excellence Erec was honored and cared for most exquisitely there. Quite profuse was the attention lavished upon both Erec and the Queen.

(7207–7231) Who now is to be his physician, to heal his wounds? For this purpose Erec had encountered two of the King's sisters there, most powerful ladies, noble and lovely. They were pleased indeed at this and glad in their hearts that Erec had come to them in such a way that he had need of their services. Such physicians as these Erec could certainly find suitable! They healed his wounds, for they were well versed in this art. The good Lady Enite likewise had him in her most faithful care. From all of this, Erec's side became pleasing to the eye and fully healed. They possessed a portion of the bandage of which I told you earlier, the one which Famurgan had fashioned there with her own hands. Lady Guinevere had sent them a piece of it as a gift, and it was that which cured this man.

(7232–7263) King Erec remained there at the castle of Penefrec exactly fourteen nights, until he was fully healed and recovered from his wound. Once his body had wholly regained its strength, he began yearning to continue his journey anew. Regardless how serene Erec's comfort was at that place, he felt most discontented there. The virtuous man's thoughts turned, in truth, towards setting forth as soon as possible, just as though he were in a forest without shelter, alone and without any comforts, where both wind and rain subjected the faithful warrior to their harsh ravages. Erec's thoughts sprang from his conviction that no worldly thing was for him preferable to the comfort of that place where he found knightly deeds and where he was forced to practice such deeds mightily with his own hand. This was the life which Erec had chosen. It was perhaps even more to him than that;[4] it was his sleep and his nourishment. Those fourteen nights, this is true, were to him as many long years. He wanted to tarry there no longer and would have been off sooner, had he been able.

⊗ XIII ⊗
ENITE'S HORSE AND SADDLE

(7264–7285) Alas, Lady Enite! What indeed is she now to ride, this lovely, kind and high-born lady? For she had lost her horse, as you have heard full well before, when Count Oringles was slain at Limors and Erec barely escaped there with her. Certainly she ought to be compensated for having lost it. And she will be nicely indemnified, for they shall replace it for her, in such a way that she can never raise a complaint about it, with a horse so fine (as I shall describe for you) that indeed no man has ever owned or even seen a more excellent horse. The ladies, the two sisters of the King, gave Enite this animal, and they were most pleased that she deigned to accept it from them. Likewise, Enite found the horse most worthy.

(7286–7335) Is someone asking whether this horse was finer than the one which Enite had hitherto ridden? They were altogether different in kind. This is how it was adorned: it was of quite contrasting colors. On the left side, where the shield was held, it was entirely white in color—so white that nothing could be any whiter, and so lovely that its radiance reflected in the beholder's eyes. No one could gaze upon it intently for any time. (This I have heard the Master[1] say of it.) And the other side had spared no pains in offsetting the white side. Just as thoroughly white as that shield-side was (about which I have just read to you now), every bit as black was this other side here, where the whiteness ended. Black and white was the horse, and this disparate contrast was exquisitely divided: between the two colors a line was emblazoned, perhaps the breadth of half a finger. This stripe was green, and bright as a blade of grass. It began at the horse's mouth and continued on, like a brush-stroke, between the ears, quite evenly down over the mane and along the back, toward the flanks and up to the horse's rump. Underneath, it was the same, running down the middle of the chest, as was indeed well fitting. This was all quite remarkable! Around each eye, this is true, was a ring of the same color. Soft and curly was the horse's mane, and it was gathered on the side where it hung down. It was of just the right thickness and not long: it flowed down in curls not quite to the knees. The forelock was long, half black and half white, just as the green color separated it. The tail was just like this in its appearance.

(7336–7365) Since I have now told of the horse's appearance, you shall also be apprised of how it looked otherwise. It was perfectly formed, in the following fashion: it was neither too low nor too tall, neither too short nor too long, neither too fat nor too thin. It rightfully bore its lean head high indeed, with prominent, but not long ears, one black, the other white. A white ring encircled the black ear, a black ring surrounded the white one. Its neck was thick and erect, with just the right amount of curvature, and slender where it joined the head. Seen from any side, it was fashioned so as to be well pleasing to your eye. Its chest was strong and broad, and it had slender legs, neither too large nor too small. They were smooth and straight, and lean as those of a deer.[2] It had— since it is my duty to praise it—a high foot and a short pastern.[3] The feet, moreover, were just right, all black in color throughout. Even if that horse were never cleaned by any groom, it would still remain beautiful and sleek.

(7366–7388) Such was this horse's nature that a man acclaimed wise by all the world, a man who understands the essence of all things, could not, by drawing upon all his learning,[4] conceive of anything more excellent than that beast, even if he were to sit eight full years engrossed in his thoughts and if he were to leave no stone unturned in giving birth in his mind to a horse beautiful and excellent in every regard. Such was Enite's horse. And if this same man then had the power to wish into existence whatever qualities he ascribed to the horse in his mind, and if once he completed it, he placed it before his eyes and then had the power to remove from the horse whatever features were unbecoming to it—so perfect was Enite's horse that such a man would not take away so much as a hair from it.

(7389–7425) If anyone says: "He is making up lies!" I shall explain matters to him more clearly, that he might recognize that this story is not invented: the horse was not bred here at home! I shall tell you how it came to be there. The host himself had taken it from a wild dwarf at the foot of a hollow mountain one day as he rode, as was his wont, into the forest in search of adventure. The dwarf had tethered it quite securely to a tree branch and had then gone off. This is how the man found it. He then untied it from the tree branch, and great was the dwarf's vexation when he returned and failed to find his horse at the tree where he had secured it. When he spotted the horse in another man's hands, his screaming and his weeping grew most loud indeed, and he gave good evidence of how precious that horse was. With great chagrin he fell into a most furious rage. He offered Guivreiz three thousand marks in gold in return for the horse, but Guivreiz refused everything he offered. He had no need of the dwarf's possessions, and so he took the horse away. At this, the little man, out of misery, raised so loud a din that the mountain resounded with his cry.

(7426–7432) As for the horse's little saddle, if someone were to take it and balance it on a scale with gold, he would fail to pay for it according to its just value. But I shall tell you no more of it, in order that I not draw out the story,[5] for it was indeed too small for a full-grown man.

(7433–7461) And after Guivreiz had then brought this horse out from the forest back to Penefrec, he gave it to the ones for whom he intended it, to his two sisters. It was quite well evident from this that he held them dear, for the horse bore its rider gently and swiftly, and I shall tell you in just what fashion: when it dropped its hoof to the ground, it pranced so softly that no man had so well-trained an ear as to be able to hear its step. Whoever sat upon that horse, I tell you in all truth that he felt quite as though he were floating. Save that it might not be proper and would be a bit unseemly to speak at such length about a horse (wherefore I wish to drop the subject), I could relate marvelous things about it. But for this reason I shall hold back with any further praise. Yet let any man say what he will, he can recount a great many tales and offer his opinion, but no one ever had so fine a horse as this in his possession. What use is there that I say any more to you about it?

(7462–7492) As the Master told us, a lady's saddle was upon the horse, a saddle which displayed much expert craftsmanship. It had been worked upon for many a day by the most skilled man ever engaged in saddle-work, by a master named Umbriz, who indeed applied all his energies to it, in truth, for a good three and a half years[6] before completing it in accordance with his plans. For me to report to you fully about this saddle, about how it was fashioned— that would become too burdensome for so simple a fellow as me. And yet even if I could relate it to you accurately now, it would be all too long a story for one mouth to tell. What is more, my poetic powers are diminished by the fact that I have never seen this saddle. On the other hand, I do wish to relate to you briefly how it was embellished, according to an account by the man from whom I obtained the story and as I read it in his book—but as briefly as I can.

(7493–7525) "Be silent now, dear Hartmann. Let me see if I can guess." All right, but speak quickly. "I must first think about it." Quickly now, I am in a hurry! "Will you then think me a wise man?" Yes, yes. For God's sake, go ahead and tell what you have to say. "This is the story which I wish to tell you." The rest I shall let you withhold! "It was made of fine hornbeam." Yes. What else might it have consisted of? "It was covered with radiant gold." Who indeed could have told you the truth of how it looked? "It was very tightly stitched." That much you have surmised correctly. "There was a fine scarlet blanket of wool on its back." At that I must certainly laugh! "Do you see that I can guess accurately?" Yes, yes. You are a man who could even divine tomorrow's weather. "You talk as though to mock me." Alas, for God's sake, no. "In truth, your lips are curled with scorn." I always like to laugh. "So, have I not guessed it after all?" Yes, but only after they have walked up with the horse in full view.[7] "Have I by chance passed over anything?" In truth, you have no idea of what you are saying today. "Then am I not right?" Not so much as a hair. "Have I then completely made up lies?" No, but as it is, you have been deceived by your childish imagination. Now let me tell you about the saddle.

(7526–7581) Behold how large a grain of sand is. There was even less wood than that in this saddle. It was crafted of ivory and precious stones and also of the finest gold ever purified in the fire. Impurities in it were hard indeed to come upon! Using these three materials, the master in his art had fashioned this saddle with great skill. At the behest of decorum, he assigned the ivory and likewise the stones their proper place. In between he then inlaid the gold in an exquisite fashion; its task was to hold the work together. Engraved on this saddle was the lengthy Song of Troy. At the very front of it was depicted the tale of how it came about that Troy was conquered and finally destroyed. With that, it ended on the one side. On the opposite side was an engraving depicting how Sir Aeneas, that most clever man, departed there to travel across the sea, and how he arrived in Carthage, and how the powerful Lady Dido accepted him into her favor, and how he then left her in a most ungallant fashion and failed to fulfill his promise to her. Thus was the lady deceived. On the rear saddle-bow was engraved on one side Dido's most poignant grief, and how she sent messengers to Aeneas, though she did little to change his mind. Here were also clearly depicted the deeds which were worthy of telling, from that time up until the day he conquered Laurentum. (To recount how he gained power over that city would take too long.) On the other side was illustrated how Aeneas took Lady Lavinia as his wife in marriage, and how Sir Aeneas ruled over that land without misfortune till the end of his days.[8]

(7582–7609) This saddle was covered with a quilt of silk and gold, a quilt finely woven, indeed as exquisitely as could be. The quilt was of just the proper length, it hung down well nigh to the ground. Individually illustrated upon it were all the wonders of the world and all that the heavens encompass. If you do not find it tiresome, then I shall recount some of these to you, though I shall keep silent about far more than I shall mention. The four elements were depicted clearly there in their individual colors, and in each of them all that is subject to it. It was expert artistry that had fabricated this! Of the four, the earth was represented with its creatures, each and every one of them—from forest or meadow, tame or wild—that any man can recognize in his mind's eye. Then a human being was depicted, wrought with such mastery as if it were about to speak and defy the properties of an image.

(7610–7641) Next to that were the waves of the ocean, therein a fish just as if it were alive; and next to it and separately depicted were all the creatures of the sea and whatever else inhabits the ocean floor. If someone would tell me their names, I would fain recognize them and be able to name them all. For that, seek out a man who can readily list for you their names. If you fail to find such a man (which will very likely be the case), then follow my advice and set out straightway and travel to the sea yourself. Therein you shall find a host of these creatures. Go and stand at the shore and bid them come out onto the sand where you are waiting; there you shall become acquainted with every species. But if even that does not help (which again will probably hold true), then go yourself and seek out the ocean floor. There they will then become known to you—though at great harm to you, and with little gain. Now my advice to all of my friends is that they drop their curiosity and remain here at home. My friends, you ought not to view as worthwhile something which can so very readily and constantly harm a man, yet which can never benefit him.

(7642–7657) Next to that then stood the third element. Are you asking which one that is? It is air, portrayed with its own properties. Birds of many species soared in the air, birds woven with such artistry as though they were living and were striving upwards towards the skies. Fire, along with its dragons and other beings which must live from fire—all of these could likewise be seen depicted on that quilt. A ribbon which led down to earth then encircled the edges. This ribbon was of a hand's breadth and was studded with precious stones.

(7658–7668) The mantle which Jupiter and the goddess Juno wore over them as they sat on the nuptial throne in their lofty realm was costly enough indeed. Yet Jupiter's mantle was no more comparable to this saddle-quilt—this I wish to tell you—than the moon is to the sun. Certainly you must grant me this much: that I am telling you the truth.

(7669–7679) Both excellent and stately were the stirrups, broad rings of gold, fashioned in the shape of two dragons. The hand of the goldsmith, who undertook his work with care, was able to shape those stirrups exquisitely! These dragons curled their tails around toward their mouths, and their wings⁹ were spread as though they were in flight. Their eyes were stones, four elegant hyacinths.

(7680–7729) Of what were each of these made, the saddle belt and the stirrup strap? You should have to inspect the work carefully before you would know what to say, whether it was embroidered with gold or lined with silk. You could not tell from the configurations that it was in fact embroidery, and you would never recognize this unless you ran your hand over it. The buckles were of silver, so that one might see a white glitter set off against the gold, and they were hard and splendid. Most excellent was the saddle-cushion, not of calfskin, as I have certainly seen on a great many cushions. On this one you could not spot even a fingernail's breadth of leather. The cushion was fine and lovely, as was becoming for that saddle and as well befitted it. This cushion was stuffed in a praiseworthy fashion, soft as cotton, so that it did not rub the horse. The part of it that could be seen protruding from underneath the saddle was thickly embroidered. To enhance its appearance there was a depiction on it of how Thisbe and Pyramus, beset by love and robbed of their good senses, met with a sorrowful end when they came to the fountain.[10] Where the fringe belonged, there was a golden net woven with gold threads, strong and durable, and spread out over the horse's rump. Placed all around it were precious stones in ample number, one at each seam where the stitches intertwined and crossed over one another. Wherever there was to be a button, a ruby was mounted in an azure-colored setting. The stones all sparkled uniformly from these settings, full of brilliant color.

(7730–7766) Fine and graceful was the harness. Sturdy and very elegant, it consisted of a strap two fingers wide whose rich embroidery extended even to the reins[11] by which the horse was led. The eleven precious stones were set in this strap with beautiful artistry.[12] The twelfth was mounted alone at the front of the reins on a broad disk which extended down in front of the forelock and hung before the horse's head. That brilliant almandine thus fulfilled its calling in this position, for brightness is its natural property, so that if a man ever had to ride out on a dark night, he would be able to see because of that stone. The other eleven stones were inlaid in this harness and arranged along it, and in between them hung costly gold bells which could be heard ringing from far away. With such accoutrements as these the saddle was finished, and in an even finer fashion than I have conceived it. Forsooth, I also think it meet and right that it was, according to all we hear of it,[13] far more exquisite than any other saddle, for in truth it was presented to the fairest woman alive in those years, to the noble Lady Enite.

(7767–7787) And now it is time that they be off, for the horses have since arrived. Did they then take leave of the assembled company? Yes, from one young courtier and the next, as well as from the King's sisters. Never before and never since could a firmer resolve for all manner of goodness be seen in any other women. They were the caretakers of good breeding. These ladies ensured that they are justly accorded the highest ranking whenever good women are being selected. Without gall my Lady Filledamur and her sister Genteflur engaged in every manner of service proper for a woman, so as rightfully to be well pleasing to God and to the world.[14]

⬡ XIV ⬡
JOIE DE LA COURT

(7788–7807) They now rode off from there, Enite and these two men, Erec and the host himself, Guivreiz. So softly did the horse carry Lady Enite along that trail that never at any time does any man navigating calm waters fare the least bit more gently, even when he enjoys a perfect wind at his back and his ship is gliding along reassuringly. Their plan was to ride straightway to the land of Britain, to King Arthur; yet at that time they knew not at which of his castles they would in fact encounter him. As they set out, King Guivreiz spoke: "We shall find Arthur at Karidol, or else at Tintajol for certain."

(7808–7825) Thus they rode in the hope that this would be confirmed, yet without any certainty, till around mid-day. The horse-path then led them across a lovely meadow to a crossroads. Which trail went to the land of Britain they did not know. But they failed to take the right path and chose instead the one which was better travelled. And as they had, after some time, ridden a good five miles, they saw before them a fortress, large and splendidly proportioned. And once Guivreiz spotted it, he became most troubled and he sorely regretted that they had come that way.

(7826–7833) "But tell us why!" I know precisely why, and I shall tell you, but not until the proper moment. It is not yet time for that. How impatient you are! Why should a man reveal the outcome of his story? The appearance of this fortress, on the other hand, I shall not hold back from you. Listen and hear this from the story.

(7834–7863) The fortress stood on a most excellent site, which as the account of the adventure documents it for us, was twelve hides wide.[1] It stood atop a vaulted cliff on which not a single knoll could be seen anywhere. This crag was as smooth as if it had been turned on a lathe. Perfection, with all its grandeur, had had a hand in shaping it, for it jutted up from the earth far beyond the reach of catapults. A fortress wall, high and thick, had been erected to encompass that mountain, and a knightly air adorned the castle within this wall. Bristling upwards beyond the battlements were towers constructed with immense ashlars.[2] Those turrets were held together at the joints not by any sandy mortar; instead, they were girded together more firmly, with iron and lead clasps positioned three together at close intervals. In between the towers there was no shortage of living quarters, wherein the inhabitants of this fortress dwelt in a manner befitting their great majesty. With equal majesty did the castle extend outward with its turrets, of which there were thirty in number, all in all.

(7864–7883) This is how the castle was embellished:[3] the tops of the towers were decorated with capitals[4] of red gold, each of which cast its radiance far out into the land. This pointed the way for strangers travelling there, so that they saw the glitter from afar and never, during daylight, went astray on their journey to the castle. A river flowed along at the foot of that fortress and because it ran through a gorge, its falls gave off a thunderous roar. So deep was this same chasm that if anyone went to sit atop the turrets and then were to cast his glance downwards, the depth of that abyss made him feel as though he were gazing down into hell itself. Such a man's limbs grew heavy with dizziness, so that he shrank back and retreated inside.

(7884–7893) On the other side, where the castle was accessible by horseback, was an elegant square, richly crowded with buildings, which at one end faced onto the water. On the other end it was bordered by an arbor[5] lovely and broad, such that never, either before or since, has a more beautiful garden been seen. This is how I heard the Master describe it.

(7894–7910) Once Erec espied this castle, he asked his comrade whether he were familiar with the fortress, and he also asked him its name. Such was that lord's reply to him: "I do recognize it. We have wandered far off from our path. May God curse it! Despite the many times I have ridden this trail, I have made an unfortunate blunder. By directing us along the left-hand path I have badly erred. The land of Britain," he continued, "lies in the distant yonder. Let us turn back in time. I shall lead you back onto our trail."

(7911–7925) King Erec then spoke: "How would that befit us, most noble man, if we were to ride off like this? Since we have come so close, for my sake follow me, that I might behold this fortress. Indeed, I shall not have it any other way. This castle is so delightful and so exquisite that I can readily tell from the outside that, if the inside is full of anything at all pleasing to the eye, then it is certainly not without its ladies. I wish to learn more about the castle. This much you will surely not begrudge me."

(7926–7951) "It is with regret that I must grant you this request. Woe be to the day when you find out what is here!" "What do you mean, King Guivreiz?" "I mean nothing more than what I know." "For God's sake, tell me what it is!"

"Turn back now, and we shall be better off." "But I am curious to know what you mean." "You shall readily find out if you refuse to turn back." "Forsooth, I must investigate this; it cannot be anything worse than death." "Then you will surely meet with a fate which your friends shall never cease to lament." "Will you now finally, for God's sake, reveal this to me? I am curious to hear what it is all about." "For my sake, turn back. I shall forever requite you for this with my service, as I well ought to do." "That would be unbecoming to me. For in this way you could be deluded into thinking that I had forgone the journey out of fear. Moreover, there is no danger which you must conceal from me. Even if it turned out to be something that gave me good cause to turn back, I would find it in me to do just that."

(7952–7981) "Sir King," spoke Guivreiz, "I shall tell you all that I know. The peril is none too slight, and I shall apprise you of it, in the hope that you will forgo the journey, as you have spoken with your own lips. This castle is called Brandigan, and a great many valiant knights have travelled here boldy in search of adventure. Each and every one of them—the finest from all lands— has, as a result, been accorded injury along with disgrace. For a long time now no man has been victorious, rather they have all shared the same fate and have been slain here in a lamentable fashion. What more can I tell you? For I am both willing and obligated to throw myself at your feet in order that you take my advice and turn back. Such are the stakes awaiting you with this adventure, that my heart beats with the fear that you might fare just as have all others who have come to this place."

(7982–7996) Erec spoke up in reply: "I would be a coward and would reap nothing but disgrace if I were to turn back now and not see this matter through to the end. Will you disclose to me what this adventure is, or how it is called? I would surely be forever beset with shame were I to fear something which I do not even know. Now why are you doing this? Why have you concealed this from me for so long and not given me a full accounting of what is at stake? For regardless what befalls me as a result, in truth I shall not turn back until I have a better knowledge of this affair."

(7997–8027) King Guivreiz then answered: "In that case I shall tell you of this adventure and of just what must be done, since you insist upon it. It is called *joie de la court.*" (Since this phrase is unfamiliar to Germans, I shall translate it for you: it means joy of the court.) Guivreiz then continued, saying: "Look closely over yonder. Do you see the arbor standing at the foot of the castle? In that garden a knight has been abiding for a very long time now. I shall tell you exactly what the stakes are in this adventure. Any man who is to win victory in the adventure here must do so by engaging in battle with this knight, whose uncle is the lord of the castle. As this knight has always proven, his equal in strength or in courage is not to be found anywhere in the empire. He has slain all knights who have ever ridden against him in hope of gaining victory in the adventure. No one has managed to be a match for him. Turn back now, for my sake!"

(8028–8047) At that, King Erec sent his horse galloping onto the trail, exclaiming with most hearty laughter: "Let us be off, noble knight! If it is but one man who must be overcome in order for me to triumph in the adventure, then things are certainly not hopeless! How is it that you are making so great an issue of it? What is he that he is to be so sorely feared—is he a mountain, or something equal in size to a mountain? I fancied the castle infested by dragons and wild beasts that would kill us as soon as we set foot into the place and before we could even defend ourselves! But now I have hope of coming away alive. Indeed, this knight shall not be granted reprieve, God willing, from being put to the test. If he slays me, then I am dead. Such is small cause for the world to grieve."

(8048–8055) The good King Guivreiz readily recognized Erec's determination to pursue this affair to the end without fail and not to let anyone dissuade him from it. Guivreiz was sorely troubled from the very moment he first set eyes upon the castle.[6] None of his resistance was of any avail in convincing Erec not to carry out his resolve.

(8056–8085) They now embarked upon the way. And as King Erec rode off toward Brandigan together with his beautiful wife at the risk of his very life, the square which he spotted at the foot of the castle was the scene of much joy: dancing and every manner of diversion well suited for young people. And as Erec came riding up, and they saw the comely Enite riding on ahead, with the two men behind her, they then observed the lady, and all of them exclaimed that they had until that day never beheld a lady so lovely and so splendid both in appearance and in attire, as well as in her horse and in her saddle. Yet at that very same moment they all, women and men alike, began to feel their joy slipping away in the face of distressing sorrow. And they wept most wretchedly for the blissful woman and lamented the fact that so valiant a man was to lose his life. For of that they had no doubt.

(8086–8111) "Lord and powerful God," they cried, "why have you called into being so perfect a man? You would have displayed the full measure of your grace by protecting him from this calamitous journey and by preventing him from coming, for he shall lose his life here. Alas! you most wretched woman! What torment you would inflict upon yourself if you could only know all that awaits you here! O, what gloom shall come and cause your sparkling eyes to disavow their present radiance and lack of sorrow! And how that gloom shall darken your rosy-red lips, which even here and now awaken happy laughter in the hearts of these people! And how you shall scorn your cheerfulness with grief, once you lose your husband!" Each and every one of them lamented Enite. Their plaints were not, however, uttered aloud, but rather in a murmur, lest any of it should fall upon Erec's ears.

(8112–8140) They continued their talking at great length. Many a woman beat her breast, and the others wept bitter tears. The virtuous Erec knew what they meant by that, yet he acted in a manner as though he knew nothing of it. Imperturbable as always, Erec contemplated things with a happy and certain mind, as should a brave man who cannot be easily unnerved by mere words. He nurtured no superstitious beliefs, and he expected neither good nor ill to come his way from the secretive murmuring of those women. Erec paid no heed whatever to anything he saw in his dreams, and never did he entertain superstitious notions about the weather. He was just as glad in the morning to see an owl fly past as a mouse-falcon. Nor did he ever order a fire made out of twigs, in order to have his fortune told from it. Erec practiced no ritual crafts: he was of such a bent that he cared not whether the palm of his hand was narrow or wide, and he paid no attention to things arising from superstition.[7]

(8141–8153) So steadfast a man was Erec that, regardless of how the people there were discouraging him, this failed to dishearten him the least bit in his valiant resolve, and he took it all as a mere joke. "As long as God deigns to have me in His care," he thought, "I cannot fare but well. And if it is His will to allow me no more time here, then I can just as gladly die right now, since the body must indeed one day perish."

(8154–8169) Erec's heart was free of distress. He rode up and greeted them with a smile, and then he raised his voice in a most joyful song. Now the people whispered amongst themselves once more: "It seems you do not altogether understand what is to happen to you here. Alas! it shall not be long now indeed before your merry song will end most sorrowfully. Before this same hour tomorrow it shall come to pass. If you and your wife could only know that you shall enjoy your happy life for but so short a time, then you would put a stop to your singing."

(8170–8187) Thus did that most fearless man ride off from them and up to the castle of Brandigan. There he was accorded his just dues, such ·that they received him most excellently. The lord of the castle proceeded far out before the gates to meet him. He greeted Erec before the portal, as did the courtiers along with him. That Erec was his guest was a source of both joy and sorrow to him: though he sorely feared that Erec would lose his life there, he was otherwise glad to bid him welcome. The lord demonstrated this full well to the two men and to the Queen, for he lavished quite proper hospitality upon them. At that time it was still broad daylight.

(8188–8207) After these noble guests were quartered in the fortress, the host and his courtiers entertained them as excellently as they were able, recounting numerous tales so that all boredom was banished from their midst. After a time he inquired whether they would like to go to the company of the ladies. They were pleased to hear this question posed, and so he led them off, the lady and the two men, up a staircase and (if the Master does not lie) into a palace so lovely that in the days when the goddess Pallas ruled here on earth, if she had been provided with such an edifice, it would have been sufficient to match her grandeur.[8]

(8208–8220) The palace was most finely decorated, it was round in shape and not rectangular, excellent and free of blemish. As was well fitting for their eyes and as perfection had dictated, it was constructed of a costly stone—of marble, which, when hewn, always yielded more fine blocks than any other material. The stones showed hues of yellow, green, brown, red, black, white and blue. So smooth[9] and so well burnished was the kaleidoscopic radiance of these blocks that they all sparkled in the manner of exquisitely fashioned glass.

(8221–8249) They saw seated in this palace the paragon of all women. Who could describe them to you and still render them all the praise they deserved? Never could human eyes behold anything comparable to this most pleasing array. There were eighty ladies, all dressed alike. They were wearing rich, yet somber clothing, of a most costly fashion. With this they were most likely showing that their hearts were beset by some sort of gloom, for they could seldom if ever be seen laughing. Their dresses and their mantles were of black velvet. Neither their sleeves nor their sides were gathered. As I am told concerning this, all haughtiness and pride were repugnant to them at that time. They had bound their heads as best they could, with wimples which were white. No great care was evident in the making of those wimples save that of a plain and common hand, and they were without any gold adornment.

(8250–8259) As the strangers entered, these ladies welcomed them with a warmth which belied their state of mind, just as is often the conduct of a shrewd man, who causes no one else to suffer for his own sorrow, whenever he can prevent it. The lord of the castle went and sat down with these ladies, and the guests were then seated over here: Erec with Lady Enite and Guivreiz at his side.

(8260–8291) Erec cast his gaze across the way and was struck by the beauty of one of those ladies, but then the next one seemed even lovelier. The third, however, caused that one to pale. Greater yet was the beauty of the fourth. Erec praised the fifth, until he caught sight of the sixth. The seventh lady outshone this one altogether, till he noticed the eighth. The ninth lady he then thought crowned with loveliness, but God's zeal had even more finely endowed the tenth with beauty. The eleventh was such as to put that one to shame, if only the twelfth had stayed away.[10] The thirteenth would have been perfect, had the fourteenth not robbed her of that distinction. The fifteenth was the ideal of a young maiden, yet all her beauty was nothing alongside the sixteenth lady. With ever greater joy were Erec's eyes able to rest upon the seventeenth one seated there. Yet the eighteenth pleased him more than any of these ladies, until the nineteenth caught his eye. The twentieth he then had no choice but to find more pleasing than all the others. What man could render a full account of them all? The very least among those women would exquisitely embellish a whole empire with her beauty.

(8292–8320) Once Erec had fully surveyed this delightful company, he thought to himself: "Powerful and benevolent God, from this I see that you are rightfully called the most wonderful God, because your power and your command have assembled in so small a place so many women who would (as you yourself know) most beautifully adorn a great many vast lands—lands which you now deprive of all joy." Erec kept these thoughts to himself. In the meantime, the host was telling those ladies news of why the stranger had come there together with his wife. Once the ladies had heard this, they were reminded at once of the sorrow which had stricken each of them. They now disowned altogether the hue of joy with which they had been delightfully flushed before. The blood left their faces,[11] and their noses and cheeks became pale from the flood of tears pouring forth from their eyes.

(8321–8333) Now the hero Erec did not know what this was all about, until Guivreiz apprised him of it, saying: "Do you see how these noble ladies are racked with grief? They were the wives of the knights who have been slain here. O why could I not find the words with which to dissuade you from this journey? If you fare badly in your duel, the fair Lady Enite must remain here like this."

(8334–8349) Since the hand of joy had striven so zealously to help shape these ladies' beauty, Erec's heart was now most acutely moved by their affliction and by the fact that their youth and their lives were so thoroughly given over to distress. For loyalty to their dead husbands made their grief seem just as fresh as when it had first beset them. With eyes discolored by woe they glanced now and again at the courageous man and bewailed him, winsome knight that he was. And they felt pity that his wife was to remain there in their company; for of this they were certain beyond all doubt.

(8350–8358) The valiant Erec thought to himself: "May God prevent my faring in such a way that I add my wife to this joyless throng by meeting my death here!" Both the strangers had a most grievous sight to behold here, for they were harrowed by the ladies' woe.

(8359–8389) Now it is time for them to leave. The lord of the house then led them off to the banquet, where he did not neglect to show them a full measure of everything which is called hospitality in that land. When they had finished dining, they then sat there conversing about all manner of things. The King of the land inquired whether they had heard any news along the way, whereupon the guests related to him whatever newsworthy happenings each of them knew. Erec then addressed his host: "Dear sir and host, people near and far have recounted to me a great many marvelous tales about the magnificence of this castle.[12] I shall ask no more questions concerning this now, for I have seen it with my own eyes and must rightfully concur: they are indeed correct in what they say. I have likewise heard tell that there is an adventure here with the chance to reap vast winnings from the hand of a fine knight. Now I should like to know just what is at stake in this. Tell me, sir host, of this matter."

(8390–8423) For a time the King gave no answer. His head drooped and he sat there very much in gloom, which was born of his own goodness of character. And in truth because of his own uprightness, he was troubled by the stranger's question, for he had already heard tell that Erec was come there in search of the winnings from that adventure. This grieved his spirit, and his thoughts ran to the many ways whereby he could prevent this and whereby he might conceive of advice such that Erec's life would be spared and he could dissuade Erec from his resolve in a manner fitting to them both. At long last he looked at Erec and finally addressed him: "My lord, I wish to give you good counsel, as well I should to a guest of mine, indeed to the dearest guest I have ever had, since I wish you nothing but well: forgo your question and drop your curiosity about this adventure once and for all. Last year and this year and for a good twelve years now—as I say to you in all truth—great harm has come from this. Moreover, we have both seen so many other things which are able to entertain us well enough indeed. Now let us talk of other matters."

(8424–8457) Erec spoke up in reply as an undaunted man whose heart was most steadfast and indeed stronger than a diamond, to which such strength as this is ascribed: if it were placed between two mountains made of steel (how could this be made any more marvelous?), the diamond would crush them both to dust before damage could be discerned anywhere on the stone. Yet this man was even more firmly set in his bold courage, because there is a certain kind of blood which can soften this stone,[13] and nothing short of a death-blow could overcome Erec's resolve, or lead him onto the path of cowardice. Erec laughed at the words of his host, saying: "If there is anything about which I dare not even ask, then it is indeed all too dreadful! My questioning was not at all undertaken in the hope of gaining some special fame unattained by all others who ever ventured here before. Rather, it vexes me not to be able to relate anything about this place, if people, both women and men, should ask me about it, despite the fact that I have been here. For this will lead them to accuse me of falsehood."

(8458–8473) The host fancied that Erec meant these words. Hence he then began to relate to him this whole matter, as I have described to you before, in just as much detail as Erec's comrade had told him along the way. And if Guivreiz had left anything out, the host recounted all of it to him and explained it more fully. He said that the arbor was strongly fortified and that although it was not enclosed, no one whose life and honor were at all dear to him should aspire to enter it.

(8474–8519) "There dwells in that garden," he said, "together with his lady-love, a knight so courageous that he has, with his strength, slain all who, at the urging of their foolish hearts, have insisted upon seeking out adventure. Let me tell you this: any good knight coming here with this intention need only go to the gate. As soon as he utters his first word, he will find it standing open.[14] He can enter on foot or on horseback; all others remain outside. Then the gate will close. The matter must then be settled between the two of them, for regardless what happens to either of them, they will have no referee. How things now shall turn out, I do not know. It has been a good half a year or more since anyone has come to him; at that time he killed knights whose names I can tell you. Forsooth, he slew three men here, the finest known in any land. One was called Venegus, who never neglected the chance to perform a deed of valor; then there was Opinaus, who had never turned away in flight; and the third man was Libaut, who had already acquired great fame, and who was from the land of the Wends.[15] And if those men have lost their lives, then you must not try your luck. And if you will permit me, I shall give you the best advice, which is that you refrain from fighting. This powerful man is of such a bent that he has beheaded all whom he has ever defeated. If you fail to believe this, and if you wish to see for yourself, then the same fate shall perforce await you as well."

(8520–8575) King Erec then replied: "I was fully aware that the path of Good Fortune lay somewhere in this world, but I did not know quite where, save that I rode out in search of it with great uncertainty; but now I have found it! God has favored me by showing me the way to this place, where I find quite the perfect contest to satisfy the yearning of my heart: a contest in which I can, with one attempt, risk little in hopes of gaining much. Up until this very day I have been seeking out just this. Praise be to God! Now I have found the chance to wager a penny in order to win a thousand pounds. This is a sign of favor, that I encounter such a bout here. Let me explain this to you more fully. I heard from you before that this lord is unparalleled in bold courage. Thus his honor is quite widespread and his name is accorded full praise throughout all these lands, for he has performed marvelous feats. On the other hand, I have not, alas! accomplished such deeds, and my honor carries little weight. My hand has thus far acquired for me very little of what brings recognition to a knight. I have been starving for lack of fame, up until this day. For this reason I shall gladly risk my meager honor, such that it might either be increased here to a full measure of praise or that it might go entirely to ruin. If God grants me the glory of defeating this man, then I shall become rich in fame. And note what unequal importance this contest bears for the two of us. To him it is nowhere near one twelfth as crucial as it is to me. He is staking his excellence against my imperfection, and his glittering gold against my dull iron.[16] It will bring him scarcely any praise at all if he is accorded the victory over me, for such has been his lot many a time and with greater winnings. Furthermore, any tears shed for me will dry up quickly. Let this be said to you in all truth: he shall not be spared my desire to do battle with him!"

(8576–8590) "Tell me, my lord," said the host, "why ought I to be more concerned for you than you are for yourself? Let us now be off to bed, for the time has come. If we live to see the morrow, I shall take you to where he is, if I am able. Yet in all loyalty I counsel you to reconsider this once more. This would be prudent, it seems to me, for once you enter the arbor, I shall mourn bitterly for you, since by doing this you shall never again set eyes upon us. Fail not to pay heed to what I say." "My lord, it shall all turn out as God wills it," spoke Sir Erec.

(8591–8613) With that they went off to their chambers to sleep. Erec and Enite's room was well stocked with rich bed-linen and with other appointments. All the walls were hung with fine tapestries, which were embellished with costly gold. In addition, precious carpets covered the stone floor, such as the host's wealth could readily produce and as befitted his fame, for he was lord over this land, and King Ivreins was his name. He instructed the chamberlains to be attentive to their every wish, as one ought to do with powerful kings. Thus these three guests were accorded luxurious and splendid honors. King Guivreiz lay nearby in a chamber where he was shown the hospitality that was his due.

(8614–8631) Erec and Lady Enite enjoyed pleasant hours as they lay together and pursued precious love till the first light of dawn intruded upon them. Erec's heart was not altogether free of manly worries, for they say that anyone who does not know fear is not a wholly perfect man, and he is numbered amongst the fools. Never was there a heart so valiant that a proper measure of fear was unbecoming to it. Whereas a man should willingly fear that which places his life in the balance, nonetheless he ought to renounce all timidity which is born of cowardice. By such fear as this was Erec's heart untainted.

⛨ XV ⛨
THE RED KNIGHT MABONAGRIN

(8632–8659) Since this was the day on which Erec was to do battle, he conducted himself in the manner of wise men, for fear was a proper part of this. He rose at a very early hour. Together with Lady Enite he went to hear the Mass of the Holy Spirit, and he entreated God most fervently to preserve his life. His wife likewise offered up the same petition. Erec was careful to partake of the Eucharist, quite in the manner of a knight who is to go off into battle against a stout-hearted man. He left after the Mass, whereupon a repast awaited them, a great feast which Erec avoided altogether. Gluttony was hardly what he practiced; rather, he took three bites from a chicken, which seemed to him sufficient. He was brought a dram, and he quaffed a farewell drink, invoking the blessing of St. John.[1] That warrior then armed himself at once and made all the necessary preparations to ride straight off into the arbor. Lady Enite's worries were never as great as now, and the tears poured down in a rain from her eyes.

(8660–8679) The place was now astir with the news. All the people knew full well, as you have heard before, that a knight was come there—one who had declared himself ready to challenge the knight in the arbor. King Ivreins of Brandigan was to witness this, nor did his courtiers wish to remain behind either. The fortress was left void of all people, save for the sorrowful throng of ladies, all of whom remained there. For they were so beset by woe that they had no yearning to behold a thing which would weigh them down with yet greater distress. Of all their heartache, however, their deepest source of anguish was that death refused to lay his hand upon them.

(8680–8697) The streets in that place, as well as all the rooftops, were now teeming with people waiting for Erec to come riding by. He rode down the very middle of the castle road, which brought him up to the arbor. Along the way he heard ample words of discouragement as well as all their silent murmuring. No less ominous or dire an affliction did the people augur for him than that death itself was certain to be his lot. In such profusion did they offer these words of warning that, if Erec ever were about to lose his courage in the face of sinister predictions or evil threats, he would have done so then. Yet he took their words as a mere joke on their part and paid them not even the slightest heed.

(8698–8714) If the book does not lie to us, then this arbor was contrived in a way such that we can all (both the astute and the dull-witted amongst us) be thoroughly amazed by it. Let me tell you this: neither a wall nor a moat encircled it, nor did a fence encompass it, nor a body of water nor a hedge, nor anything tangible. A smooth pathway went all the way around the arbor, and yet no man could enter, either on foot or on horseback, except off on one side, at a very secret spot. At this place there was a narrow path, of which few of the people were aware.

(8715–8729) Anyone entering by chance at this passage found inside all manner of delightful and pleasing things. There were trees of many species which bore fruit on one side and hung heavy with delightful blossoms on the other. The sweet strains of birds likewise brought joy into the heart of any intruder. Furthermore, the ground there was not bare for as much as a hand's breadth at any point, but rather was sprinkled with flowers of all the colors of the rainbow, flowers which breathed a sweet aroma.

(8730–8744) So exquisite was the fragrance of the fruit and the blossoms, and so lovely was the constant rivalry amongst the birds, and such a sight to behold was all of this, that anyone beset by woe who came walking in upon this would perforce forget his sorrows in that place. The fruit could be eaten wherever one wished—and as much as one wanted. The rest was to be left behind; indeed there was no other choice, for things were devised such that no one could carry the fruit out with him.[2]

(8745–8753) Would you perchance like to hear tell of how this garden was sealed off so tightly? I know full well that few men now alive have knowledge of the sorcery whereby this was accomplished. A cloud could be seen encircling the arbor—a cloud through which no one was able to pass, except as I have described to you before.

(8754–8776) Now the host himself rode on ahead of them toward the arbor, in order to guide Erec, as he had requested, to the hidden entrance[3] where he could encounter the knight. All the people remained outside that passage, save for Lady Enite and Sir Guivreiz, who was likewise allowed to accompany them.

There were these four people, and no more, in their company. In but a short time they came to a spot where they caught sight of something which they rightfully had to agree was extraordinary. A wide circle was fashioned here with oaken stakes. Erec marveled at the sight of this, for each of these stakes was topped by a man's head impaled upon it, save for one stake which was empty. Why was this? There was a large horn hanging on that stake.

(8777–8816) Erec then began to inquire as to what all of this meant. "You would be better off to have forborne this," spoke the host to his guest, "and it shall become a source of deep regret to you that you have ventured here. Your instinct for competition has led you astray. Now see for yourself the truth, that I have not spoken falsely. But if you still believe so, then look: these are the heads which the knight has severed. And I have more to say to you: the stake which is still standing there empty has been awaiting you. Onto it your head is to be affixed. However, should you or any other man who might defeat this knight be absolved of that fate—which certainly cannot happen (so many a day now has been passed in waiting for just that)—then that victor is to blow thrice into this horn very loudly (such is its purpose), so as to proclaim that he has been victorious. Such a man's fame would become lasting and would be made known throughout all these lands, surpassing that of all other men. But of what use is such talk? It is a waste of time! The man destined to blow this horn has, I fancy, never been born in all the world. All the knights now living are nothing compared to the one here. Yet inasmuch as you are unwilling to forgo this contest, noble knight, may God be your shield, and may He watch over your soul. There is no one who can prevent you from losing your life."

(8817–8835) Once the fair woman had taken note of this peril and had likewise heard these words of discouragement, her heart was robbed of all happiness and joy, if indeed she brought either of those with her there. Her strength subsided along with her coloring, and she turned pale and took on the appearance of death, falling unconscious with grief. The bright day became to Enite as the night, for she neither heard nor saw a thing. Though she had been beset many a time by woe, never had her heart's anguish been any greater in all her life, as was betokened by her mien. The host and her lord then moistened Enite's brow and shared her tribulation.

(8836–8873) As she opened her eyes and came to her senses, Erec spoke most valiantly: "My lady, sweet Enite, be not distressed any longer. This is not the time for weeping. Why do you have need of such lament? Am I either sick or dead? In truth, I am standing here by you quite in fine health. You ought to wait until such time as you see me red with blood or my shield hacked to pieces from top to bottom or my helmet chopped to shreds, with me lying dead beneath it. Yet even then you would have ample time for your lament. Now, however, a duel is in the offing, a duel which is to take place between myself and another man.[4] We have no way of knowing for certain who will be acclaimed the victor. Yet I have been told in good sooth that God is as benevolent as He ever was. O, how full many a time it has come to pass that a man to whom He was willing to grant His mercy has been saved! If such is His will, then I trust to the full that I shall come away unharmed. Your weeping vexes me, and if you knew my frame of mind, you would not continue your lament so bitterly. For I wish to tell you in truth, if I possessed not the slightest shred of courage save that bit which I derive from you, then I could never go wrong. Whenever my thoughts turn to you, my hand is blessed with victory, for your love is the fount of my strength, so that nothing can trouble me the whole day long."

(8874–8895) At this point Erec had to depart from his two comrades and ride on alone. Very deeply did this distress them, Enite and the good King, and their thoughts were clouded by concern for Sir Erec. The host himself pointed the way to Erec, past the stakes and onto a grassy, narrow path which he found there. With that they all remained behind, while Erec rode forth alone. How things turned out for him, I do not know.[5] Never had a knight been subjected to more words of determent than was Erec. He trod a perilous path, which gave rise to mourning amongst his followers. May God's power now protect him, so that his life may be spared! Therefore, assist his wife, all of you, in asking God that victory may fall to Erec!

(8896–8925) King Erec rode alone along the grassy trail, through flowers and through the singing of the birds, off into that garden about thrice the distance a horse could cover in a single charge. Now he saw ahead of him there a pavilion, luxurious and beautiful, and both high and broad in dimension. It was of two kinds of velvet fashioned in stripes of black and white and brightly decorated with attention to all detail. On this tent were illustrations both of women and of men, and of birds, depicted as if in flight, whereby they appeared deceptively realistic to the eye, and of animals wild and tame; above each of these was inscribed its name. The figures themselves were fabricated of gold. In place of the capital[6] there was a finely crafted eagle trimmed all over with gold. The tent was pitched on the grass and an aura of honor and of merit surrounded it. The ropes to this pavilion were of pure silk and not of just one single color: they were woven into rolls with strands of red, green, white, yellow and brown.

(8926–8957) Beneath this tent Erec espied a woman sitting, such that (as his heart told him) he had never in all his days beheld a more beautiful woman, save for Lady Enite. For it had to be conceded to Enite that she was praised above all women living either then or now for her delightful beauty. Enite was the child of Perfection, which had left nothing wanting in her. The lady who was now sitting here was most exquisitely dressed. She wore a long cloak of ermine, in which she had wrapped herself. Her mantle was of a fine velvet, the color of brown glass and excellently trimmed with sable at the cuffs. A wimple bound her hair together. You ask how her tunic looked? Inquire of her chamberlains![7] God knows I never saw it, for I was not often in her presence. Nor could Erec see it[8] either. It was of necessity so, for the mantle in which she was dressed hung down before it on all sides. Moreover, the couch whereon this lady was seated was finely constructed: the posts were large and were crafted of silver, and its appearance betrayed elegant craftsmanship.

(8958–8989) As he watched her sitting there, the stranger dismounted with gentility. His horse he tied to a tree branch, leaning both shield and lance against the trunk. He unbuckled his helmet and placed it over the top of the shield. Erec then removed the helmet cap from his head, for his good breeding was most abundant.[9] Thus did he go and stand before her. She would fain have seen this not happen, for she feared that it might cause her chagrin. Yet she greeted the lord, for custom allowed her no other choice. She welcomed him with such words as these: "My lord, I would fain greet you warmly, save that one ought not to offer insincere salutations. Except for the fact that harm and disgrace shall—indeed must!—befall you here, I would have gladly received you. At whose advice have you journeyed here? Or have you come upon this idea yourself, at the urging of your own heart? If so, then you carry a faithless counsellor within your breast, for it has betrayed your very life. My lord, for God's sake, be gone from here! It shall of needs cost you your life if my lord catches sight of you. He is not far away from us now."

(8990–9023) Before she had finished speaking these words and had warned him, Erec heard a voice loud and fierce, which resounded like the blaring of a horn, for the man to whom that voice belonged had an enormous throat. This was the lady's husband. Armed such that he was lacking nothing and outfitted just as finely as the intruder Erec, he had ridden off from the lady through this arbor to roam about for pleasure and to see whether he might find something wherewith to occupy himself. At this moment he then spotted the stranger standing before his wife. This struck him as foolhardy and aroused his displeasure; he turned back in haste toward the intruder. Erec had now espied him riding up in the distance. The lord of the arbor was tall and big, well nigh the equal of a giant. He then began growling with loud threats. His horse was large and tall and bright red, the color of fire. Of this same color was his shield all over, as was likewise his battle tunic. According to what I have read, he himself was clad in red armor, much in keeping with his spirit. So bloodthirsty was that man's hand, I fancy, that his heart bled whenever he failed to find occasion to do battle.

(9024–9048) He now rode up to the stranger and greeted him rather brusquely, in the manner of an evil man, saying: "Tell me, knave, who told you to approach the lady so closely?" "How have I done wrong by that?" "It is most foolhardy." "My lord, wherefore are you reprimanding me?" "You strike me as impudent towards the lady!" "My lord, your words give evidence of your violent nature." "Tell me, who brought you here?" "Good friends." "Tell me now, who?" "My heart and my determination." "Then they have failed to render you good advice." "Thus far they have guided me well." "That shall come to an end here." "No, it shall not!" "For what reason do I see that you are armed?" "Because, my lord, this armor is indeed mine." "Do you desire to do battle with me?" "If you wish so, then I am also willing." "What notions have you put into your head, stupid fool?" "That you shall find out full well." "It shall turn out to be a most grievous bout for you." "You neglect to say: 'God willing!'" "How is it that you are so contemptuous of my words?"

(9049–9069) "I shall pay no heed to your threats, and I liken them unto two big mountains. In all their wisdom these mountains swore that they would beget a fitting offspring for themselves, a large one, just as they likewise were. God then let this come to pass in such a way that it became the object of the people's scorn: those two mountains gave birth to a field mouse! What is more, great castles have been burnt to the ground by small fires. Those who foam so at the mouth have but a pittance of courage. This very point shall be illustrated here. Before we part company this day, one of us or both of us shall see his boasting ended once and for all." "Yes, of that I wish to assure you,"[10] exclaimed the red knight. With these words Erec turned and left him.

(9070–9102) With great dispatch he returned to where he had left his horse standing. He strapped on his helmet and prepared himself straightway. Then he mounted his horse without delay. Nor did the other man neglect to make the same preparations. Each of them took up his shield and strapped it tightly to himself. The shanks of both men's horses—the host's and the stranger's—began to fly. They displayed beyond question a furious wrath, giving spur to their horses and lunging toward one another most boldly and with all their strength. The ash-wood lances were then lowered and aimed straight at the four nails where their opponent's hand grasped the shield.[11] Their aim was well executed, for both weapons hit their mark. The lances thrust right through both shields all the way up to their hands, but failed to touch either man's body. The sturdy shafts remained whole, though they had been propelled with great force. They then pulled back their lances with valiant zeal and rode apart, those two like-minded men, in order to continue the joust.

(9103–9133) Once more the horses were painfully and sharply urged on with spurs and sent together again. Here began a most fervent love, a love which strove after high stakes, and one which they pursued without the aid of a bed. They vied with one another to win this love, and the specter of death hung over whichever of them were to be defeated. It was with the shafts of their lances that they kissed, plunging right through the shields toward one another's chest with such passion that the ash-wood shafts split apart into little pieces all the way back to each man's hand, and the splinters flew up into the air. So fiercely did the horses come ramming together with the burden of both men that the two adversaries were most mightily stunned, and the horses each reared back and fell onto their haunches. At this, they dropped the reins and dismounted onto the turf. Lord God, vouchsafe to watch over King Erec! For he is going into battle with a warrior possessed of courage and strength, which enkindles in me fear for Erec's safety.

(9134–9168) They now both drew the swords from out of their scabbards and reached back with them, brandishing the blades in the air. They now bashed at one another's shields as they faced off. Furious blows did those men mete out! They held forth their shields, which then became so completely hacked apart, right down to the frames, that they could no longer carry them on their arms, and the shields were of no avail in defending them. With that, they threw the shields off from their hands. Now the armor shielded them time and again from death. Their weapons gave off hot sparks of fire whenever they met. So many a fierce blow was dealt out here that the world can well marvel at their helmets and swords for fending off these thrusts. Time after time it came to pass that this most enormous man struck viciously at his smaller opponent and repelled him a good distance indeed. Yet Erec would then beat him back again across the same path. Back and forth they struggled so many times that they altogether trampled both the flowers and the grass, such that nothing remained there that was any greener than in the midst of wintertime. In that same fashion did this battle continue from morning till after the noon hour.

(9169–9187) "Hartmann, my friend, tell us now, how were their bodies able to endure that?" It was their wives who gave them their strength. The one who was actually sitting there did this for her husband: if he was beset by any uncertainty, whenever he glanced back at her, her beauty renewed his strength, such that he undauntedly regained his vigor and fought on as a rested man. Hence he could not lose his courage. Of Erec let me tell you this: whenever he thought of Lady Enite, her love imbued his heart as well as his senses with such vitality that he too fought with renewed strength, in pursuit of manly excellence.

(9188–9218) After they had persisted in battle for a long time indeed and yet both remained unharmed, the huge man thought to himself: "It angers me that this little man is holding his ground so long before me." In a fury he clutched his sword with the intention of cutting down his opponent. He reared back with it and whipped the blade through the air. This most enormous devil was unable to feel any mercy. His heart pumped a full measure of powerful strength into his arms. With firm resolve he brandished his sword, striking Erec on the helmet right over the middle of his scalp, and he came down so hard with it that a wide, fiery flame shot out from the blow, such that a wisp of straw could have caught fire from it. May God reward all who believe this, for I cannot swear to it! This furious clout resounded in Erec's head, so that he very barely avoided falling. His ears and his eyes began to fail him, such that he could neither hear nor see. Save for the fact that the sword broke in two, it would have been the end of Erec.

(9219–9246) In an instant, however, the intruder Erec recovered his strength, so that his sight, his senses and his hearing were just as before. He was aggrieved by hurt and shame that any man had ever gained such an advantage over him. Yet now Erec extracted revenge for having slipped from his superiority[12] into such great feebleness of body. The thought of his fair wife breathed vigor into his muscles. He began to avenge his injury, and he brandished the sword furiously with both hands and fought so as to draw blood from his opponent, slamming down onto the hard steel of his armor. Although this knight loomed as a mountain alongside Erec, once his defenses ran out, he had to yield ground in the face of Erec's sword blows. This he did without any tinge of disgrace. For of this I am certain, indeed more certain than of anything else: had Mabonagrin's sword but remained in one piece, Erec could not have struck at him freely without seeing each such stroke returned in self-defense.

(9247–9269) Thus he was driven back with force by the intruder, who set about madly avenging that powerful blow. No longer did Erec strike out in the same manner as before: his blows were now more ferocious, not at all like those of a coward. He countered blow with blow, so that the blow of one man's sword met the blow of the other's. Thus did Erec beat at that iron armor, until the sword which he held forth glowed from all the dints, and its blade lost much of its sharpness. Its sparkling color became dull, and it broke perforce, just as had the other man's sword before. What else do you expect Erec to do, but this: with what was left of that sword in his hand he struck his retreating opponent on the chest so powerfully that the red knight well nigh stumbled and fell to the turf from the impact.

(9270–9295) Nonetheless that devilish creature regained his balance and caught sight of Erec's empty hand and of his broken sword. "Now I shall be avenged," thought the red knight to himself. With a fury he lunged at Erec, intending to grab hold of him all at once, and to lift him up and batter him with his great strength, so that Erec's limbs would fly off in pieces. Much to his advantage, however, Erec had—during his youth in England, as the story has it— also learned quite thoroughly the art of wrestling, along with other useful skills. What is more, Erec was aided by the fact that it is most difficult to obtain a firm grip on a man wearing armor. Hence Erec slipped out of his grasp, so that the man's design was thwarted. At that, he grabbed Erec in front by his belt, but Erec slipped out from under him. The other man was hard pressed to catch hold of Erec, but such was not to be.

(9296–9315) Erec then made a show of his strength. As his opponent bent over, Erec thrust his shoulder before the red knight's chest, so that the man could not get at him. With great might Erec shoved him away and jerked him back again so swiftly that the huge fellow began to fall. Because of his weight he could not regain his balance, but toppled to the ground instead. At this point the noble Erec pounced upon him. Erec, that performer of amazing feats, inflicted upon his opponent every bit as much distress as he himself felt delight.[13] He knelt upon his chest and pelted him so many times that the knight, as he lay there beneath Erec, grew weary of living. He altogether ceased to offer any defense.

(9316–9337) Once he had yielded to despair, the red knight requested a truce from his smaller opponent, saying: "Sir knight, let me live for a short time, and then take my life." "Are you willing to concede the victory to me?" "That cannot yet occur." "What is it then that you wish?" "Noble knight, leave off and tell me your name." Erec, who is still on top of him, answered thus: "Seldom if ever have you heard of such a thing before, nor shall I be the one to let it happen. For it would be a strange thing indeed if the victor were forced to surrender to the vanquished. If you wish to live for any time, then follow my good advice and tell me forthwith where you are from and who you are, as well as whatever else I desire to know."

(9338–9365) The red knight answered him thus: "You are deceived if you expect that to happen. Though you have defeated me and you now prevail with force, I would sooner be slain than not hear from your lips either your name or your lineage. In truth, this disgrace of mine may have befallen me at the hand of someone who is a stranger to victory, and if so, I prefer to let myself be killed. If a man of less than noble birth has done this, then I should not wish to live on, not for anyone's sake. On the other hand, if God has granted to me that you are worthy of this by birth, then deign to drop all animosity, for in that case I shall swear an oath of surrender to you, that I am gladly willing to follow your every command. In God's name I beg you to display your goodness! And know this also: that if you are of ignoble lineage, then my life shall come to an end on this very spot, for in that event I am overwhelmed by disgrace. I am quite convinced that it is less injurious for me to die with honor than to see my honor die."

(9366–9386) The good Erec then answered him with a laugh: "In this case I am quite willing to comply. Though it be done contrary to custom, I am willing to inform you of this: my father is a powerful king who rules over the land of Destrigales, my mother is readily his equal, and I am called Erec." "Shall I be certain of this?" "Indeed you shall." "Then spare my life, and accept my vow of surrender. Behold, I am prepared to swear it to you. In this fashion you can have my service, which you must forfeit if you kill me. I wish to tell you my name: Mabonagrin I am called." Erec then felt compassion, such that he spared the man's life.

(9387–9400) Once Erec had received his oath of surrender, he extended his hand to help him up. Each of them untied the laces of the other's armor, for no one else assisted them, and they then removed their helmets. At this point they lost all animosity. They withheld no words of praise for one another's honor and excellence, just as one should when in the company of a friend and comrade. They sat down together on the grass, for each of them was most exhausted from the battle.

(9401–9442) During this time they talked on at length and about many things, of each man's circumstances and of what had just happened to the two of them. King Erec spoke: "I have heard full well of your situation, that the King of Brandigan here, the lord of the castle, is your uncle. There is no affair of yours about which I have not heard some detail, and I have not failed to elicit from this a full understanding of your circumstances. But one thing remains unknown to me: for as long as you have been in this garden, tell me, how have you passed the time without having more people in your midst? Although it is delightful in here, and though no manner of good thing so gladdens the heart as when two lovers lie side by side—as is so with you and your wife—nonetheless, one ought, in truth, to escape upon occasion from the women. I have secretly heard from the lips of a woman that they do not object to our coming and going. Although they do not say it openly, they want us to remain new to them and not to be ever under foot. Moreover, it would better befit this lady, who has sat in here all these years, to be in the company of other women. O, I can never cease to be amazed at how you have managed to remain so stately a man![14] For it is so good to be out amongst other people. Have you taken on this attitude at someone else's behest? Or do you hope to be rewarded for it by God? Or is it ordained that you remain in this garden forever?"

(9443–9485) Mabonagrin answered him thus: "All of this I shall reveal to you. I did not freely choose this way of life, for there was never a man born who enjoyed the company of others more than I. Listen now to the strange tale of why I have elected this lifestyle. Unless I had been willing to break my word, I had no choice but to maintain this routine, even if I should have grown old while in here—lest God were to free me from it, as He has done by His mercy. Today this all ends, somewhat with misfortune to be sure, but that I shall easily cease to lament. My lord, I shall now tell you to whom I have pledged my word in exchange for this way of life. It came about that prior to this I had ridden forth in my youth to another land, where I found this lady in her mother's keeping—a child, perhaps eleven years of age and of noble lineage. What is more, I have never perceived greater comeliness in a child, whether boy or girl. All my intuition told me this. And once my eye caught sight of her, so noble and so enrapturing, my heart embraced her, for we were then both equally young in years. At once I sued for her love. This courtship, moreover, was not without success, for she absconded together with me. After I had then taken her away and brought her home to this castle, my uncle would grant me no further respite before I was to be dubbed a knight.

(9486–9509) "Thereupon I took the sword of knighthood in this arbor. Then as my lady-love and I once sat dining, about half-way through the meal she bound me ever so tightly by an oath. 'Think, dear sir,' she said, 'of all which I have done for your sake,' and she asked to be requited for that. She exhorted me most urgently, and she made me promise upon her hand[15] to fulfill whatever she requested. I pledged my constancy to her in doing this, compelled as I was by love. Nor did it ever occur to me that she would ask anything of me other than that which I could do without misgivings. Yet I would still have granted my lady her every wish, insofar as I could have accomplished it or it would have been proper for me to do so. Moreover, to this day I still perform whatever she requests of me. I can rely upon her to do the very same for me. Whatever she desires I also desire, and whatever I wish she grants me.

(9510–9531) "How could the union between a man and a woman ever enjoy the fullness of love when both appear only outwardly to be good spouses, and when inwardly they are so different that the one wants, to one degree or another, that which the other does not desire? Between the two of us this impropriety does not exist. From this day forth for the next hundred years I would never deviate in the least from acknowledging her will as my best source of happiness, for such is the greatest portion of the true joy which is mine: to see to it, whenever I can, that her will is carried out. Nor does she depart from this same course towards me. Hence if I did not gladly do her bidding, I would be acting far more wrongly towards myself than towards her.

(9532–9561) "And once this pledge was given, she embraced me out of joy, saying, 'How well it is for me that I experience so delightful a gift as God has bestowed upon me. I have embraced all which my heart desires. I have indeed fared well. Moreover, I wish to be so bold as to assert that we are sitting in a second Paradise. This very spot here I praise before all other gardens. As you can perceive for yourself, there is great splendor in here, splendor from birds of all species and from the many-colored blossoms. To remain here would be good.' She continued: 'This is the gift which I request: I wish to relish fully your love here in this arbor. With this favor I shall indeed see to it that I can remain yours, without fear of other women. This I shall accomplish by your remaining in here with me, the two of us together, until such time as a man, fighting single-handedly, shall defeat you in this arbor, such that it happens before my very eyes so that I myself might see the truth of it.'

(9562–9589) "Now why was it that she did this? I shall explain that to you more fully. She had no idea that this could ever come about, or that the man could be found anywhere who would conquer me. So very excellent did she think me! Indeed, up until this very day I have been spared that, a fact which I can quite readily verify if you do not believe it fully. Do you see those heads? Each one of them I have severed. And I wish to tell you furthermore: the stake which stands there empty, without a head upon it, and on which the horn is hanging, awaits the arrival of a new man. I was to have used it for you and to have set your head upon it. God has absolved us both of this. I have acquired today, I believe, disgrace without injury, since your hand has freed me from this fetter. It was God who sent you here. Today marks the end of my ordeal; now I shall leave this place and go wherever I wish.

(9590–9627) "And let this be said to you in all truth: you have come here bringing a great measure of good fortune to this court, for because of me it had lost every vestige of its gladness and was bereft of its splendid joy. In all the time they have been without me, they have not once engaged here in merriment of any sort. Because my youth and my high birth were, for them, buried alive, the *joie de la court* has died out altogether. Now they shall pursue it once more, for they have their protector back.[16] Your bold hand has freed this most sorrowful land from great suffering and has restored it entirely to a state of joy. For this you shall be forever honored. My lord, you must now arise and go with good cheer to blow into yonder horn, for it is intended such that if anyone should conquer me, he would inform the people of that at once by blowing into it thrice. It has hung there unblown for many a day now, to the point where I can well grow weary of it, while I have called this place my home." He then removed it from the stake and bade Erec blow into it. Erec put it to his lips straightway. Most powerful indeed was the sound from that horn, for it was long and massive.

(9628–9651) When all of the people (those who were to keep watch outside the arbor for the victory) heard this blast from the horn, they each looked at one another, for there was not a man amongst them who nurtured any hope that things had transpired such that Sir Mabonagrin had been defeated. And the courtiers fancied that it was a trick, until Erec gave notice a second time with the horn, and then a third. Without delay they now proceeded contrary to long-standing custom. King Ivreins of Brandigan took Lady Enite and led her aside into the arbor. Save for him, no one present knew how to enter it, if he himself did not lead the way.

(9652–9678) With a merry din they all rushed up to where they spotted the two lords standing. At that point these two men, Erec and Mabonagrin, were splendidly greeted by all the throng, and the day was crowned with a joyful battle song.[17] In atonement for their long period of heartache, they now pursued joy and heaped fine praise upon Erec and greatly augmented his glory. With a single voice they cried out at once, both men and women: "Sir knight, all fame be to you! May you ever be blessed with good fortune! God has given you to us and has sent you into this land to be our protector. May you be gladdened and praised, o pillar of all knighthood! In truth, God, together with your own courageous hand, has placed upon your head a crown over all lands for evermore. May you grow old with all happiness!"

(9679–9711) Unabated joy held sway in that garden. Nor was the fair Lady Enite stricken by any sorrow at that time. This I readily swear and wish to proclaim: that the spirits of these two women—the one who was seated beneath the tent and the other one, whose lot had been enhanced there in battle— were busied by very different thoughts. Both ladies' lips were silent, but Enite's[18] heart sang out. The one was crowned with joy, the other had a burden of heartache added to her ample bitterness, for she was no longer to be together with her lover Mabonagrin in the garden. She wrung her hands, moreover, at such misfortune as had befallen her husband. Lady Enite, once she had espied her sitting there weeping, displayed a womanly heart. Enite's immense kindness compelled the lovely lady to greet her, despite her great distress. Thereupon they both exchanged many tales back and forth, of joy as well as of sorrow, and they bound themselves together in friendship thereby, as is the custom amongst women.

(9712–9743) They began to inquire as to each other's land and kinsmen and to become acquainted through their conversation, and each recounted as much as she knew. Before long they had established that they were cousins close in blood. How, given this, could their relationship be any closer? For Duke Imain, the lord of Tulmein and the brother of Lady Enite's mother, was also the brother of this lady's father. Moreover, as I have read, both were born in the same place, in Lute.[19] Behold, at this point all mourning was forgotten. With that, they embraced and were both happy at the sight of one another, which they proved by weeping tears of joy. The crying, however, ended quickly, and they laughed, as befitted them better. The ladies then clasped hands and walked over to join their lords. Compelled by joy, they could no longer keep silent or fail to proclaim openly that they were cousins. Upon hearing these new tidings, all agreed that God had brought them together in a marvelous fashion in such a foreign land as this.

(9744–9765) Thereupon the women and the men departed from that arbor. The skulls, which, as you have heard tell, had been severed in there, were removed from their stakes, and messengers were dispatched into the land to summon priests, that they might be buried with all propriety. May God honor Erec for that! Only now did the joy at Brandigan begin to bourgeon, and rightly so. For as soon as word of these happenings spread so rapidly into all the land (word that the joy of the court, which they had seen wither away, was now restored), the King's kinsmen and vassals all journeyed to the court along with the ladies of the land, in order to witness this new gladness.

(9766–9778) The finest of all men gathered there. The host—along with his guests, whom he was able to assemble there by request or by coercion—staged a festival which lasted with convival merriment from that day onward for four weeks' time. The sorrowful routine which King Ivreins has suffered on account of his nephew is cast aside in favor of joy. Now he is indemnified for all of this, and in its place he is well surrounded by a great abundance of bliss.

(9779–9815) Erec was in attendance there at the festival, together with all his company, for the King refused to let them be off. Yet Erec's stay here was bare of all joy, such that he never unburdened his heart of its woeful sorrow. Whenever he thought of this, all his cheerfulness vanished, as is the way with men of compassion, whose eyes often well up with tears, in public as well as in private, whenever they behold something which rightfully awakens pity in their hearts. And this predicament was pitiful enough indeed. Never did there live a man so rich in joys, a man whose heart was so closed to compassion (this I can say with full certainty!) that he could have held back his tears once he had witnessed that tribulation. It was that wretched throng which awakened the pity in Erec's heart: the eighty ladies who were altogether bereft of their joy there, as could be seen most pathetically from their demeanor—those women whose lovers the red knight Mabonagrin had slain. Their calling was both to mourn and to lament, day in and day out. Quite in the same manner as the hare avoids its food while being hunted, they too, pressed by sorrow, shunned the very sounds of joy. Moreover, they did not wish, for the rest of their lives, ever again to set eyes willingly on that man who had caused their sorrow.

(9816–9825) Erec now helped them vent their grief. Indeed, this was quite evident from the fact that he, together with Lady Enite, never willingly [20] left their side. Through his kind words of consolation Erec relieved them of some measure of their heartache. What is of greater avail to a man than someone to offer him tender words of comfort after distress has stricken him? This is the duty which one friend owes another.

(9826–9857) Moreover, Erec advised them—advice which they gladly heeded—to tarry there no longer, but to spend their years in better surroundings and to take leave and accompany him to King Arthur's court, for they ever wished to remain strangers to happiness here at this court. With that, they requested leave. The lord of the house was not offended by this, for he had been well apprised of their declaration that they had incurred such suffering there that they could never know any joy at the castle of Brandigan. Hence he was quite willing to grant them leave if they could improve their lives. Yet had they been able to take on a joyous air at his court, Ivreins would have been loath to see them grow old anywhere save there, in his own care. Most willingly did he then equip them for their journey. The host was solicitous as to their wishes, for he furnished them with garb suitable for mourning, as befitted their spirits; and he then likewise outfitted horses such that the color of both, horses as well as clothing, was the same and well-matched: a sorrowful black from top to bottom.

(9858–9875) The festival came to an end, and the foreigner Erec departed with these women. It was an act of courtliness on Erec's part that he took them away from that place, where it was unfitting for them to be. The lord of Brandigan mounted a handsome Castilian horse, and his men climbed onto their own swift steeds, the finest that they had, and they escorted the guests a good distance from the castle. Sir Erec then bade them remain there with all good fortune. With that, he rode off together with the women and took them to King Arthur's court.

☗ XVI ☗
HONOR RESTORED

(9876–9902) Erec was most heartily welcomed there, and they all took good note of the fact that the women were outfitted with such similar clothing and horses. And they rightfully exclaimed that never had they beheld a more remarkable throng, nor so many ladies attired in one single color. And those who knew nothing of it inquired of those guests as to their circumstances, until Erec advised them of what had happened. At this point, Erec, that man free of all deceit, was crowned with esteem by all the assembled company as a reward for his ordeal. So great was his praise that they proclaimed that no man of great valor had ever been born more excellent or more winsome that he. For, as they all asserted, no man from any land had ever reaped such great success from high adventure. This never could have come about, save for the fact that Fortuna[1] had lent her hand to the nurse who cared for Erec as he lay in the cradle.

(9903–9909) The sight of these ladies seemed to them an extraordinary thing. The most noble Queen Guinevere now led them off to comfortable quarters. May her soul be blessed, for she acted quite willingly and of her own accord in an altogether virtuous manner.

(9910–9931) King Arthur was likewise pleased to hear that these guests were at his court. And when he had allowed them time enough that he thought it appropriate to go to visit them, Erec and Walwan and also Guivreiz, these three, as well as the rest of the company, were most happy amongst themselves at this prospect. The King then addressed them: "My lords, let us go to visit our newly-arrived ladies and console them after all their suffering." Thereupon they both stood up, King Arthur and Erec, and went at once to their chamber, which was more exquisitely furnished with ladies than ever before. The host went and sat down with them; the others likewise took seats forthwith, some of them over here, others over there.

(9932–9962) And as the King observed them enduring the same lament and the same woe because of their hardship—those women who were of the same constancy, the same fidelity, the same beauty, the same youthfulness, the same good breeding, the same virtue, the same attire, the same kindness, the same circumstances and the same state of mind—he found this to be well fitting for women, and he deemed it good. It moved his heart and could not fail to please him well. Standing before them all, he spoke: "Erec, my dear kinsman, you shall justly be praised and honored forever, for you have indeed enhanced the splendor of our court. May any man who begrudges you his favor be evermore a stranger to happiness!" "Amen!" they all cried out, for they had good words of praise for Erec. The others, those most sorrowful women, were then persuaded to welcome joy into their hearts and into their lives, and to honor the King by permitting him to replace their attire, which was ill-fitting for happiness, with such garb as is best suited for joy, vestments of silk and of gold.

(9963–9979) Both honor and hospitality were then lavished with all zeal upon Erec, that friend of honor, and upon Guivreiz le Petit, and they were attended to in a fashion well befitting their standing—until word came to Erec that his father had died. It was now imperative for Erec's realm that he demonstrate his loyalty by travelling home, for his lands and his people would benefit from his presence. Thereupon he took his leave and departed there from King Arthur's court in order to begin the journey to his homeland.

(9980–10,001) As he left the court, Erec gladdened the hearts of the needy ones amongst them by offering them his charity (even if they had never sought it), all in accordance with each man's circumstances and with the resources which Erec had at hand. Wherefore they faithfully uttered a common blessing over the hero, that God might watch over his good name and preserve his soul. The little man, King Guivreiz, likewise departed then together with Erec in order to return to his own empire. In a grand fashion they were now both escorted to the point where their paths diverged. With that and in the company of the others, Erec and Guivreiz took leave of one another, a farewell free of all jealous enmity and unsurpassed, I am certain, by that of any other two comrades. Guivreiz then journeyed toward Ireland and Erec toward Karnant.

(10,002–10,036) Now Erec's people were well informed of both the day and the hour when he was to arrive in the land. Six thousand or more of them, men numbered amongst the finest in the realm, had assembled at once. With haste they rode out a good three days' march towards him in order to welcome him, all for the sake of their lord, for they were pleased to see him. Lest he were to report falsely, no man can claim ever to have witnessed any more fervent a reception. Spurred on by their pledged loyalty, they all welcomed Erec on their blanket-draped horses with a din tempered by good breeding. And all those who were of sufficient means and who called themselves knights carried their respective banners in their hands: banners which were costly, which matched the horses' blankets and which were artfully embroidered with uncommon craft. The fields here were speckled red, white, yellow and grassy-green by their silken garb, the finest in all the world. Thus did the men of Karnant from the land of Destrigales welcome their returning lord to his kingdom, in a way befitting a powerful king.

(10,037–10,053) Blessed with good fortune, Erec had accomplished feats in many a land, such that—as the truthful story tells us of him—no man living in those days was as highly praised for his valiant deeds. Such is his fame that he was called Erec the performer of marvelous feats. Thus it was with Erec that his presence and his figure were felt far and wide, across all lands. Are you asking how that was possible? This is how: even if he was only in this place or that in person, his fame was everywhere. So full of his praise[2] was all the world that no man was spoken of so highly in those days.

(10,054–10,076) After God had returned him to his home, Erec commanded that a festival be held for the joy of his land, a festival such that there never was, before or since, a celebration in that realm so delightful or attended by such mighty lords. A great host of Erec's peers journeyed there, men whom I would fain enumerate for you if only I knew their names. At this time Erec received the crown of the realm in a praiseworthy fashion—the crown which his father, King Lac, had worn honorably before him, for he had accomplished a great many deeds of goodness. Never did a son, moreover, replace his excellent father with greater propriety. What man would be more fitting to assume King Lac's throne? May God bestow His blessing upon Erec's rule, for he justly deserves as much. Nor shall we begrudge him this, for he has made a propitious beginning to his reign, with joy and with a show of hospitality.

(10,077–10,106) For a good six weeks' time a great company of knights and ladies could be seen there. And for the whole duration of that festival, all of them found there an abundance of every sort of pleasure they desired. Thus did Erec arrange the affairs of his land[3] such that peace held full sway over it. Erec acted in the manner of wise men, who give thanks to God for whatever honor they acquire and who acknowledge that it comes to them from Him. Many men, on the other hand, are led astray by a false notion which truly deceives them, once arrogance has gained the upper hand: the notion that, if anything good falls to their lot, then it is granted to them only because of their own excellence. And such men fail to render thanks to God, yet how easily does such good fortune vanish! It was not in this manner, however, that King Erec comported himself. Since God had blessed him with honor, Erec in turn offered praise to Him day and night. For this, he was an illustrious man in the eyes of others, just as his heart desired. For his fame endured untainted until his death, in accordance with the Heavenly Ruler's decree.

(10,107–10,114) While off in foreign lands, Lady Enite had endured times of hardship. Yet this she has certainly seen transformed, for all of that is ended here and yields perforce to comfort and honor and to splendor of many sorts.

(10,115–10,118) Both Koralus and Karsinefite grew old in perfect happiness, for God had sent Enite's father and mother back into their own land, much to their joy.[4]

(10,119–10,129) Whenever possible, King Erec was attentive to Enite's wishes himself, and yet in a way proper for him—not as once had been his wont, when he had lain about idly on Enite's account.[5] For Erec conducted his life in accordance with honor, and in such a way that God, after conferring upon him the worldly crown, then granted the fatherly reward of everlasting life to both Erec and his wife.

(10,130–10,135) For the sake of God, raise your prayer, all of you, that we may, after our wanderings in this place of exile, reap the reward which brings us closer to God, for this is greater in value than gold! Here this story[6] shall have its end.

COMMENTARY

COMMENTARY

Throughout the following notes, full bibliographical citations are given only for wórks not listed in the bibliography. Frequently recurring abbreviations are: BMZ = Benecke, Müller, Zarncke, *Mittelhochdeutsches Wörterbuch;* Leitzmann (ATB) = Leitzmann, ed., *Erec* (Altdeutsche Textbibliothek); Lexer = Lexer, *Mittelhochdeutsches Handwörterbuch;* MHG = Middle High German; PMS = Paul, Moser, Schröbler, *Mittelhochdeutsche Grammatik.*

CHAPTER I. THE CONTEST FOR THE SPARROW-HAWK

1. Because the first 150 or so lines are missing from the Ambras Manuscript, the only surviving document to transmit a more or less complete version of Hartmann's *Erec,* I have placed at the beginning of the story a summary (the first three paragraphs, which are set off in italics) of the initial verses of Chrétien de Troyes' *Erec et Enide.* Hartmann's story proper then commences with the following paragraph, beginning in mid-sentence, as does the text of the Ambras Manuscript.

2. (94) The MHG text reads: "und hebe dich der sunnen haz." Cramer (p. 10) mistakenly places a comma after *dich* in this line and translates: "and be gone, you object of the sun's abhorrence" ("und mache dich fort, du Abscheu der Sonne"). Instead of being a vocative phrase, the second half of this verse must be taken together with the verb *heben* as part of a vulgar expression meaning "to go to the Devil." See BMZ (I, 641) and Blosen ("Bemerkungen," p. 61).

3. (189) The bird in question is a small species of the falcon which feeds on sparrows. The sparrow-hawk is a short-winged bird which can fly more easily in heavily wooded terrain than can long-winged hawks, which, technically speaking, are the only true falcons. See Joseph and Frances Gies, *Life in A Medieval Castle* (New York, Hagerstown, San Francisco, London: Harper & Row, 1974), p. 128.

4. (210–17) Unlike Cramer (p. 14) and Thomas (p. 33), I have placed the verbs in these lines in the past perfect tense. Clearly Hartmann is referring not to the contest at hand (which does not begin until v. 621), but to the two previous contests, in which Iders has emerged victorious. Hartmann's use of the pret-

erite with pluperfect meaning is not uncommon in MHG (see PMS, par. 302c).

5. (310) The MHG text reads: "diu was ein diu schœniste maget." Both Cramer (p. 19) and Thomas (p. 34) treat this as an absolute superlative ("the most beautiful maiden"). The same construction in the *Nibelungenlied* (1233, 4), however, is translated by A. T. Hatto (trans., *The Nibelungenlied* [Harmondsworth: Penguin, 1965], p. 159) and Karl Simrock (trans., *Das Nibelungenlied* [Berlin, Darmstadt, Vienna: Deutsche Buch-Gemeinschaft, 1965], p. 331) in a fashion parallel to my rendition here (i.e. "*one of the* fairest maidens"). Interestingly, Cramer (p. 75) and Thomas (p. 49) both render v. 1626 ("one still counts him [Gawein] *among the finest men* at the Round Table") as they ought to have treated v. 310. Unfortunately, PMS (par. 294) is curiously unclear on this point.

6. (403) Hartmann's text reads: "vil gar unlasterlîche." Both Cramer (p. 23) and Thomas (p. 36) read "through no fault of his own." Hartmann, however, speaks in the ensuing verses not only of Koralus' innocence in this political conflict, but also of the adroitness with which he and his family have borne their misfortune. Hence "honor" more adequately covers both aspects (innocence and adroitness) of Koralus' circumstances. Furthermore, Lexer (II, 1906) renders the adverb *lasterlîche* as "with unimpaired honor" ("unbeschadet der ehre").

7. (507) Another possible reading for "ich behabete den strît" is: "I would prove through battle ("Ich würde durch Kampf beweisen," Cramer, p. 29), although *strît* can mean a battle with weapons or with words (Lexer [II, 1240]); see also Schwarz (p. 668).

8. (601) It is not entirely clear whether this line ("unz mirs got gunnen wolde") belongs together with the preceding text ("as long as God granted me the armor") or with the following verses ("as long as God granted me the strength to fight in this armor"). Unlike Leitzmann (ATB), whose punctuation (p. 16) argues for the former interpretation, I have chosen to connect v. 601 with the question of Koralus' infirmity (i.e., that God and old age have made it no longer possible for him to engage in battle). Both syntactically and grammatically, however, either reading is possible. For a thorough discussion of this passage, see Blosen ("Bemerkungen," pp. 63–68), who adheres in general to Leitzmann's reading, while proposing some other changes in the MHG text.

9. (750) The reference is to Enite's father Koralus, although Erec and Enite are not yet married at this point.

10. (762) Both Cramer (p. 39) and Thomas (p. 40) take *schenkel* to refer to the knights' legs (which have just given spur to their horses), and not to the horses' legs or shanks. Grammatically and syntactically, either reading is admissible, but context would seem to favor the latter interpretation, as the "flying" of the horses' shanks follows more logically from the application of spurs,

which takes place in the preceding verse. Furthermore, the verb "fly" more accurately describes the charging horses than the knights' application of spurs.

11. (826) Both Cramer (p. 41) and Thomas (p. 40) ignore the adjective *hôher* and thereby the notion that Erec, who has unhorsed Iders, now enjoys the advantage of being above his opponent.

12. (869–90) Hartmann's use of arcane gaming terminology in this difficult passage necessitates a somewhat free rendition. As Haupt (*Erec*, pp. 338–43) points out, Hartmann metaphorically employs various phrases from games of dice and from board games to describe the duel between Erec and Iders. Because of the unfamiliarity of these games to the modern reader, certain of Hartmann's nuances are inevitably lost in the translation. For more detailed treatment of these verses, see also Pfeiffer (pp. 196–99) and Bech (*Germania*, p. 432), the latter of whom suggests minor textual changes, but offers, oddly, no interpretation of this passage.

13. (922) Cramer (p. 45) translates Hartmann's "witzige unde tumbe" as: "the intelligent and stupid" ("Kluge und Dumme"), thereby missing Hartmann's point that the two opponents were so evenly matched that even those among the onlookers who knew something about the art of dueling were unable to distinguish which of the two men had the upper hand.

14. (935–37) This is a common motif in Arthurian literature. The notion that a knight gains succor in battle from the very sight of his lady also occurs in *Erec* vv. 9171–79, when Mabonagrin renews his strength by glancing back at his wife during the duel with Erec. Furthermore, the same salutary effect can even be achieved (cf. vv. 8868–73 and 9182–87) by the knight's merely thinking of his lady in her absence.

15. (942–49) The full MHG text reads: "doch jener die besten würfe warf / der kein zabelære bedarf, / dô half disen daz ern nie / ûz den slegen komen lie, / und gewan ez eine wîle / so sêre mit der île / unz er doch daz spil verlôs / und gelac vor im sigelôs." Because Hartmann employs only personal and demonstrative pronouns in these verses (and not a single proper name), it is not always clear to which of the two knights he is referring at any given point. Although Thomas (p. 42) appears at first glance to be correct in assuming that *jener* of v. 942 refers to Iders and *disen* of v. 944 to Erec, Cramer's reversal (p. 47) of these pronouns is the only possible means of rendering Erec the ultimate victor, which—based upon all that follows—is obviously Hartmann's intention.

16. (952) This is not the hooded part of a suit of chain mail, but rather a separate hood or cap worn beneath the helmet. This soft, padded cap served both to alleviate the pressure of the helmet, which was heavy, and to diminish the force of an opponent's sword-blow; see Schultz (II, 50f.).

CHAPTER II. EREC'S ACCLAIM

1. (1101) Or Cardigan, the Norman name for Aberteivi in Wales.

2. (1125) Cramer (p. 55) translates the curious adverbial phrase *sus und sô* as "so und so." Another possible alternative to my rendition ("most severely") is Thomas' "just as I told you" (p. 44), though Guinevere is at this point only beginning her account of Erec's misfortune and has in fact not yet told Arthur anything at all.

3. (1152) A Latinate form of Gawein. Hartmann uses the two names interchangeably.

4. (1153) The duties of the seneschal at a medieval court entailed administering justice, overseeing certain domestic affairs, and representing his lord in court.

5. (1338) Because of the vagueness of many of the Germanic terms for familial relationships, the noun *geswîe* can be applied broadly to designate various relatives by marriage. It could, in other words, refer here to either Enite or Koralus, despite the fact that the form used in this verse is masculine. Indeed, Cramer (p. 63) assumes it to designate Enite. Were it not for the occurrence in v. 1370 of the noun *sweher*, which according to both BMZ (II/2, 766f.) and Lexer (II, 1350) means only father-in-law, we might assume that Koralus is not present at Imain's court. Since Koralus is, however, clearly at hand, it is probably best to read *geswîe* as also designating Koralus in v. 1338.

6. (1341f.) Or, with Thomas (p. 46) and Cramer (p. 63): "how could I do this? Should I abandon my host [. . .]?"

7. (1370) Cramer (p. 65) mistakenly reads: "his [Imain's] niece" ("sein Schwesterkind"), i.e. Enite. However, since BMZ (II/2, 766f.) and Lexer (II, 1350) both give "father-in-law" as the only meaning of *sweher*, Hartmann must be referring here not to Enite but rather to Koralus, who is also present at Imain's court (see Chapter II, Note 5).

8. (1446–50) Hartmann's narrator displays considerable success here in reining himself in and not engaging in overly long description of the horse and saddle—an instance of brevity which stands in marked contrast to the greatly detailed account (vv. 7278ff.) of Enite's second horse and saddle.

9. (1558) That is, Ireland.

10. (1566) Both Thomas (p. 48) and Cramer (p. 73) disregard the participle *bevangen* ("gathered in").

11. (1590–1603) Hartmann's narrator engages here in a modesty formula common to medieval literature. See Introduction (p. 27).

12. (1675) A lacuna occurs at this point in the Ambras Manuscript.

13. (1617–97) Hartmann does not actually list so many knights. The lacuna following v. 1674 may account for some of the discrepancy. Other textual problems surround Hartmann's catalogue of knights. Haupt (*Erec*, pp. 351–53)

points out, for instance, that it is virtually impossible to reconstruct many of these names in their original spelling as intended by Hartmann. Moreover, it is altogether possible that Hartmann misunderstood certain of the names he adopted from Chrétien's version (other names Hartmann appears to have invented freely, as they are not present at all in Chrétien's story). Finally, in certain instances (e.g. v. 1693) it is not entirely clear whether Hartmann is listing an additional knight, or whether he is merely giving an appositional phrase describing the preceding knight (on this difficult point see Blosen ["Bemerkungen," p. 68]).

14. (1701–06) Hartmann employs entirely conventional colors to describe Enite. Both in the MHG song poetry and in the MHG courtly romance, ladies of the court commonly have a pure white complexion punctuated by the red of their lips and cheeks.

15. (1787) Geoffrey of Monmouth first names this figure as the father of King Arthur. The name is of Welsh origin: Welsh *Uthr* = "terrible"; *pen* = "head chief"; *dragon* = "dragon" or "leader."

CHAPTER III. THE WEDDING FESTIVAL

1. (1860) The notion that love, while potentially sweet and beautiful, can also be the source of great suffering, was a common motif in the courtly literature of the MHG age. First introduced to the German literary public by Heinrich von Veldeke in his *Eneit*, this concept was to play a central role in much of the important literature written in the German tongue during the high Middle Ages.

2. (1901) Pentecost (or Whitsunday), which marks the descent of the Holy Spirit upon the Apostles, falls on the seventh Sunday after Easter, hence normally in late May. In Arthurian literature this is the time at which the great knightly festivals typically take place. The association of Pentecost with the full advent of spring's flowers and greenery doubtless gave rise to the tradition that these outdoor festivals were held at this time of year.

3. (1925) MHG *wurm* has a broad field of meaning and can signify, among other things, "spider," "worm," "fly," and "snake," in addition to "dragon"; see Lexer (III, 1008f.). While the surrounding context does not, in and of itself, clearly suggest any single one of these meanings, a dragon would seem to be the animal most capable of disturbing the "tranquillity" in this or any land. Schwarz (p. 683) explains Hartmann's various uses of this word.

4. (1931) In Arthurian tradition Avalon is the island to which the mortally wounded King Arthur is taken, although Hartmann makes no reference here to this legend. While much uncertainty surrounds both the etymological origins and the actual geographical site of Avalon, it is frequently associated with

Glastonbury in Somerset, England. In Celtic mythology, Avalon is the blissful underworld of the deceased.

5. (1949) Or this verse ("diu mâze wart behalten") may be joined to the preceding sentence: "as was fitting"; see Cramer (p. 89) and Thomas (p. 52).

6. (1966) These birds were therefore four years old.

7. (2003–09) Conne or Conneland has been identified with the ancient city of Iconium, which lies in present-day Turkey. Since it is known that Iconium was captured by German Crusaders in May of 1190, and that Emperor Friedrich Barbarossa passed through it on his way to the Holy Land (hence its position, as Hartmann states, between the land of the Greeks and that of the heathens), this passage has been cited to support the theory that Hartmann took part in the Crusade of 1189–90. (The mention of Conneland might be used to advance the argument that this passage of *Erec* was composed after the Crusade of 1189–90, since reports of this realm would have filtered back into Germany and would be likely to show up in the literature as a distant, exotic place.) However, as Rosenhagen (pp. 301f.) argues, it is not in fact very likely that Hartmann took part in this Crusade (but rather in that of 1197–98), since several of the details Hartmann offers concerning Conneland are inaccurate and therefore indicate that he had not seen the land with his own eyes. Most notable among the discrepancies in Hartmann's account is his claim (vv. 2010f.) that Conneland is especially known for its sable—a highly improbable notion given the rocky and warm nature of the country; concerning sable, see Schwarz (pp. 683f.). For a full discussion of the question of Hartmann's Crusading, see Introduction (p. 13).

8. (2049) The bustard is a large bird which is related to the crane and plover.

9. (2145–47) Or this passage ("sô wart dâ trûren bedaht. / alsô si des verdrôz, / sô was ir vreude sus grôz") may be read, with Cramer (p. 97): "Sorrow disappeared there. If they had had any woe, now their happiness became great" ("Trauer verschwand da. / Hatten sie einen Kummer gehabt, / so wurde jetzt ihr Glück groß."). Thomas (p. 54) seems to ignore the enigmatic v. 2146 in his translation.

10. (2155) Instead of "swift footraces," both Thomas (p. 54) and Cramer (p. 99) translate *snelleclîchen springen* as "dancing," though Cramer indicates his uncertainty by means of a question mark in parentheses. Either reading may be correct.

11. (2166–68) Hartmann's text reads: "swaz der diete dar kam, / die guot umbe êre nam, / der entete man niht eines rât." These verses present considerable difficulty for the translator. Thomas (p. 55) translates (up to the colon in my text): "Not one of those people who entertain for pay was turned away." Cramer (p. 99) reads the passage in a similar fashion. The source of uncertainty in these verses is the antecedent of the genitive indefinite pronoun *eines* in v.

2168. Other than *guot* (v. 2167), there is no grammatically possible masculine or neuter antecedent; it appears unlikely that the (in this sense) innumerable noun *guot* would be replaced by any form of the pronoun *einez*. Instead, *eines* must be translated "of one thing," whereby a semicolon after *rât* in v. 2168 would neatly introduce Hartmann's explanation of the "one thing" (namely the supposed jealousy of minstrels). Hence *der* (v. 2168) is the dative of the person (antecedent: *der diete* of v. 2166). BMZ (II/1, 572) gives examples of Hartmann's use of similar constructions, none of which speaks against my reading of the passage. Also the word order *(niht eines* instead of *eines niht)*, though partially necessitated by metrical considerations, seems to achieve the special emphasis required by such a reading; Bech (*Germania*, pp. 438f.) deals with the position of *niht*, but declines to suggest a meaning for this verse. Haupt (*Erec*, p. 364) correctly identifies as minstrels the persons described in vv. 2166f., but also fails to explain v. 2168.

CHAPTER IV. THE TOURNAMENT

1. (2224) Hartmann's text actually reads: "if so fine a man should depart," but the use of the singular here seems to point specifically to Erec, in whose honor the festival has been held. Hence I have added the name "Erec" to the sentence.

2. (2267) MHG *gast* means both "guest" and "stranger." Since each meaning is appropriate in the context, I have included both in the translation.

3. (2293) It was not uncommon for a lady to present her knight with an article of her clothing prior to his going into battle. A sleeve from the lady's dress was often affixed to the knight's shield (or sometimes to his helmet or lance) and was symbolic in function, acting as a sign that he was fighting in her honor. Such sleeves were usually very broadly cut so as to hang down nearly to the ground. They were not sewn on permanently, but rather were simply laced onto the dress, so they could be given separately from the dress itself. See Schultz (I, 603–05).

4. (2356) The MHG reads: "dâ was ouch turneies zil." Both Cramer (p. 107) and Thomas (p. 57) read *zil* as a chronological (and not geographical) reference to the tournament ("the time for the tournament was at hand"). As is evident from Lexer (III, 1112f.), however, this noun has both a temporal and a spatial dimension. In fact, Lexer specifically lists this verse from *Erec* as an example of the latter. Furthermore, Hartmann has just reintroduced the locale (not the timetable) for the tournament in the previous lines.

5. (2454) As is the case here, the *vespereide* consists of individual knights jousting on the eve of the actual tournament, which commences on the following day.

6. (2531) The MHG text states: "got gebe im heil swenne ers gert." Cramer's translation (p. 115) of this line: "May God protect any man with whom he [Erec] wishes to fight!" ("Gott möge den schützen, mit dem er kämpfen will"), is questionable. Had he wished to say this, Hartmann would likely have employed the demonstrative pronoun *dem* (to anticipate the ensuing clause) in place of the personal pronoun *im*.

7. (2544–46) Or this passage ("ein lützel âz er unde tranc: / vil enliez in der gedanc / den er hin wider hâte") may be read with Cramer (p. 115) and Thomas (p. 59): "He had a little to eat and drink, but his desire to return to the field kept him from taking much."

8. (2580f.) Hartmann's text reads "daz man in nande / zem besten in sînem lande." Cramer (p. 117) mistakes this construction for that discussed above (Chapter I, Note 5) and erroneously translates: "that he was considered *one of the best* in his land" ("daß man ihn für einen der besten / in seinem Lande hielt").

9. (2699) I have translated literally "three parts of a mile," as it is not entirely certain just what fraction Hartmann intended here. Both Lexer (II, 1414) and BMZ (III, 20) translate *diu zwei teil* as "two thirds," but neither treats Hartmann's *driu teil.* Cramer (p. 121) and Thomas (p. 60) both give "one third," but Mohr (p. 65) reads "three quarters" ("Dreiviertel-").

10. (2703) The abatis was a form of defensive barricade which consisted of sharpened tree branches arranged to point outward so as to prevent the enemy from mounting it.

11. (2773–75) In a duel such as this, the two combatants did not fight to the death. Instead, the victor won the right to take the other man as his prisoner. The latter, however, could buy his liberty by paying a ransom; see Haupt (*Erec,* p. 373).

12. (2795) The jousting knight aimed his lance either at the throat of his opponent or at the umbo (the stud or knob) of his shield. The four nails mentioned in this passage were located near the umbo and served to hold together the shield and the strap with which the knight grasped the shield with his left arm. See Schultz (I, 166f.).

CHAPTER V. HONOR LOST

1. (2887) It was customary in medieval times to accord special hospitality to messengers, who were often allowed to be seated and to drink a cup of wine before presenting their message. Regardless of the content of their tidings, messengers were protected against any retribution, even by the recipient of a hostile message, for they were, after all, merely speaking according to the wishes of their lords. Only barbarians are portrayed in the literature as acting contrary to

this custom. When the message was a joyous one, as here in *Erec*, the messenger was usually offered a reward, which could take the form of a monetary gift or of clothing or other finery, even perhaps a horse or riding accoutrements. See Schulz (I, 176–78).

2. (2971) This is Erec's major mistake, the one which sets in motion the rest of the romance; see Introduction (pp. 18, 21, 24 and 31). Hartmann uses the reflexive verb *sich verligen* to describe Erec's knightly inactivity. This verb is somewhat difficult to translate directly into English, but it means something like "to mis-lay oneself," "to spend too much time lying about."

3. (3047) Or the phrase "mit gedinge" may be translated, with Thomas (p. 65) and Cramer (p. 137): "on the condition." This reading, however, would make Erec guilty of breaking his word to Enite, for certainly he does go on to pursue the matter in what is almost a vendetta against Enite.

CHAPTER VI. FOREST ROBBERS

1. (3107) Both Cramer (p. 139) and Thomas (p. 66) translate Hartmann's text ("riten [. . .] / âne holz niuwan heide"): "rode through fields and woods." The MHG text might have been smoother had the demands of the rhyme not constrained Hartmann to reverse the two elements in this line. The result would have been: "niuwan heide âne holz." Nonetheless, Erec and Enite are clearly riding over a moorland without (âne) any forestation. It is later (in vv. 3113f.) explicitly stated that the two of them enter into a forest, thus rendering Cramer's and Thomas' reading of the verse improbable, if not altogether impossible.

2. (3263) The MHG text states: "welt ir nû daz ez mich riuwe." Cramer (p. 145) and Thomas (p. 67) read: "If you think that I was wrong." Not only is the apodosis ("then forgive me") rendered somewhat illogical by this protasis, the verb *riuwen* does not mean "to commit a wrong"; see Lexer (II, 474f.).

3. (3460) The personification of good luck or fortune.

CHAPTER VII. THE TREACHEROUS COUNT

1. (3645) Thomas (p. 72) and Cramer (p. 161) read *stat* as "city," "town." Although the noun *stat* can indeed have this meaning (see Lexer [II, 1144]), it is often used in the more generalized sense of "place," "site." While the presence of a castle with a marketplace and perhaps several inns might well justify the word "town" here, it is equally possible to read the verse: "to the site of the finest innkeeper" (i.e., "to the finest inn nearby").

2. (3651) In the Christian tradition the Archangel Michael, who is widely venerated in Roman Catholicism and in the Eastern Church, is portrayed as the military leader of God's heavenly host and as the conqueror of Satan. Hence the notion, expressed here, that St. Michael is empowered to free souls from hell.

3. (3694–708) Hartmann states in this passage the fundamental dichotomy of love, which seems to have made this particular emotion so very intriguing to the poets of the courtly age.

4. (3768f.) In other words, Enite would be a suitable consort for the Emperor, who, at the most likely time of composition of *Erec*, was the illustrious Friedrich Barbarossa.

5. (3809f.) Enite of course actually possesses both. In lying here to the Count, she is attempting to use to her advantage two important prerequisites for the prospective wife of a nobleman such as the Count: that she be of acceptable social rank and that she bring with her a substantial dowry.

6. (3890) Cramer (p. 173) mistakes the conditional subjunctive *vergulte* for a hortatory subjunctive and translates: "may God reward" ("Gott möge [. . .] lohnen").

7. (3900–05) The exact format of the oath-swearing is not entirely clear from the MHG text. Apparently, however, it consists of two stages. First, the Count raises certain fingers (most likely the index and middle fingers of his right hand), then the two parties in effect shake hands. Despite the formality of this oath, the reader certainly does not, given the circumstances, expect Enite to adhere to its terms. Yet Thomas (p. 75) goes too far in anticipating the outcome (i.e. her breaking of the oath) by translating *ein ungewissez phant* of v. 3904 (in my version: "a vague and dubious token of her obedience") as "a pledge, which proved to be unreliable." Hartmann at this particular juncture is strongly hinting, but not yet stating quite so openly as Thomas, that Enite will break her pledge.

8. (4019–21) St. Gertrude is the patron saint of travellers. Invocation of her protection is fairly commonplace in the MHG literature, particularly when someone is about to set out on a journey. See Schulz (I, 578f.).

9. (4033) Vv. 4028–33 read: "ê daz sich Êrec / ûf machete ûf den wec, / dô gedâhte dar an / der vil ungetriuwe man, / wenne er zer vrouwen solde komen, / ob er si wolde hân genomen." Both Cramer (p. 179) and Thomas (p. 76) mistakenly assume the Count (and not Erec) to be the antecedent of *er* in v. 4033. Thomas translates vv. 4028–33: "Even before Erec set out, the traitor [the Count] was thinking of how he would seize the lady when the time came to go to her." However, under examination in this passage is the Count's fear (which manifests itself in his dream) that Erec might carry Enite off before he (the Count) arrives to carry out his planned abduction of her. Why otherwise would the Count be frightened (v. 4034) out of his sleep? Certainly not by the dream

of having Enite to himself, as Cramer and Thomas appear to think! In this context, therefore, the conjunction *ob* of v. 4033 means "whether or not," and not "how."

10. (4214) Hartmann's text reads: "dar zuo im abe der arm brach." The word *abe* is of uncertain significance in this verse. Its most obvious meaning is "off," i.e. "one of his arms was also broken off." But if this were the case, it would seem odd to list so serious an injury last, almost as an afterthought. Also, would an arm not be "ripped" or "torn" off, and not "broken" off? Mohr (p. 99), Cramer (p. 185) and Thomas (p. 79) all read—correctly, as it would appear—that the Count merely broke one of his arms. Hence *abe* may best be regarded as an abbreviated form of *aber*, which can be used (see Lexer [I, 11]) as a filler particle to indicate the continued flow of the narrative. By this reading, then, *abe* would not require an exact equivalent in the English translation.

CHAPTER VIII. GUIVREIZ LE PETIT

1. (4294) A fathom is a measure of length equal to six feet. Such a man would therefore be seventy-two feet tall.

2. (4317) A lacuna occurs at this point in the Ambras Manuscript.

3. (4455) This is a most puzzling line (the MHG text states: "dehein edel dich vervienge") which might also be read, with Thomas (pp. 81f.): "no matter how high your station might be"; or, with Cramer (p. 197): "no other man of nobility would commit himself to you" ("kein Adliger würde sich dir sonst verpflichten"); or, with Mohr (p. 107): "your rank would not compel me to recognize you" ("Dein Rang würde mich nicht zwingen, daß ich dich anerkenne").

4. (4461) Hartmann's text actually reads: "until the time of nones." In medieval times the indication of the time of day was given by referring to the canonical hours; nones occurs at about 3 p.m. Thomas (p. 82) mistranslates this passage as: "Now the combat had lasted for nearly three hours."

5. (4553–56) Or this passage ("ouch sult ir mich geniezen lân / daz ich iu stæte triuwe / leiste âne riuwe / al die wîle daz ich lebe") may be read with Thomas (p. 83): "Now you must reward my freely given oath of lifelong fealty by granting me a favor which I greatly desire of you."

6. (4629) At this point in the story a lacuna appears in the Ambras Manuscript. Through a stroke of considerable luck, however, this gap is filled by the Wolfenbüttel Fragment, a manuscript which contains *inter alia* vv. 4549–4832, along with the fifty-eight verses missing in the Ambras Manuscript between vv. 4629 and 4630. When the first leaves of the Wolfenbüttel Fragment were discovered in 1898, the line-numbering in *Erec* was already long established.

Hence, so as not to upset the traditional numbering, it has since been customary to designate these fifty-seven "new" lines from the Wolfenbüttel Fragment with superscript numbers.

7. (4629 [5]) A lacuna occurs here in the Wolfenbüttel Fragment.

8. (4629 [12]) This is the only passage in which Hartmann refers by name to the Old French poet Chrétien de Troyes (ca. 1135–ca. 1190), whose *Erec et Enide* was his source. For a full discussion of this, see Introduction (pp. 19–22).

9. (4629 [15-17]) This passage ("[si] lâgen bî der strâze / alsô ze mâze / ein vierteil einer mîle") might also be translated: "Their camp was about a quarter of a league from the road," with Thomas (p. 84) and Cramer (p. 205). Mohr (pp. 111f.), however, reads this passage as do I.

CHAPTER IX. KING ARTHUR'S ENCAMPMENT

1. (4629 [19]) For this form of the name Gawein, see Chapter II, Note 3.

2. (4629 [43]) A lacuna occurs after this verse in the Wolfenbüttel Fragment.

3. (4636) This verse reads in MHG: "sin herze was gevieret." Paul (p. 195) deals with the possible meanings of (and possible textual alternatives to) the participle *gevieret* ("divided into four parts"). The word is problematical, for although Hartmann lists four qualities of Keii in the ensuing verses (integrity, wickedness, courage and cowardice), it is really Keii's two-sided nature that is of interest. The four attributes listed here are actually two pairs of opposites, each virtue being set off by a corresponding vice. At any rate, Hartmann's depiction of Keii in *Erec* is entirely in keeping with his role throughout Arthurian literature as the roguish seneschal who is generally disliked by the other knights of the Round Table.

4. (4693) Thomas ("if you are brave enough," p. 85) and Cramer ("for then I will be in your power" ["denn dann bin ich in Eurer Gewalt"], p. 209) both miss the point of this last clause ("wan ich iu wol gewunnen bin"), namely that Erec, without revealing his identity, is teasing Keii with the notion that it would be much to Keii's credit if he could manage to take Erec captive. In other words, the other members of the Round Table, Erec implies, would be much impressed by such a prize catch.

5. (4751) Cramer (p. 211) misinterprets this last clause ("ez enmac dir niht gewerren") as: "Nothing will be of any avail to you [in resisting my request to learn your name]" ("Es hilft dir nichts").

6. (5015) Cramer (p. 223) and Thomas (p. 88) offer a possible alternative rendition of the apodosis ("daz sol mit guotem willen sîn") of this sentence: "[then] I'll be glad to help."

7. (5216–18) The most famous of the various sibyls of classical mythology is the Cumaean Sibyl, whom Vergil describes in the *Aeneid*. Because of the

prophetic powers of the Sibyl, Hartmann associates her here with the art of magic. The Latin poet Lucan (A.D. 39–65), a nephew of the philosopher Seneca, is most noted for his epic *Bellum Civile*, in which he documents the civil war between Caesar and Pompey. In Book VI Lucan describes the magical powers of Erichtho, a Thessalian witch who is consulted by Sextus Pompeius following the battle of Dyrrhachium in the year 48 B.C.

CHAPTER X. SIR CADOC AND THE GIANTS

1. (5315f.) On the courtly motif of the lamenting voice, see Wilhelm Frenzen, "Klagebilder und Klagegebärden in der deutschen Dichtung des höfischen Mittelalters," Diss. Bonn 1936, pp. 30f. Haupt (*Erec*, p. 391) points out the similarity between this passage and *Iwein* 3828.

2. (5337) For a discussion of Erec's reaction to the lady's distress in this passage, see Endres (pp. 118f.).

3. (5347) Cramer's reading (p. 237) of "senses" ("Sinne") instead of "voice" ("Stimme") presumably represents only an editorial oversight.

4. (5381) In courtly literature, giants most often tend to appear in groups of two (as here) and twelve; see Ernst Herwig Ahrendt, *Der Riese in der mittelhochdeutschen Epik*, Diss. Rostock 1923 (Güstrow: Michaal'sche Hof- und Ratsbibliothek, 1923), p. 93.

5. (5386) As Haupt (*Erec*, p. 391) points out, Hartmann employs the same sort of indirect question addressed to the reader/listener in vv. 6554, 8775 and 8946.

6. (5402–05) Haupt (*Erec*, p. 391) notes the similarity to *Iwein* 4937.

7. (5426) Hartmann's use of the preposition *âne* in the phrase "âne tôt" is somewhat ambiguous. The possible meanings (see Lexer [I, 66]) are "aside from" and "without (incurring)." An alternative reading might be: "[. . .] that never could a man endure greater affliction than befell him and still live (to tell of it)." See Helmut de Boor, *Mittelalter. Texte und Zeugnisse* (Munich: Bech, 1965), II, 1087, note to v. 139; de Boor glosses *âne tôt* as "abgesehen vom Tode," which corresponds to my preferred reading of this prepositional phrase.

8. (5429–34) Concerning the psychological factors contributing to Erec's decision to intercede for the knight, see Endres (pp. 120f.). Bernhard von Jacobi ("Rechts- und Hausaltertümer in Hartmanns Erec. Eine germanistische Studie," Diss. Göttingen 1903, p. 95) lists other passages in which Erec's complexion is described as changing color as an outward response to inner emotions. Although in this particular passage Hartmann does not state that his protagonist turns pale, it is clear that, in this situation, his turning red (with anger) would be incongruous with the surrounding lines.

9. (5436–42) See Endres (p. 88) for discussion of Hartmann's use of as-

surances of good intentions accompanying a request for information. See also Kuhn ("Erec," p. 131) on the significance of Erec's almost exaggerated politeness to the giants.

10. (5459) Hartmann's text reads: "und wânde in sô gevristen." The ambiguous pronoun *in* causes some uncertainty in this verse. If it refers to the giant, then *gevristen* must mean "to delay," "to put off." On the other hand, if *in* refers to the knight, then the verb must be rendered "to save." Cramer (p. 241) chooses the former and translates *gevristen* "to delay" ("aufhalten"). While Lexer (I, 966) lists both meanings for *gevristen*, the examples given indicate that persons are often the object of *gevristen* in the sense of "protect" or "save," and that things are used with this verb when it means "to put off." Hence my reading of *gevristen* as "to save," whereby the personal pronoun *in* must refer to the knight.

11. (5485f.) The notion that Erec would fight to defend a stranger is clearly alien to the uncourtly giant, whom only the bonds of kinship would move to such action. Hartmann portrays Erec here outside of the Arthurian court and, in an inward sense, outside of the world in which the chivalric code is supreme.

12. (5502f.) See Friedrich Bode (*Die Kampfesschilderungen in den mittelhochdeutschen Epen*, Diss. Greifswald 1909 [Greifswald: Hans Adler, 1909], pp. 15f.) on the placement of the lance under the (right) arm and on the various MHG expressions for this part of the battle preparations.

13. (5515) The verb *erougen* means "to bring before (others') eyes," i.e. "to show." The root derives from *ouge* ("eye"), so that Hartmann clearly intends a pun on the eye which the giant has just lost to Erec's lance. Unfortunately the wordplay fails to survive the translation into English, or into modern German, for that matter.

14. (5534) The shield was grasped in the left hand during combat; see Friedrich Bode (*Die Kampfesschilderungen in den mittelhochdeutschen Epen*, Diss. Greifswald 1909 [Greifswald: Hans Adler, 1909], pp. 18f.) on the use of different MHG expressions for holding forth the shield.

15. (5561–65) See Ohly (pp. 74f.) on the significance of God's coming to the aid of Erec in battle. On the same topic Willson (p. 6) states that in Hartmann's world "the things of God and the things of man, His favorite creature, are not irreconcilably separate, but analogically related." On the comparison to Goliath, see Ernst Herwig Ahrendt, *Der Riese in der mittelhochdeutschen Epik*, Diss. Rostock 1923 (Güstrow: Michaal'sche Hof- und Ratsbibliothek, 1923), p. 104.

CHAPTER XI. COUNT ORINGLES

1. (5799) Cramer (p. 255) translates here: "I accuse" ("so klage ich [. . .] an"); but the form here is *zige*, the subjunctive, and not the present indicative, *zîhe*. See PMS, par. 55 (p. 84) and Lexer (III, 1110f.).

2. (5811) Or, with Cramer (p. 257) and Thomas (p. 97): "by thought or deed."

3. (6275) The phrase *über lant* might also be rendered: "about the country"; see Thomas (p. 102) and Cramer (p. 277). The uncertainty arises from the fact that *lant*, while it can also pluralize to *lender* (see Lexer [I, 1822]), generally has a zero ending in the plural in MHG. Furthermore, the preposition *über* could be used to support either reading.

4. (6348) Vv. 6346–48 read as follows: "swiez der vrouwen wære / widermüete und swære, / si wart im sunder danc gegeben." Despite the unambiguously indicative nature of the verb *wart gegeben*, Cramer (p. 279) translates the verbs in both clauses as past subjunctives: "Regardless how repugnant and grievous it would have been to the lady, she would have been married to him against her will" ("Wie sehr es auch der Dame / zuwider und kummervoll gewesen wäre, / sie wäre ihm gegen ihren Willen verheiratet worden"). Enite is indeed wedded to the Count, although Erec's subsequent appearance renders the union null and void. Cramer is perhaps misled here by the presence in the first clause (v. 6346) of the subjunctive verb *wære*. However, the use of the subjunctive (as in this verse) with the conjunction *swie* ("although") is commonplace even when the concessive clause involves a factual circumstance; see PMS, par. 353:2 (p. 437).

5. (6451–56) The MHG text reads as follows: "und enwæret ir niht ein kint, / ir mühet iuwer klage lân, / und kundet ir iuch rehte entstân, / wie rehte schône in kurzer vrist / iuwer dinc gehœhet ist, / doch iuch lützel noch bedrôz." Cramer (p. 283) mistakenly translates the verb *enwaeret* (v. 6451) as an indicative, although his free rendering of *möhtet* [. . .] *lân* in the following verse as an imperative is altogether justifiable. Both Cramer (p. 283) and Thomas (p. 104) view v. 6453 as a protasis (and not, as in my text, as a second, parallel apodosis dependent upon v. 6451) having v. 6456 as its apodosis. While the word order ("und kundet ir iuch") of v. 6453 might initially appear to speak in favor of Thomas and Cramer, their reading ignores the concessive role of the conjunction *doch* (see PMS, par. 353:1 [pp. 436f.]) in v. 6456, which makes it virtually impossible that this verse (6456) could be an apodosis to v. 6453.

6. (6583) Or this line ("si wânde ir wille ergienge") may be read, with Thomas (p. 106) and Cramer (p. 289): "She hoped to have her wish fulfilled."

7. (6632) Literally: "However highly he might be shorn." The reference is to the tonsure or shaving, usually by a bishop, of the crown of a priest's head. The tonsure marks a priest's entrance into holy orders.

8. (6641) A pun by Hartmann contained in the MHG noun *brûtlouft* ("wedding") is unfortunately lost in translation. The word is a compound noun which literally means "bride's run," thus playing on the fact that Oringles' courtiers are *running* madly from the hall. The word *brûtlouft* may derive from the custom born in ancient times whereby a footrace was held to win the woman's hand in marriage (see Lexer [I, 374]). Schwarz (pp. 636f.) offers various other

explanations of this word, suggesting that it may have signified (1) the procession of the bride and groom to their new home, (2) a wedding dance, (3) a wedding procession, (4) the wedding itself, (5) the banquet held to dedicate a new home, and (6) the sexual union of male and female dogs.

9. (6718) This is a direct loan word from the Old French *rotruenge*, which designated a certain style of singing. In music, as in so many other spheres of chivalry, German knights of the twelfth and thirteenth centuries proved themselves most eager to imitate their French counterparts. It is not surprising that so many loan translations and loan words from Old French are to be found in MHG. See Schwarz (pp. 663f.).

CHAPTER XII. RECONCILIATION AND HEALING

1. (6840) While the verb *entslâfen* literally means "to fall asleep," it can also, as Lexer (I, 587) points out, be used figuratively, here in the negated sense of "not fall asleep (on the job)," "not be lazy." Cramer (p. 301) and Thomas (p. 109) both interpret this verse quite literally: "[Guivreiz], who had not yet gone to bed." This reading, while by no means incorrect, yields information about Guivreiz that seems at best irrelevant. More probably, Hartmann intends to allude here with ironic understatement to Guivreiz' eagerness to come to Erec's aid.

2. (7169) Carmer (p. 315) erroneously translates: "their *first* tack" ("so rannte es zuerst"). The MHG text actually reads: "sô was sîn jungeste [i.e. "youngest," "most recent," "last," "final"] vart."

3. (7181) In part because Hartmann has already made explicit reference (in vv. 7155–57) to hunting dogs, R. Sprenger ("Zu Hartmanns Erec," *Germania*, 27 [1882], pp. 374f.) reads in the MHG noun *hasenwinden* not "harriers" (a breed of dogs trained to hunt hares and rabbits), but rather certain unspecified instruments used in such hunts. For lack of any definitive external lexicographical supporting evidence, Sprenger's suggestion cannot be viewed as compelling.

4. (7258) The exact meaning of this verse ("im was dâ mite lîhte baz") is unclear. Cramer (p. 319) reads: "He felt at ease in it" ("Dabei fühlte er sich wohl"); Thomas (p. 113) interprets it: "and he liked it." Both, however, ignore the comparative nature of the adverb *baz* ("better," "more"), which I have incorporated into my translation by means of the phrase "more [. . .] than that."

CHAPTER XIII. ENITE'S HORSE AND SADDLE

1. (7299) As in vv. 7462, 7893 and 8201, Hartmann's mention of "the Master" is a reference to Chrétien de Troyes, whose *Erec et Enide* served as

the model for Hartmann's *Erec*. See also note to v. 4629[12] and Introduction (pp. 19–22).

2. (7359) The MHG noun *tier* can signify, as does modern German *Tier*, an animal in general or, specifically (and unlike modern German) a deer; see Lexer (II, 1433f.). The present context appears to suggest the latter meaning.

3. (7361) The pastern is the part of the horse's foot located above the hoof and below the fetlock (or tuft of hair which grows on the lower back part of the leg).

4. (7367) It is uncertain as to whether the prepositional phrase *von sîner meisterschaft* refers to the horse or to the learned man being described here. Thomas (p. 114) fails to translate the phrase at all, while Cramer (p. 323) sees the horse as the antecedent of the possessive adjective *sîner:* "in regard to its [the horse's] perfection" ("in bezug auf seine Vollkommenheit"). This is both grammatically and logically plausible, but the context is probably better served by my reading, whereby *sîner* has as its antecedent the learned man: "by drawing upon all his [the learned man's] learning."

5. (7429f.) Unlike his earlier (vv. 1446–50) successful attempt at narratorial self-restraint, this profession of brevity by Hartmann's narrator is to prove spectacularly fruitless, for he will, despite what he says in these verses, talk on for another 335 odd lines about the various attributes of Enite's horse and saddle.

6. (7473) Cramer (p. 327) mistakenly translates *vierdehalbez jâr* as "for four years" ("vier Jahre lang") instead of "for three and a half years."

7. (7517) Despite Haupt's assertion (*Erec*, pp. 410f.) that this verse ("jâ, dâ si dâ trâten") defies translation, despite Cramer's question mark (p. 329) which is presumably intended as a disclaimer of his translation, and despite Thomas' silent omission (p. 116) of this and the following verse, the meaning is actually quite evident. Hartmann's text reads literally: "Yes, when they stepped there." The narrator is responding here with sarcasm to the listener's question (v. 7516), saying in effect that the listener has taken so very long to begin his account of the saddle that the story-telling has come to a halt and has, paradoxically, been overtaken by the ongoing events of the story itself; in other words, that the courtiers have, during this long period of narratorial squabbling, already brought forth the horse for all (including the listener/would-be narrator) to see.

8. (7545–81) The allusions in this passage are to Vergil's (70–19 B.C.) *Aeneid*, which exerted a strong, if indirect, influence upon the courtly literature of Germany. Hartmann most likely knew not the original Latin epic of Vergil, but rather an adaptation (called *Eneit*) composed roughly between 1170 and 1190 by the German poet Heinrich von Veldeke. Heinrich's story, in turn, was based upon the Old French *Roman d'Eneas*, which was written during the 1170s in northern France. Since *Erec* was written around 1185, Hartmann may have been acquainted with an only partially completed *Eneit*.

9. (7677) MHG *vedere* can mean either "wing" or "feather"; see Lexer (III, 38). Because dragons are not customarily depicted as feathered animals and because the same verse contains, in the form of a simile, an allusion to flight, I have chosen to translate *vedern* as "wings."

10. (7707–13) Hartmann alludes here to the two young ill-fated lovers of classical mythology whose union is opposed by their parents. One evening they arrange to meet secretly, and the maiden Thisbe, arriving first at the rendezvous place, is frightened away by a lion. Its jaws bloody with earlier prey, the lion picks up the mantle which Thisbe has left behind, bloodying and tearing it and thus convincing the arriving Pyramus that his beloved has been killed. Wracked with grief, Pyramus kills himself; when Thisbe returns, she finds him dead, and takes her own life.

11. (7734) This verse ("nâch dem zoume vollekomen") is problematical, chiefly because of questions surrounding the role of *nâch*, which could be either a dative preposition meaning here "corresponding to," "according to" or a dative adjective meaning "close to." The precise function of the participial adjective *vollekomen* is likewise uncertain. As a result, this verse is rendered in markedly divergent ways in the various translations. Cramer (p. 339) reads: a strap "lay along the reins" ("saß an dem Zaum"); Thomas (p. 118): "like the reins"; and Mohr (p. 183): "as it [the strap] is well suited to the reins" ("wie dem Zaume sie gebührt"). None of these readings appears clearly preferable to my interpretation of v. 7734, which, at any rate, remains somewhat enigmatic.

12. (7738) Hartmann refers in this passage, as Haupt (*Erec*, p. 416) points out, to the twelve (eleven here, the twelfth being introduced in the following verse) precious stones of Aaron's priestly robe which are listed in Exodus 28, 17ff.

13. (7760) The prepositional phrase *mit vollem mære* (literally "with full report") is of ambiguous meaning and presents certain difficulties in translation. Thomas (p. 119) translates: "all in all." Cramer (p. 339) allows the phrase to flow anonymously into his text, without translating it directly. Neither solution seems demonstrably superior to my rendition: "according to all we hear of it."

14. (7783f.) The task of pleasing both God and the world—that is, of finding a satisfactory position within the secular realm while also ensuring one's heavenly salvation—was perhaps the most daunting dilemma facing medieval man; see Introduction (Note 27).

CHAPTER XIV. JOIE DE LA COURT

1. (7837) A hide is a portion of land which can vary, depending upon local custom, from eighty to 120 acres. The area of land upon which the fortress stood was therefore quite considerable.

2. (7850) An ashlar is either a square stone hewn for building purposes or a facing constructed of thin slabs and employed to cover brick walls. The context seems to call for the former meaning.

3. (7864) Hartmann's text reads: "sus was daz hûs gevieret." MHG has two weak verbs *vieren*. One means "to quadruple," "to square," or "to divide up into quarters"; the other "to make beautiful" (from the adjective *fier* "stately," "beautiful"). Both Thomas (p. 121) and Cramer (p. 343) interpret the participle *gevieret* as deriving from the former verb. Since both verbs are weak, this reading is grammatically possible. However, nowhere does the surrounding context support the notion that this castle is in any way laid out in four parts. Rather, Hartmann is about to describe the way in which it is decorated. Also, the verbs *vieren* and *zieren* ("to decorate") are, as Lexer (III, 340) points out, frequently used together as near synonyms in MHG literature because of their obvious rhyme possibilities; Hartmann's rhyme in vv. 7864f. is, in fact, precisely this (*gevieret : gezieret*).

4. (7866) In architecture a capital is the uppermost section of a column or pillar (here, of the castle towers). The capital serves as the decorative head or crown at the top of the vertical part of these towers and just below the entablature, or horizontal superstructure.

5. (7890) Hartmann uses the MHG noun *boumgarte*, which literally means "orchard" or "tree-nursery." In my translation I render *boumgarte* variously as "arbor" or "garden."

6. (8052f.) In these verses ("dâ von geschach im ungemach. /dô erz hûs von êrste ane sach,") I have followed Cramer's (p. 351) example in altering the punctuation of the Leitzmann (ATB) edition: the period after v. 8052 becomes a comma, and the comma after v. 8053 becomes a period. As Blosen ("Bemerkungen," pp. 68f.) correctly points out, this change causes the pronouns *im* (v. 8052) and *er* (v. 8053) to refer to Guivreiz. Not until v. 8055, then, does a personal pronoun (here *er*) within this immediate passage make reference to Erec.

7. (8126–40) In documenting Erec's levelheadedness, Hartmann makes reference here to various acts of witchcraft and superstitious beliefs in common circulation during the Middle Ages. For more on certain of these superstitions, see Schultz (I, 459 and 650f.).

8. (8203–07) In classical mythology, Pallas is the name given to the goddess Athena after she accidentally kills a youthful playmate called Pallas (or, in other legends, because she kills a giant by the same name). In addition to being the goddess of war, of peace and of wisdom, Athena was also a guardian of cities, especially Athens, where the Parthenon was built in her honor. Hence, perhaps, Hartmann's connection of Pallas Athena with the imposing structure at Brandigan.

9. (8218) Neither Thomas (p. 125) nor Cramer (p. 359) translates *gebent*

("smooth"), which is a syncopated (from *geebenet*) form of the past participle of the verb *ebenen* ("to make even," "to smooth").

10. (8275) Both Thomas (p. 125) and Cramer (p. 361) mistranslate this last clause ("hæte si diu zwelfte lân") as: "and she by the twelfth." Hartmann's text reads literally: "had the twelfth left her [alone]," i.e. "had the twelfth not been present [to outshine her]."

11. (8318) Hartmann uses a synonym (*hiufel*, "cheek") here for *wengel* of the following line. Since English does not have a close synonym for "cheek," I have translated *hiufel* as "face."

12. (8375–78) If Erec has heard of Brandigan before coming there with Guivreiz, it is not evident in the passage (vv. 8028–47) in which he first responds to Guivreiz' description of it. Erec's claim to familiarity with the wonders of this place must be viewed as rhetorical hyperbole.

13. (8437f.) Hartmann refers here to the medieval belief that diamond, the hardest natural substance known, could be softened by ram's blood. See Bech (*Erec der wunderære*, p. 275, note to v. 8436 [sic]).

14. (8482–86) King Ivreins' mention here of a gateway leading into the arbor is curiously inconsistent, both with what has been said earlier (v. 8470, which states that the arbor is not enclosed by any wall) and with other information still to be given concerning the arbor (vv. 8704–07: "neither a wall nor a moat encircled it, nor did a fence encompass it, nor a body of water nor a hedge, nor anything tangible"; and vv. 8751–53: "A cloud could be seen encircling the arbor—a cloud through which no one was able to pass, except as I have described to you before"). To be sure, in the passage (vv. 8754–58) in which they enter the arbor, Hartmann uses a word (*bürgetor*) which literally means "castle gate" or "city gate"; however, as Lexer (I, 393) points out, *bürgetor* can also be used figuratively and in a more generalized sense. Hence, I have translated it in v. 8758 simply as "entrance." The present passage (vv. 8482–86), in which the entrance is portrayed in more concrete terms (as a gate which will open itself when addressed), must probably be viewed as an inconsistency on the part of Hartmann.

15. (8508) The Wends, or Sorbs, are a Slavic people living in Lusatia (in present-day East Germany). In medieval times, however, the term "Wends" was used loosely by speakers of German to designate all of the Slavs living between the Oder River in the east and the Elbe and Saale Rivers in the west.

16. (8567f.) The MHG text reads here: "er setzet wider valsche guot, / sîn golt wider êre." Cramer (p. 373) mistranslates *êre* as "honor" and wrongly alters Leitzmann's (ATB) punctuation in an attempt to accommodate this misprision. The noun that Hartmann employs here is *êr/êre* ("ore," "iron") and not its homograph *êre* ("honor"). I have added the adjectives (not present in Hartmann's text) "glittering" and "dull" in order to underscore the intended contrast between these two metals. The chief cause of the many misreadings centering

on these two verses is the not-so-obvious fact that there are two pairs of noun opposites expressed here: in v. 8567 *valsche* (this is not an adjective modifying *guot*) and *guot;* and in v. 8568 *golt* and *êre.* See Blosen ("Bemerkungen," pp. 61–63) and Haupt (*Erec,* p. 428).

CHAPTER XV. THE RED KNIGHT MABONAGRIN

1. (8652) The reference is to St. John the Evangelist (often called "St. John the Divine"), who was one of the twelve Disciples and is traditionally considered the author of the fourth Gospel, of three epistles and of the Revelation. It was into John's care that Christ committed the Virgin Mary in his final moments. On the custom of drinking and invoking the blessing of a saint in MHG literature, see Schultz (I, 578f.).

2. (8715–44) Hartmann's depiction of the arbor is a conventionalized account of a *locus amoenus* (literally "pleasant place") common to much of older literature.

3. (8758) See note to vv. 8482–86 (Chapter XIV, Note 14).

4. (8852) Hartmann's text literally reads: "a duel which is to take place *between us.*"

5. (8886) This sort of narratorial disclaimer of knowledge as to the ultimate outcome is typical of the way in which Hartmann's narrator assumes a pose of non-omniscience so as to heighten suspense in his audience; see Introduction (pp. 27f.).

6. (8915) See Chapter XIV, Note 4.

7. (8947) Or, with Thomas (p. 132): "chamberlain" (singular). Since the noun *kameræere* has a zero ending in the plural, and since the possessive adjective *ir* ("her") modifying *kameræere* is undeclined here, it is not possible to determine whether Hartmann intended singular or plural.

8. (8950) Here Cramer (pp. 390f.) wisely alters Leitzmann's (ATB) MHG text ("ouch enmohte si Êrec niht gesehen"), which would have yielded the reading: "Nor could Erec see her [Mabonagrin's lady] either." Not only is Leitzmann's text inconsistent (Hartmann is speaking here not of the lady, but specifically of the tunic which she is wearing), it runs counter to the text of the Ambras Manuscript, which reads: "auch mocht es Ereck nit gesehen." As Blosen ("Bemerkungen," pp. 69f.) points out, Cramer's change ought to have been not (from Leitzmann's *enmohte si*) to *enmohtez,* but rather to *enmohtes* (genitive singular dependent upon the negator *niht*).

9. (8967) For a knight such as Erec to approach a lady while fully armed would have constituted a breach of good manners; see Haupt (*Erec,* p. 430).

10. (9067) Or this line ("jâ, des wil ich dir verphlegen") may be translated, with Cramer (p. 395): "I shall [or "I wish to"] see to that" ("dafür will ich sorgen").

11. (9090) On the function of the nails, see Chapter IV, Note 12.

12. (9226) As in v. 7367 (see Chapter XIII, Note 4), the prepositional phrase *von sîner meisterschaft* is the source of some confusion. Both Thomas (p. 136) and Cramer (p. 401) see the possessive adjective *sîner* as referring to Mabonagrin and not to Erec. Instead of my rendition ("from his [Erec's] superiority"), they would read: "as a result of [*von*] his [Mabonagrin's] skill." Either reading may be correct.

13. (9308–10) Hartmann's text reads: "Êrec der wunderære / machete im sô swære / als et in wol luste." Cramer (p. 405) translates this: "Erec the amazing one made himself as heavy as he wanted" ("Erec, der Erstaunliche, / machte sich so schwer / wie er wollte"). Not only does this yield a somewhat illogical reading, Cramer ignores the fact that Hartmann's pronoun *im* ("to him" or, reflexively, "to himself") is in the dative and not the accusative, as Cramer's rendition requires. Thomas (p. 137) follows Cramer's interpretation in translating these verses: "At this the surprising Erec dropped down upon him with all his weight." While the verb *lüsten* can mean (see Lexer [I, 1992]) "to wish," "to want" (as per Cramer/Thomas) or "to be happy" (as in my reading), the pronoun (if used reflexively, as Cramer/Thomas read it) in v. 9309 would have to be in the accusative (i.e. *sich* instead of *im*) in order for *swære* to be an adjective meaning "heavy," and not, as in my reading, a noun meaning "distress." Hence v. 9309 must be translated: Erec "caused as much distress to him [Mabonagrin]," i.e. "inflicted upon his opponent every bit as much distress."

14. (9435–37) The MHG text reads: "wie ir mohtet belîben / ein alsô wætlîcher man, / wie mich des niht verwundern kan!" Both Cramer (p. 411) and Thomas (p. 138) mistakenly translate: "I am really surprised that such a handsome knight as you could remain here." Hartmann's text does not contain the adverb "here." The verb *belîben* ("to remain") does not signify *where* Mabonagrin has remained (since there is no locational adverb to complement the verb), but rather (as a predicate noun phrase) *what* he has remained, namely a stately man, despite his lengthy stay in the arbor.

15. (9495) The promise appears to have taken much the same outward form as did Enite's pledge to the Count; see Chapter VII, Note 7.

16. (9603f.) Although Hartmann's text ("nû suln si ir aber phlegen, / wan nû hânt si wider ir trôst") contains in v. 9603 a nominative third person plural personal pronoun (*si*), Cramer (p. 417) inexplicably gives as the subject of this sentence "we" instead of "they." Also, in v. 9604 Cramer (p. 417) translates: "for now they are consoled" ("denn jetzt sind sie getröstet"). While this is not an incorrect rendition of Hartmann's text (which literally reads: "for now they again have their comfort"), the noun *trôst* ("comfort") can also be personified (see Lexer [II, 1527]), as in my version (*trôst* = "protector") and in Thomas' translation (p. 140): "because they have their favorite [= *trôst*] back."

17. (9660) In this verse Hartmann uses an antiquated word for "battle

song": *wîcsanc*. (Traces of Latin *vincere* ["to conquer"] can be found in *wîc*, the first part of the compound.) By this point in the history of the German language, many such older words, which were common to the Germanic heroic epic, had already begun to be replaced by newer words based on Old French models. In the MHG courtly romance, much of the terminology centering on chivalry and warfare has its roots in words from the literature which was coming into Germany from France during these years; see Schwarz (pp. 680f.). Used within the parameters of Hartmann's courtly Arthurian romance *Erec*, a word such as *wîcsanc* must have seemed markedly out of place to audiences of the late twelfth and early thirteenth centuries.

18. (9689) The MHG text ("in sweic der munt, ir herze sanc") reads quite literally: "The mouth was silent for them, her [or "their"] heart sang." In the first clause it is clear (because of the unambiguously plural personal pronoun *in* ["to them," "for them"]) that Hartmann means both ladies. In the second clause, however, Hartmann uses the possessive adjective *ir* which, as in modern German *ihr*, can mean either "her" or "their." Furthermore, MHG syntax parallels modern German usage in not normally pluralizing parts of the body even when they are ascribed to more than one person; hence the singular subject *herze* ("heart") and its singular verb *sanc* ("sang") are of no help in eliminating the possibility that, as in the initial clause, both ladies are intended. Context alone dictates that, under the circumstances, only one of these two ladies (namely Enite, whose husband has just won the duel) has reason to let her heart sing out for joy. Thomas (p. 141) apparently comes to the same conclusion, while Cramer (p. 421) circumvents the problem by adapting his modern German translation to parallel Hartmann's ambiguous syntax.

19. (9716–24) This sort of coincidental blood relationship anticipates, on a much smaller scale, the vastly complex series of interrelationships among many of the characters in Wolfram von Eschenbach's *Parzival*. There as here, the fact that two persons are related to one another often comes out only after some sort of adversarial relationship has established itself. James V. McMahon ("Enite's Relatives: The Girl in the Garden," *Modern Language Notes*, 85 [1970], pp. 367–72) argues in favor of a textual emendation in v. 9722 which would knit together the characters in *Erec* even more tightly. McMahon would change Hartmann's *veter* (whose primary meanings are "father's brother" and "male cousin," though it can also signify "brother's son," i.e. "nephew"; see Lexer [III, 331]; its modern German descendent, *Vetter*, only means "male cousin") to *vater* ("father"). This would make Mabonagrin's lady the daughter (and not the niece) of Duke Imain. (By either reading, this lady and Enite would be first cousins.) McMahon cites (1) the well-known unreliability of the Ambras scribe, Hans Ried (who might easily have copied *veter* in place of Hartmann's original *vater*), and (2) the fact that the change of *veter* to *vater* would bring Hartmann's version into line with Chrétien's story. However, Hart-

mann differs from his source (Chrétien's *Erec et Enide*) in countless small details (see Introduction, pp. 19–22) and may have simply misunderstood Chrétien's text on this particular point. At any rate, McMahon's proposed emendation lacks any direct textual evidence and must be rejected as speculative.

20. (9820) Or the phrase "sînes dankes" may be rendered, instead of "willingly": "if it could be avoided," Thomas (p. 142); or "if/whenever he could arrange things so" ("wenn er es einrichten konnte"), Cramer (p. 427).

CHAPTER XVI. HONOR RESTORED

1. (9899) As in v. 3460 (see Chapter VI, Note 3), Fortuna (MHG *vrou Sælde*) is the personification of good luck or fortune.

2. (10,052) Or, with Thomas (p. 145) and Cramer (p. 437), this line ("alsô was sîn diu werlt vol") may be connected to the preceding sentence: "so that the world was filled with him [Erec]." (This leaves the following verse to stand as an independent sentence: "none other received like acclaim" [Thomas, p. 145].) Hartmann's text reads literally: "The world was so full of him [or "of it"]." Because the genitive personal pronoun *sîn* can be either masculine ("of him," i.e. "of Erec") or neuter ("of it," i.e. "of Erec's praise"), either reading may be accepted.

3. (10,083) Or this verse ("hie sazte er sô sîn lant") may be translated, with Thomas (p. 145): "Erec ruled the land"; or, with Cramer (p. 439): "He [Erec] gave his country such laws" ("Er gab seinem Lande solche Gesetze"). Because the MHG verb *setzen* has, as in modern German, a very broad field of meaning (see Lexer [II, 894–96]), Hartmann's phrase *sîn lant setzen* may be translated freely in a number of divergent ways.

4. (10,115–18) These lines are rife with ambiguity. Hartmann's text ("zu wunsche wurden si beide alt, / wan si got hâte gesant / ze vreuden in ir eigen lant, / ir vater und ir muoter") reads literally:

115   In perfect happiness (or "having all they could wish for")
     they both became old,
116   for God had sent them (or "her")
117   for joy into their (or "her") own land,
118   her father and her mother.

As so often before, problems arise here as a result of the ambiguity of certain MHG personal pronouns and possessive adjectives. Not surprisingly, widely divergent translations of these verses have resulted. Unfortunately, some of the same ambiguities of the MHG original often survive into the modern German translations. Mohr (p. 237), for instance, renders this passage: "They [presumably "Erec and Enite"] grew old in thankfulness, for God had sent them [again, "Erec and Enite"] home for joy into their [or "her"] own land to her [not "their," since Erec's father is already dead (cf. vv. 9969f.)] father and her mother" ("Sie wurden alt in Dankbarkeit, / denn Gott hatte sie heimgesandt / zur Freude in ihr eigenes Land / ihrem Vater und ihrer Mutter"). Several problems are evident here. First, why would Erec and Enite be dispatched to a different land after Erec has so arduously conquered his own realms? Second, why would Hartmann call this their (or her) "own" land? It would belong to Koralus and Karsinefite, who seem to be still alive and therefore in possession of it. (Furthermore, when and how was this land, which Enite's parents had lost through no fault of their own [cf. vv. 400–10], reconquered?) And third, why would Hartmann use the pluperfect ("had sent") when speaking of what was still to happen to Erec and Enite? Would he not more likely employ the preterite (or the perfect) for this, while reserving the pluperfect for events in his story which are already completed but which, as here, have not yet been related (such as the news that Koralus and Karsinefite had regained their land at God's command)?

Cramer's (p. 439) interpretation comes closer to providing clarity; he translates: "In perfect happiness they [apparently "Erec and Enite"] had a long life, for God had sent, much to her [Enite's] joy, her father and her mother into [their] own land" ("In vollkommenem Glück hatten sie ein langes Leben, / denn Gott hatte ihr / zur Freude ins eigene Land / ihren Vater und ihre Mutter geschickt"). Unlike Mohr, who views v. 10,118 as a dative indirect object, Cramer sees it as an appositive to the accusative direct object personal pronoun *si* of v. 10,116. The only serious objection to this reading lies in the lack of any motivational correlation between the first verse and the final three verses. Why, in other words, should Enite's (and, as it seems, Erec's) happiness be dependent upon (or at least brought to full fruition by) the fact that Enite's parents regain possession of their lost territory, and not, for example, by her parents spending their last days together with Erec and Enite?

Thomas (p. 146) translates these lines: "She too had all she wanted for the rest of her life, because, to her great joy, God had sent her father and mother to live in her land." Here, apparently, Koralus and Karsinefite have been delivered not into their former land, but to Erec's realm. Seen purely from the standpoint of plot, this yields what might be the most satisfactory outcome. However, two egregious errors are evident in Thomas' translation. First, he mistranslates *si* of v. 10,115 as "she" (i.e. "Enite") instead of "they" (be this couple Erec and Enite, or Koralus and Karsinefite). While *si* can serve both as the nominative feminine singular and as the nominative plural of the personal pronoun, the verb *wurden* (whose subject is *si*) is unmistakably plural. Second, Thomas circumvents the problem posed by the adjective *eigen* ("one's own") by simply disregarding it altogether. Given these two major errors, Thomas' rendition cannot stand up to any further contentual analysis.

Finally, my own translation: "Both Koralus and Karsinefite grew old in perfect happiness, for God had sent Enite's father and mother back into their own land, much to their joy." I adhere most closely to Cramer's reading, with one major exception: I take v. 10,118 to be a belatedly introduced appositive to *si* ("they") of v. 10,115 (and/or to *si* ["them"] of v. 10,116). By this interpretation, all of the ambiguous forms in this passage must refer to Koralus and Karsinefite, and not once to Enite or to Erec and Enite. As Mohr and Cramer seem to believe, Enite's parents have managed (just when and in what fashion is never divulged), by God's help, to repossess their own realm, where they live on into old age. Erec and Enite live out their years not together with Enite's parents, but in Erec's realm. The one problem with this reading is the abruptness with which Hartmann first broaches then disposes of the subject of Enite's parents. But then, the same sense of abruptness is evident regardless how one interprets Hartmann's fleeting mention here of Koralus and Karsinefite. Furthermore, at this point in his story, Hartmann is intent upon tying together in summary form the final threads of his tale.

    5. (10,123) Once again, as in v. 2971 (see Chapter V, Note 2), Hartmann reiterates Erec's great mistake: *sich verligen*, or lying about immoderately instead of pursing the call of knightly adventure. That mistake (and all its attendant failings) now rectified and the golden mean reestablished, Hartmann's story can finally come to a close.

    6. (10,135) Hartmann uses here the noun *liet*, which can also mean (see Lexer [I, 1913f.]) "song" or "stanza."

SELECTED BIBLIOGRAPHY

It is not within the scope of this bibliography to present a full and complete catalogue of all the literature pertaining to Hartmann's *Erec*. Readers wishing to gain access to this rather considerable body of scholarship are referred to Elfriede Neubuhr's *Bibliographie zu Hartmann von Aue* (cited below). Users of the present bibliography can expect to find listed, first and foremost, those works which have had the most enduring impact upon *Erec* scholarship over the years. In addition, a greater measure of completeness is attempted in two further areas: (1) contributions which have appeared since Neubuhr's bibliography was published in 1977 and (2) works written in the English language.

CRITICAL EDITIONS AND TRANSLATIONS

Bech, Fedor, ed. *Hartmann von Aue. Erster Teil. Erec der wunderære*. Deutsche Klassiker des Mittelalters, 4. 3rd. ed. Leipzig: Brockhaus, 1893.

Comfort, W. W., trans. *Erec et Enide*. In *Chrétien de Troyes: Arthurian Romances*. Introd. and notes by D. D. R. Owen. Everyman's Library. London and Toronto: Dent, 1914; rpt. New York: Dutton, 1977.

Cramer, Thomas, trans. *Hartmann von Aue. Erec. Mittelhochdeutscher Text und Übertragung*. Fischer Taschenbuch, 6017. Frankfurt: Fischer, 1972.

Haupt, Moriz, ed. *Erec. Eine Erzählung von Hartmann von Aue*. 2nd ed. Leipzig: Hirzel, 1871; rpt. Hildesheim and New York: Olms, 1979.

Leitzmann, Albert, ed. *Hartmann von Aue. Erec*. 6th rev. ed., by Christoph Cormeau and Kurt Gärtner. Altdeutsche Textbibliothek, 39. Tübingen: Niemeyer, 1985.

Mohr, Wolfgang, trans. *Hartmann von Aue. Erec*. Göppinger Arbeiten zur Germanistik, 291. Göppingen: Kümmerle, 1980.

Naumann, Hans, and Hans Steinger, eds. *Hartmann von Aue. Erec—Iwein*. Deutsche Literatur in Entwicklungsreihen. Höfische Dichtung, 3. Leipzig: Reclam, 1933; rpt. Darmstadt: Wissenschaftliche Buchgesellschaft, 1964.

Schwarz, Ernst, trans. *Erec. Iwein. Text, Nacherzählung, Worterklärungen*. Darmstadt: Wissenschaftliche Buchgesellschaft, 1967.

Thomas, J. W., trans. *Erec by Hartmann von Aue*. Lincoln and London: University of Nebraska Press, 1982.

Unterkirchner, Franz, ed. *Ambraser Heldenbuch. Vollständige Faksimile-Ausgabe.* Codices selecti, 42. Graz: Akademische Druck- und Verlagsanstalt, 1973.

SECONDARY LITERATURE ON *EREC*

Bayer, Hans. " 'bî den liuten ist sô guot': Die *meine* des *Erec* Hartmanns von Aue." *Euphorion,* 73 (1979), 272–85.

Bech, Fedor. "Zu Hartmanns Erek." *Germania, 7* (1862), 429–469.

Bechstein, Reinhold. "Zu Hartmanns Erec. 14. Aventiure. Conjecturen und Restitutionen." *Germania,* 25 (1880), 319–329.

Blosen, Hans. " 'Assumptions about lost manuscripts?' Zur Erec-Diskussion." *Orbis Litterarum,* 37 (1982), 367.

————. "Bemerkungen zur Textkritik in Thomas Cramers Erec-Ausgabe mit Übertragung." *Kopenhagener Beiträge zur germanistischen Linguistik, 7* (1976), 59–72.

————. "Hartmanns Erec als eifersüchtiger Ehemann. Nachtragsnotiz zu meinem Aufsatz: Noch einmal: Zu Enites Schuld in Hartmanns *Erec, Orbis Litterarum,* 31 (1976), 81–109." *Orbis Litterarum,* 33 (1978), 1–3.

————. "Noch einmal: Zu Enites Schuld in Hartmanns *Erec.* Mit Ausblicken auf Chrétiens Roman und das Mabinogi von Gereint." *Orbis Litterarum,* 31 (1976), 81–109.

Boggs, Roy A. "Hartmann's *Erec.*" In *Innovation in Medieval Literature: Essays to the Memory of Alan Markman.* Pittsburgh: University of Pittsburgh Press, 1971, pp. 49–62.

Brommer, Peter. "Ein unbekanntes «Erec»-Fragment in Koblenz." *Zeitschrift für deutsches Altertum,* 105 (1976), 186–194.

Carne, Eva Marie. "Hartmann von Aue's *Erec:* A Hero's Conduct Reexamined." *Selecta,* 4 (1983), 59–63.

Clark, S. L. "Hartmann's *Erec:* Language, Perception and Transformation." *Germanic Review,* 56 (1981), 81–94.

Cormeau, Christoph. *"Joie de la curt:* Bedeutungssetzung und ethische Erkenntnis." In *Formen und Funktionen der Allegorie.* Ed. W. Haug. Stuttgart: Metzler, 1979, pp. 194–205.

Cramer, Thomas. "Soziale Motivation in der Schuld-Sühne-Problematik von Hartmanns Erec." *Euphorion,* 66 (1972), 97–112.

Ehrismann, Gustav. "Textkritische Bemerkungen. 1. Zum Erec." *Beiträge zur Geschichte der deutschen Sprache und Literatur,* 24 (1899), 384–386.

Ehrismann, Otfried. "Handlungsbegründungen in Hartmanns von Aue 'Erec'." *Zeitschrift für deutsche Philologie,* 98 (1979), 321–344.

Endres, Rolf. *Studien zum Stil von Hartmanns Erec.* Munich: UNI–Druck, 1961.

Fisher, Rodney. "Erecs Schuld und Enitens Unschuld bei Hartmann." *Euphorion,* 69 (1975), 160–174.

Freytag, Wibke. "Zu Hartmanns Methode der Adaptation im 'Erec'." *Euphorion,* 72 (1978), 227–239.

Gärtner, Kurt. "Der Text der Wolfenbütteler Erec-Fragmente und seine Bedeutung für die Erec-Forschung." *Beiträge zur Geschichte der deutschen Sprache und Literatur*, 104 (1982), 207–230 and 359–430.

———. "Probleme einer Neuausgabe von Hartmanns «Erec»." In *Germanistik. Forschungsstand und Perspektiven*. Ed. Georg Stötzel. Vorträge des Deutschen Germanistentages 1984. Berlin: de Gruyter, 1984.

———. "Zur Rezeption des Artusromans im Spätmittelalter und den Erec-Entlehnungen im «Friedrich von Schwaben»." In *Artusrittertum im späten Mittelalter. Ethos und Ideologie*. Ed. Friedrich Wolfzettel. Beiträge zur deutschen Philologie, 57. Gießen: Schmitz, 1984, pp. 60–72.

Goebel, Ulrich. "Concerning the Promotion of Hartmann's *Erec*." *Semasia*, 2 (1975), 75–81.

Green, Dennis H. "Hartmann's Ironic Praise of Erec." *Modern Language Review*, 70 (1975), 795–807.

Hatto, Arthur T. "Enid's Best Dress. A Contribution to the Understanding of Chrétien's and Hartmann's Erec and the Welsh Gereint." *Euphorion*, 54 (1960), 437–441.

Haug, Walter. "Erec, Enite und Evelyne B." In *Festschrift für Kurt Ruh zum 65. Geburtstag*. Ed. D. Huschenbett, K. Matzel, G. Steer and N. Wagner. Medium ævum, Beiträge zur deutschen Literatur des hohen und späten Mittelalters. Tübingen: Niemeyer, 1979.

———. "Die Symbolstruktur des höfischen Epos und ihre Auflösung bei Wolfram von Eschenbach." *Deutsche Vierteljahrsschrift*, 45 (1971), 668–705.

Haupt, Moriz. "Zu Hartmann von Aue. Berichtigungen und Nachträge zum Erec." *Zeitschrift für deutsches Altertum*, 3 (1843), 266–273.

Heine, Thomas. "Shifting Perspectives. The Narrative Strategy in Hartmann's 'Erec'." *Orbis litterarum*, 36 (1981), 95–115.

von Heinemann, Otto. "Wolfenbütteler Bruchstücke des Erec." *Zeitschrift für deutsches Altertum*, 42 (1898), 259–267.

Höhler, Gertrud. "Der Kampf im Garten. Studien zur Brandigan-Episode in Hartmanns Erec." *Euphorion*, 68 (1974), 371–419.

Hrubý, Antonín. "Moralphilosophie und Moraltheologie in Hartmanns *Erec*." In *The Epic in Medieval Society: Aesthetic and Moral Values*. Ed. Harald Scholler. Tübingen: Niemeyer, 1977, pp. 193–213.

———. "Die Problemstellung in Chrétiens und Hartmanns 'Erec'." *Deutsche Vierteljahrsschrift*, 38 (1964), 337–360. Rpt. in *Hartmann von Aue*. Ed. Hugo Kuhn and Christoph Cormeau. Wege der Forschung, 309. Darmstadt: Wissenschaftliche Buchgesellschaft, 1973, pp. 342–372.

Huby, Michel. *L'adaptation des romans courtois en Allemagne au XIIe et au XIIIe siècle*. Paris: Klincksíeck, 1968.

———. "L'approfondissement psychologique dans *Erec* de Hartmann." *Études germaniques*, 22 (1967), 13–26.

———. "Hat Hartmann von Aue im *Erec* das Eheproblem neu gedeutet?" *Recherches germaniques*, 6 (1976), 3–17.

Jackson, William H. "Some Observations on the Status of the Narrator in Hartmann von Aue's *Erec* and *Iwein*." *Forum for Modern Language Studies*, 6 (1970), 65–82; rpt. in *Arthurian Romance: Seven Essays*. Ed. D. D. R. Owen. New York: Barnes & Noble, 1971, pp. 65–82.

Jillings, Lewis. "The Ideal of Queenship in Hartmann's *Erec.*" In *The Legend of Arthur in the Middle Ages: Studies Presented to A. H. Diverres by Colleagues, Pupils, and Friends.* Ed. P. B. Grout, R. A. Lodge, C. E. Pickford and E. K. C. Varty. Cambridge: Brewer, 1983, pp. 113–128.

Kalinke, Marianne. "Vorhte in Hartmanns *Erec.*" *Amsterdamer Beiträge zur älteren Germanistik,* 11 (1976), 67–80.

Kellermann, Wilhelm. "Die Bearbeitung des 'Erec-und-Enide'-Romans Chrestiens von Troyes durch Hartmann von Aue." In *Hartmann von Aue.* Ed. Hugo Kuhn and Christoph Cormeau. Wege der Forschung, 309. Darmstadt: Wissenschaftliche Buchgesellschaft, 1973, pp. 511–531.

Knapp, F. P. "Enites Totenklage und Selbstmordversuch in Hartmanns *Erec:* eine quellenkritische Analyse." *Germanisch-romanische Monatsschrift,* NS 26 (1976), 83–90.

Kramer, Hans-Peter. *Erzählerbemerkungen und Erzählerkommentare in Chrestiens und Hartmanns Erec und Iwein.* Göppinger Arbeiten zur Germanistik, 35. Göppingen: Kümmerle, 1971.

Kuhn, Hugo. "Erec." In *Festschrift für P. Kluckhohn und H. Schneider.* Tübingen: Mohr, 1948, pp. 122–147. Rpt. in Hugo Kuhn. *Dichtung und Welt im Mittelalter.* 2nd ed. Tübingen: Metzler, 1969, pp. 133–150; also in *Hartmann von Aue.* Ed. Hugo Kuhn and Christoph Cormeau. Wege der Forschung, 309. Darmstadt: Wissenschaftliche Buchgesellschaft, 1973, pp. 17–48.

Kuttner, Ursula. *Das Erzählen des Erzählten. Eine Studie zum Stil in Hartmanns 'Erec' und 'Iwein.'* Studien zur Germanistik, Anglistik und Komparatistik, 70. Bonn: Bouvier, 1978.

Leitzmann, Albert. "Die Ambraser Erecüberlieferung." *Beiträge zur Geschichte der deutschen Sprache und Literatur,* 59 (1935), 143–234.

Lewis, Robert E. "Erec's Knightly Imperfections." *Res Publica Litterarum,* 5 (1982), 151–158.

Mayer, Hartwig. "Ein 'vil vriuntliches spil': Erecs und Enites gemeinsame Schuld." In *Festschrift zu Ehren von Hermann Boeschenstein.* Ed. A. Arnold, H. Eichner, E. Heier and S. Hoefert. Analecta Helvetica et Germanica. Bonn: Bouvier, 1979.

Meng, Arnim. *Vom Sinn des rittlerlichen Abenteuers bei Hartmann von Aue.* Zurich: Juris, 1967.

Middleton, Roger. "Studies in the Textual Relationships of the Erec/Gereint Stories." Diss. Oxford 1976.

Milde, Wolfgang. "'daz ih minne an uch suche': Neue Wolfenbütteler Bruchstücke des *Erec.*" *Wolfenbütteler Beiträge,* 3 (1978), 43–58.

———. "Zur Kodikologie der neuen und alten Wolfenbütteler Erec-Fragmente und zum Umfang des darin überlieferten Erec-Textes." *Beiträge zur Geschichte der deutschen Sprache und Literatur,* 104 (1982), 190–206.

Müller, Wilhelm. "Zu Hartmann's Erek." *Germania,* 7 (1862), 129–140.

Naumann, Hans. "Zu Hartmanns Erec." *Zeitschrift für deutsche Philologie,* 47 (1918), 360–372.

Nellmann, Eberhard. "Diplomatischer Abdruck der neuen Erec-Fragmente: Berichtigung zum Abdruck in ZfdPh 101, Seite 35–40." *Zeitschrift für deutsche Philologie,* 101 (1982), 436–441.

———. "Ein zweiter Erec-Roman? Zu den neugefundenen Wolfenbütteler Fragmenten." *Zeitschrift für deutsche Philologie*, 101 (1982), 28–78 and 436–441.

Neumann, Friedrich. "Connelant in Hartmanns Erec." *Zeitschrift für deutsches Altertum*, 83 (1951/52), 271–287.

Ohly, Walter. *Die heilsgeschichtliche Struktur der Epen Hartmanns von Aue.* Berlin: Reuter, 1958.

Paul, Hermann. "Zum Erec." *Beiträge zur Geschichte der deutschen Sprache und Literatur*, 3 (1876), 192–197.

Pérennec, René. "Adaptation et societé: L'adaptation par Hartmann d'Aue du roman de Chrétien de Troyes 'Erec et Enide'." *Études germaniques*, 28 (1973), 289–303.

Peters, Ursula. "Artusroman und Fürstenhof. Darstellung und Kritik neuerer sozialgeschichtlicher Untersuchungen zu Hartmanns Erec." *Euphorion*, 69 (1975), 175–196.

Pfeiffer, Franz. "Über Hartmann von Aue. 1. Zum Erek." *Germania*, 4 (1859), 185–237.

Pickering, F. P. "The 'Fortune' of Hartmann's *Erec*." *German Life and Letters*, 30 (1977), 94–109.

Reinitzer, Heimo. "Über Beispielfiguren im 'Erec'." *Deutsche Vierteljahrsschrift*, 50 (1976), 597–639.

Rosenhagen, Gustav. "Zobel von Connelant." *Zeitschrift für deutsches Altertum*, 55 (1917), 301f.

Ruberg, Uwe. "Bildkoordinationen im 'Erec' Hartmanns von Aue." In *Gedenkschrift für W. Foerste*. Ed. Dietrich Hofmann. Cologne and Vienna: Böhlan, 1970, pp. 477–501.

Scheunemann, Ernst. *Artushof und Abenteuer. Zeichnung höfischen Daseins in Hartmanns 'Erec'.* Breslau: Maruschke & Berendt, 1937.

Schröder, Joachim. *Zu Darstellung und Funktion der Schauplätze in den Artusromanen Hartmanns von Aue.* Göppinger Arbeiten zur Germanistik, 61. Göppingen: Kümmerle, 1972.

Schulze, Ursula. "âmis und man. Die zentrale Problematik in Hartmanns 'Erec'." *Beiträge zur Geschichte der deutschen Sprache und Literatur*, 105 (1983), 14–47.

Smits, Kathryn. "Enite als christliche Ehefrau." In *Interpretation und Edition deutscher Texte des Mittelalters: Festschrift für John Asher zum 60. Geburtstag.* Ed. K. Smits, W. Besch and V. Lange. Berlin: Schmidt, 1981, pp. 13–25.

———. "Die Schönheit der Frau in Hartmanns «Erec»." *Zeitschrift für deutsche Philologie*, 101 (1982), 1–28.

Sparnaay, Hendricus. "Zu Erec-Gereint." *Zeitschrift für romanische Philologie*, 65 (1925), 53–69.

Tax, Petrus. "Der *Erec* Hartmanns von Aue: Ein Antitypus zu der *Eneit* Heinrichs von Veldeke?" In *Helen Adolf Festschrift*. Ed. S. Z. Buehne, J. L. Hodge and L. B. Pinto. New York: Ungar, 1968, pp. 47–62.

———. "Studien zum Symbolischen in Hartmanns 'Erec': Enitens Pferd." *Zeitschrift für deutsche Philologie*, 82 (1963), 29–44.

———. "Studien zum Symbolischen in Hartmanns 'Erec': Erecs ritterliche Erhöhung." *Wirkendes Wort*, 13 (1963), 277–288.

Thoran, Barbara. "'Diu ir man verrâten hât': Zum Problem von Enîtes Schuld im *Erec* Hartmanns von Aue." *Wirkendes Wort*, 25 (1975), 255–268.

Thornton, Thomas P. "Die Schreibgewohnheiten Hans Rieds im Ambraser Helden-buch." *Zeitschrift für deutsche Philologie*, 81 (1962), 52–82.

Tobin, Frank. "Hartmann's *Erec:* The Perils of Young Love." *Seminar*, 14 (1978), 1–14.

Vancsa, Kurt. "Wiener «Erec»-Bruchstück." *Jahrbuch für Landeskunde von Nieder-österreich*, NS 29 (1944/48), 411–415.

Voß, Rudolf. *Die Artusepik Hartmanns von Aue. Untersuchungen zum Wirklichkeits-begriff und zur Ästhetik eines literarischen Genres im Kräftefeld von soziokul-turellen Normen und christlicher Anthropologie.* Literatur und Leben, NS 25. Cologne and Vienna: Böhlan, 1983.

Welz,, Dieter. "Erec and the Red Knight. Some Observations on Arthurian Romance and Courtly Ideology." *Theoria. A Journal of Studies in the Arts, Humanities and Social Sciences*, 68 (1972), 85–91.

———. "Glück und Gesellschaft in den Artusromanen Hartmanns von Aue und im 'Tristan' Gottfrieds von Straßburg." *Acta Germanica*, 6 (1971), 11–40.

———. "Kabale und Liebe in Karnant. Zur Struktur des Verrats in Hartmanns *Erec.*" *Acta Germanica*, 16 (1983), 7–23.

Wiegand, Herbert Ernst. *Studien zu Minne und Ehe in Wolframs Parzival und Hart-manns Artusepik.* Berlin and New York: de Gruyter, 1972.

Wiehl, Peter. *Die Redeszene als episches Strukturelement in den Erec- und Iwein-Dichtungen Hartmanns von Aue und Chrestiens de Troyes.* Munich: Fink, 1974.

———. "Zur Komposition des *Erec* Hartmanns von Aue." *Wirkendes Wort*, 22 (1972), 89–107.

Willson, H. Bernard. "Sin and Redemption in Hartmann's 'Erec'." *Germanic Review*, 33 (1958), 5–14.

———. "*Triuwe* and *untriuwe* in Hartmann's *Erec.*" *German Quarterly*, 43 (1970), 5–23.

Wolf, Alois. "Die *adaptation» courtoise.* Kritische Anmerkungen zu einem neuen Dogma." *Germanisch-Romanische Monatsschrift*, 27 (1977), 257–283.

Zwierzina, Konrad. "Mittelhochdeutsche Studien. 13. Zur Textkritik des Erec." *Zeit-schrift für deutsches Altertum*, 45 (1901), 317–368.

GENERAL LITERATURE ON HARTMANN VON AUE AND HIS WORKS

Arndt, Paul Herbert. *Der Erzähler bei Hartmann von Aue. Formen und Funktionen seines Hervortretens und seiner Äußerungen.* Göppinger Arbeiten zur Ger-manistik, 299. Göppingen: Kümmerle, 1980.

Bayer, Hans. *Hartmann von Aue. Die theologischen und historischen Grundlagen seiner Dichtung sowie sein Verhältnis zu Gunther von Pairis.* Mittellatein-isches Jahrbuch, Beiheft 15. Kastellaun: Henn, 1978.

Carne, Eva-Marie. *Die Frauengestalten bei Hartmann von Aue. Ihre Bedeutung im Aufbau und Gehalt der Epen.* Marburger Beiträge zur Germanistik, 31. Mar-burg: Elwert, 1970.

Cormeau, Christoph. "Hartmann von Aue." *Verfasserlexikon.* Vol. 3, 2nd. ed. Berlin and New York: de Gruyter, 1982, col. 500–520.

Cormeau, Christoph and Wilhelm Störmer. *Hartmann von Aue: Epoche—Werk—Wirkung.* Munich: Beck, 1985.

Eroms, Hans Werner. *vreude bei Hartmann von Aue.* Medium Ævum, 20. Munich: Fink, 1970.

Grosse, Siegfried. "Beginn und Ende der erzählenden Dichtungen Hartmanns von Aue." *Beiträge zur Geschichte der deutschen Sprache und Literatur,* 83 (1961/ 62), 137–156; rpt. in *Hartmann von Aue.* Ed. Hugo Kuhn and Christoph Cormeau. Wege der Forschung, 309. Darmstadt: Wissenschaftliche Buchgesellschaft, 1973, pp. 172–194.

Hrubý, Antonín. "Hartmann als artifex, philosophus und præceptor der Gesellschaft." In *Deutsche Literatur im Mittelalter. Kontakte und Perspektiven. Gedenkschrift H. Kuhn.* Ed. Christoph Cormeau. Stuttgart: Metzler, 1979, pp. 254–275.

Kaiser, Gert. *Textauslegung und gesellschaftliche Selbstdeutung. Aspekte einer sozialgeschichtlichen Interpretation von Hartmanns Artusepen.* 2nd rev. ed. Wiesbaden: Athenaion, 1978.

Kramer, Hans-Peter. *Erzählerbemerkungen und Erzählerkommentare in Chrétiens und Hartmanns "Erec" und "Iwein."* Göppinger Arbeiten zur Germanistik, 35. Göppingen: Kümmerle, 1971.

Kuhn, Hugo. "Hartmann von Aue als Dichter." *Der Deutschunterricht,* 5, No. 2 (1953), 11–27; rpt. in *Hartmann von Aue.* Ed. Hugo Kuhn and Christoph Cormeau. Wege der Forschung, 309. Darmstadt: Wissenschaftliche Buchgesellschaft, 1973, pp. 68–86.

Kuhn, Hugo, and Christoph Cormeau, eds. *Hartmann von Aue.* Wege der Forschung, 309. Darmstadt: Wissenschaftliche Buchgesellschaft, 1973.

Kuttner, Ursula. *Das Erzählen des Erzählten: eine Studie zum Stil in Hartmanns Erec und Iwein.* Studien zur Germanistik, Anglistik und Komparatistik, 70. Bonn: Bouvier, 1978.

Linke, Hansjürgen. *Epische Strukturen in der Dichtung Hartmanns von Aue: Untersuchungen zur Formkritik, Werkstruktur und Vortragsgliederung.* Munich: Fink, 1968.

Mertens, Volker. *Gregorius Eremita. Eine Lebensform des Adels bei Hartmann von Aue in ihrer Problematik und ihrer Wandlung in der Rezeption.* Münchener Texte und Untersuchungen, 67. Munich: Artemis, 1978.

Müller, Karl Friedrich. *Hartmann von Aue und die Herzöge von Zähringen.* Lahr: Schauenburg, 1974.

Neumann, Friedrich. "Wann dichtete Hartmann von Aue?" In *Studien zur deutschen Philologie des Mittelalters. Festschrift F. Panzer.* Ed. Richard Kienast. Heidelberg: Winter, 1950, pp. 59–72; rpt. in Friedrich Neumann. *Kleinere Schriften zur deutschen Philologie des Mittelalters.* Berlin: de Gruyter, 1969, pp. 42–56.

Polsakiewicz, Roman. "Zur Chronologie der epischen Werke Hartmanns von Aue." *Euphorion,* 71 (1977), 82–91.

Schönbach, Anton Erich. *Über Hartmann von Aue. Drei Bücher Untersuchungen.* Graz: Leuschner & Lubensky, 1894; rpt. Hildesheim and New York: Olms, 1971.

Schröder, Werner. "Zur Chronologie der drei großen mittelhochdeutschen Epiker." *Deutsche Vierteljahrsschrift*, 31 (1957), 264–302.

Schultz, Alwin. *Das höfische Leben zur Zeit der Minnesänger*. 2 vols. Leipzig: Hirzel, 1889; rpt Osnabrück: Zeller, 1965.

Sparnaay, Hendricus. "Brauchen wir ein neues Hartmannbild?" *Deutsche Vierteljahrsschrift*, 39 (1965), 639–649.

———. "Hartmann von Aue and his Successors." In *Arthurian Literature in the Middle Ages. A Collaborative History*. Ed. Roger Sherman Loomis. Oxford: Clarendon, 1959, pp. 430–442.

———. *Hartmann von Aue. Studien zu einer Biographie*. 2 vols. Halle: Niemeyer, 1933–38; rpt. in one vol. Darmstadt: Wissenschaftliche Buchgesellschaft, 1975.

Thum, Bernd. "Politische Probleme der Stauferzeit im Werk Hartmanns von Aue. Landesherrschaft im 'Erec' und 'Iwein'. Mit einem Anhang: Hartmann von Aue, *Augia minor* und die Altdorfer Welfen." In *Stauferzeit: Geschichte, Literatur, Kunst*. Ed. R. Krohn et al. Stuttgart: Klett-Cotta, 1979, pp. 47–70.

Voß, Rudolf. "Handlungsschematismus und anthropologische Konzeption—zur Ästhetik des klassischen Artusromans am Beispiel des «Erec» und «Iwein» Hartmanns von Aue." *Amsterdamer Beiträge zur älteren Germanistik*, 18 (1982), 95–114.

Wapnewski, Peter. *Hartmann von Aue*. 7th ed. Sammlung Metzler, 17. Stuttgart: Metzler, 1979.

Wolff, Ludwig. "Hartmann von Aue." *Wirkendes Wort*, 9 (1959), 12–24.

———. "Hartmann von Aue. Vom *Büchlein* und *Erec* bis zum *Iwein*." *Der Deutschunterricht*, 20, No. 2 (1968), 43–59.

Zutt, Herta. "Die Rede bei Hartmann von Aue." *Der Deutschunterricht*, 14, No. 6 (1962), 67–79.

GENERAL SECONDARY LITERATURE

Bäuml, Franz. "Varieties and Consequences of Medieval Literacy and Illiteracy." *Speculum*, 55 (1980), 237–265.

Bertau, Karl. *Deutsche Literatur im europäischen Mittelalter*. 2 vols. Munich: Beck, 1972–73.

Borst, Arno. *Lebensformen im Mittelalter*. Frankfurt am Main, Berlin and Vienna: Ullstein, 1979.

Brogsitter, Karl Otto. *Artusepik*. Sammlung Metzler, 38. 2nd ed. Stuttgart: Metzler, 1971.

Brooke, Christopher. *The Twelfth Century Renaissance*. Norwich, England: Jarrold and Sons, 1969.

Bumke, Joachim. *Ministerialität und Ritterdichtung. Umrisse der Forschung*. Munich: Beck, 1976.

———. *Studien zum Ritterbegriff im 12. und 13. Jahrhundert*. Heidelberg: Winter, 1977; in English *The Concept of Knighthood in the Middle Ages*. Trans.

W. T. H. Jackson and Erika Jackson. AMS Studies in the Middle Ages, 2. New York: AMS Press, 1982.

Cormeau, Christoph. *"Artusroman und Märchen: Zur Beschreibung und Genese der Struktur des höfischen Romans."* In *Wolfram-Studien* V. Ed. Werner Schröder. Berlin: Schmidt, 1979, pp. 63–78.

Curschmann, Michael. "Hören—Lesen—Sehen. Buch und Schriftlichkeit im Selbstverständnis der volkssprachlichen literarischen Kultur Deutschlands um 1200." *Beiträge zur Geschichte der deutschen Sprache und Literatur,* 106 (1984), 218–257.

Curtius, Ernst Robert. *European Literatur and the Latin Middle Ages.* Trans. Willard R. Trask. Bollingen Series, 36. Princeton: Princeton University Press, 1967.

de Boor, Helmut. *Die höfische Literatur: Vorbereitung, Blüte, Ausklang, 1170–1250.* 10th ed. Vol. 2 of *Geschichte der deutschen Literatur von den Anfängen bis zur Gegenwart.* Ed. Helmut de Boor and Richard Newald. Munich: Beck, 1979.

Ehrismann, Gustav. *Geschichte der deutschen Literatur bis zum Ausgang des Mittelalters.* Part 2, vol. 2, 1st half. Handbuch des deutschen Unterrichts an höheren Schulen, 6,2,2,1. Munich: Beck, 1927.

Fisher, Rodney. *Studies in the Demonic in Selected Middle High German Epics.* Göppinger Arbeiten zur Germanistik, 132. Göppingen: Kümmerle, 1974.

Fleckenstein, Joseph. "Friedrich Barbarossa und das Rittertum. Zur Bedeutung der großen Mainzer Hoftage von 1184 und 1188." In *Das Rittertum im Mittelalter.* Ed. Arno Borst. Wege der Forschung, 349. Darmstadt: Wissenschaftliche Buchgesellschaft, 1976. Rpt. from *Festschrift für Hermann Heimpel zum 70. Geburtstag am 19.9.1971.* 2 vols. Göttingen: Vandenhoeck und Ruprecht, 1972.

Freed, John B. "Reflections on the Medieval German Nobility." *American Historical Review,* 91 (1986), 553–575.

Gies, Frances and Joseph. *Women in the Middle Ages.* New York: Crowell, 1978.

Gürttler, Karin R. *'Künec Artûs der guote': Das Artusbild der höfischen Epik des 12. und 13. Jahrhunderts.* Studien zur Germanistik, Anglistik und Komparatistik, 52. Bonn: Bouvier, 1976.

Jauss, Hans Robert. "Theorie der Gattungen und Literatur des Mittelalters." In *Grundriß der romanischen Literatur des Mittelalters.* Ed. Hans Robert Jauss and Erich Köhler. Heidelberg: Winter, 1972, vol. I, pp. 107–138.

Keen, Maurice. *Chivalry.* New Haven and London: Yale University Press, 1984.

Köhler, Erich. *Ideal und Wirklichkeit in der höfischen Epik: Studien zur Form der frühen Artus- und Graldichtung.* 2nd ed. Beihefte zur Zeitschrift für romanische Philologie, 97. Tübingen: Niemeyer, 1970.

Krauss, Henning, ed. *Europäisches Hochmittelalter.* Neues Handbuch der Literaturwissenschaft, 7. Wiesbaden: Athenaion, 1981.

Kuhn, Hugo. "Die Klassik des Rittertums in der Stauferzeit." In *Annalen der deutschen Literatur.* Ed. Heinz Otto Burger. 2nd ed. Stuttgart: Metzler, 1971, pp. 99–177.

———. "Soziale Realität und dichterische Fiktion am Beispiel der höfischen Ritterdichtung Deutschlands." In *Soziologie und Leben.* Ed. C. Brinkmann. Tübingen: Wunderlich, 1952, pp. 195–219; rpt. in Hugo Kuhn, *Dichtung und Welt im Mittelalter*. 2nd ed. Stuttgart: Metzler, 1969, pp. 22–40; also in *Das Rittertum im Mittelalter*. Ed. Arno Borst. Wege der Forschung, 349. Darmstadt: Wissenschaftliche Buchgesellschaft, 1976, pp. 172–197.

Loomis, Roger Sherman. *Arthurian Literature in the Middle Ages. A Collaborative History*. Oxford: Clarendon Press, 1959.

———. *Arthurian Tradition and Chrétien de Troyes*. New York: Columbia University Press, 1949.

Lucas, Angela. *Women in the Middle Ages: Religion, Marriage and Letters*. New York: St. Martin's Press, 1983.

Morris, Rosemary. *The Character of King Arthur in Medieval Literature*. Cambridge: Brewer; Totowa, NJ: Rowman & Littlefield, 1982.

Mundy, John. *Europe in the High Middle Ages: 1150–1309*. London: Longman, 1973.

Pörksen, Uwe. *Der Erzähler im mittelhochdeutschen Epos. Formen seines Hervortretens bei Lamprecht, Konrad, Hartmann, in Wolframs Willehalm und in den 'Spielmannsepen'*. Philologische Studien und Quellen, 58. Berlin: Schmidt, 1971.

Ruh, Kurt. *Höfische Epik des deutschen Mittelalters I: Von den Anfängen bis zu Hartmann von Aue*. Grundlagen der Germanistik, 7. 2nd. ed. Berlin: Schmidt, 1977.

Schirmer, Walter F. *Die frühen Darstellungen des Arthurstoffs*. Arbeitsgemeinschaft für Forschung des Landes Nordrhein-Westfalen Geisteswissenschaften, 73. Cologne and Opladen: Westdeutscher Verlag, 1958.

Schmolke-Hasselmann, Beate. *Der arthurische Versroman von Chrestien bis Froissart*. Beihefte zur *Zeitschrift für romanische Philologie*, 177. Tübingen: Niemeyer, 1980.

Schultz, Alwin. *Das höfische Leben zur Zeit der Minnesänger*. 2 vols. 2nd ed. Leipzig: Hirzel, 1889; rpt. Osnabrück: Zeller, 1965.

Shahar, Shulamith. *The Fourth Estate: A History of Women in the Middle Ages*. Trans. Chaya Galai. London and New York: Methuen, 1983.

Stevens, John. *Medieval Romance: Themes and Approaches*. London: Hutchinson University Library, 1973.

Stock, Brian. *The Implications of Literacy: Written Language and Models of Interpretation in the Eleventh and Twelfth Centuries*. Princeton: Princeton University Press, 1983.

Stuard, Susan Mosher, ed. *Women in Medieval Society*. Philadelphia: University of Pennsylvania Press, 1976.

Wais, Kurt. *Der arthurische Roman*. Wege der Forschung, 157. Darmstadt: Wissenschaftliche Buchgesellschaft, 1970.

Walshe, M. O'C. *Medieval German Literature*. London: Routledge & Kegan Paul, 1962.

Wehrli, Max. *Literatur im deutschen Mittelalter: eine poetologische Einführung*. Stuttgart: Reclam, 1984.

REFERENCE WORKS

Benecke, G. F., W. Müller and F. Zarncke. *Mittelhochdeutsches Wörterbuch*. 3 vols. Leipzig: Hirzel, 1854–66; rpt. Hildesheim: Olms, 1963.

Boggs, Roy A. *Hartmann von Aue. Lemmatisierte Konkordanz zum Gesamtwerk*. 2 vols. Indices zur deutschen Literatur, 12/13. Nendeln: KTO Press, 1979.

Jandebeur, Franz. *Reimwörterbücher und Reimwortverzeichnisse zum Ersten Büchlein, Erec, Gregorius, Armen Heinrich, den Liedern von Hartmann von Aue und dem sogenannten Zweiten Büchlein. Mit einem Vorwort über die Entwicklung der deutschen Reimlexikographie*. Münchener Texte, Ergänzungsreihe, 5. Munich: Callwey, 1926.

Klemt, Irmgard. *Hartmann von Aue. Eine Zusammenstellung der über ihn und sein Werk von 1927 bis 1965 erschienenen Literatur*. Bibliographische Hefte, 5. Cologne: Greven, 1968.

Lexer, Matthias. *Mittelhochdeutsches Handwörterbuch*. 3 vols. Leipzig: Hirzel, 1872–78; rpt. Stuttgart: Hirzel, 1970.

Neubuhr, Elfriede. *Bibliographie zu Hartmann von Aue*. Bibliographien zur deutschen Literatur des Mittelalters, 6. Berlin: Schmidt, 1977.

Paul, Hermann. *Mittelhochdeutsche Grammatik*. 22nd ed., by Hugo Moser, Ingeborg Schröbler and Siegfried Grosse. Tübingen: Niemeyer, 1982.

INDEX OF PROPER NAMES
FROM *EREC*

Included in this index are most of the proper names from the Translation only. Not listed here are (1) names of persons who are, strictly speaking, not characters in the story, such as God or Satan, and (2) personified abstract nouns, such as Lady Poverty, Love, etc. Certain of the proper names from this index are also listed separately in the General Index. Italicized numbers indicate references to the Introduction or Commentary.

GENERAL INDEX

Included in this index are entries from the Introduction and Commentary only. Characters from the Translation are referenced separately in the Index of Proper Names preceding this index; in addition, certain of the more important characters (such as Arthur, Erec, Enite) are listed here in the General Index as well. Finally, medieval names are alphabetized by first name, e.g., not *Vogelweide, Walther von der,* but *Walther von der Vogelweide;* similarly, not *Mons, Gislebert of,* but *Gislebert of Mons.*

Aaron, 202
Abatis, 192
Aberteivi, 188
Acrostic, 52 n.51
Adventure, knightly, 22–24, 39, 210
Aeneas, 3
Aeneid (Vergil), 3, 196–97, 201
Alexander the Great, 3
Ambras Manuscript, 18–19, 47, 48, 51 n.39, 185, 188, 195, 205, 207
Aneirin, 50 n.34
Anglo-Norman dialect, 16
Anjou, 16–17
Annales Cambriae, 50 n.34
Apostles, 189
Aquitaine, 16
Arbor at Brandigan, 21, 203, 204, 205
Arebeit (strenuous striving), 39. *See also* Virtues, courtly
Argumentum ad absurdum, 27
Aristotle, 35
Arme Heinrich, der (Hartmann von Aue). See *Henry the Leper*
Arthur, King, 15–18, 21, 39, 51 n.37, 188, 189; festivals, 3, 37; function of court, 22–24, 39–40; as historical figure, 15, 16; as literary figure, 16–18, 51 nn. 37, 40; Round Table, 4, 15, 23. *See also* Arthurian legend; Arthurian romance
Arthurian legend, 15, 16, 17, 50–51 n.35, 51 n.37

Arthurian romance, 4, 7, 13, 14, 40, 187; character development, 27; chronological parameters, 15, 17; claims of source, 29–30; classical Arthurian romances, 22; development of, 15–18; disfavor and rediscovery, 51 n.38; festivals, 189; geography of, 17; God and the Church, 40, 53 n.72; humor, 42; introduction of to Germany, 18–19, 50–51 n.35, 51 n.37; Keii, 196; marriage, 32; optimism, 18, 40–41, 45; reception of, 50 n.29; as reflection of real life, 35–36, 41–42, 45–47; structure of, 22–24; women, 36, 53 n.71
Ashlar, 203
Asia Minor, 8
Athena, 203
Athens, 203
Auctoritas, 29–30
Audience of courtly literature, 10–11, 15, 18, 19, 20, 22, 23, 25–30, 35, 42–43, 50 n.29, 52 n.54
Aue: Hartmann's lord at, 12; location of, 4, 12
Avalon, 189–90

Babenberg, dukes of, 8
Barbarossa. *See* Friedrich I (Holy Roman Emperor)
Bäuml, Franz, 52 n.49
Beatrix, Empress, 8
Bellum Civile (Lucan), 197
Benoît de Sainte-Maure, 17

UNIVERSITY OF PENNSYLVANIA PRESS

MIDDLE AGES SERIES

EDWARD PETERS,
General Editor

Edward Peters, ed. *Christian Society and the Crusades, 1198–1229.* Sources in Translation, including The Capture of Damietta by Oliver of Paderborn. 1971

Edward Peters, ed. *The First Crusade: The Chronicle of Fulcher of Chartres and Other Source Materials.* 1971

Katherine Fischer Drew, trans. *The Burgundian Code: The Book of Constitutions or Law of Gundobad and Additional Enactments.* 1972

G. G. Coulton. *From St. Francis to Dante: Translations from the Chronicle of the Franciscan Salimbene (1221–1288).* 1972

Alan C. Kors and Edward Peters, eds. *Witchcraft in Europe, 1110–1700: A Documentary History.* 1972

Richard C. Dales. *The Scientific Achievement of the Middle Ages.* 1973

Katherine Fischer Drew, trans. *The Lombard Laws.* 1973

Henry Charles Lea. *The Ordeal.* Part III of Superstition and Force. 1973

Henry Charles Lea. *Torture.* Part IV of Superstition and Force. 1973

Henry Charles Lea (Edward Peters, ed.). *The Duel and the Oath.* Parts I and II of Superstition and Force. 1974

Edward Peters, ed. *Monks, Bishops, and Pagans: Christian Culture in Gaul and Italy, 500–700.* 1975

Jeanne Krochalis and Edward Peters, ed. and trans. *The World of Piers Plowman.* 1975

Julius Goebel, Jr. *Felony and Misdemeanor: A Study in the History of Criminal Law.* 1976

Susan Mosher Stuard, ed. *Women in Medieval Society.* 1976

James Muldoon, ed. *The Expansion of Europe: The First Phase.* 1977

Clifford Peterson. *Saint Erkenwald.* 1977

Robert Somerville and Kenneth Pennington, eds. *Law, Church, and Society: Essays in Honor of Stephan Kuttner.* 1977

Donald E. Queller. *The Fourth Crusade: The Conquest of Constantinople, 1201–1204.* 1977

Pierre Riché (Jo Ann McNamara, trans.). *Daily Life in the World of Charlemagne.* 1978

Charles R. Young. *The Royal Forests of Medieval England.* 1979

Edward Peters, ed. *Heresy and Authority in Medieval Europe.* 1980

Suzanne Fonay Wemple. *Women in Frankish Society: Marriage and the Cloister, 500–900.* 1981

R. G. Davies and J. H. Denton, eds. *The English Parliament in the Middle Ages.* 1981

Edward Peters. *The Magician, the Witch, and the Law.* 1982

Barbara H. Rosenwein. *Rhinoceros Bound: Cluny in the Tenth Century.* 1982

Steven D. Sargent, ed. and trans. *On the Threshold of Exact Science: Selected Writings of Anneliese Maier on Late Medieval Natural Philosophy.* 1982

Benedicta Ward. *Miracles and the Medieval Mind: Theory, Record, and Event, 1000–1215.* 1982

Harry Turtledove, trans. *The Chronicle of Theophanes: An English Translation of anni mundi 6095–6305 (A.D. 602–813).* 1982

Leonard Cantor, ed. *The English Medieval Landscape.* 1982

Charles T. Davis. *Dante's Italy and Other Essays.* 1984

George T. Dennis, trans. *Maurice's Strategikon: Handbook of Byzantine Military Strategy.* 1984

Thomas F. X. Noble. *The Republic of St. Peter: The Birth of the Papal State, 680–825.* 1984

Kenneth Pennington. *Pope and Bishops: The Papal Monarchy in the Twelfth and Thirteenth Centuries.* 1984

Patrick J. Geary. *Aristocracy in Provence: The Rhône Basin at the Dawn of the Carolingian Age.* 1985

C. Stephen Jaeger. *The Origins of Courtliness: Civilizing Trends and the Formation of Courtly Ideals, 939–1210.* 1985

J. N. Hillgarth, ed. *Christianity and Paganism, 350–750: The Conversion of Western Europe.* 1986

William Chester Jordan. *From Servitude to Freedom: Manumission in the Sénonais in the Thirteenth Century.* 1986

James William Brodman. *Ransoming Captives in Crusader Spain: The Order of Merced on the Christian-Islamic Frontier.* 1986

Frank Tobin. *Meister Eckhart: Thought and Language.* 1986

Daniel Bornstein, trans. *Dino Compagni's Chronicle of Florence.* 1986

James M. Powell. *Anatomy of a Crusade, 1213–1221.* 1986

Jonathan Riley-Smith. *The First Crusade and the Idea of Crusading.* 1986

Susan Mosher Stuard, ed. *Women in Medieval History and Historiography.* 1987

Avril Henry, ed. *The Mirour of Mans Saluacioune.* 1987

María Menocal. *The Arabic Role in Medieval Literary History.* 1987

Margaret J. Ehrhart. *The Judgment of the Trojan Prince Paris in Medieval Literature.* 1987

Betsy Bowden. *Chaucer Aloud: The Varieties of Textual Interpretation.* 1987

Felipe Fernández-Armesto. *Before Columbus: Exploration and Colonization from the Mediterranean to the Atlantic, 1229–1492.* 1987

Michael Resler, trans. *EREC by Hartmann von Aue.* 1987

A. J. Minnis. *Medieval Theory of Authorship.* 1987

EREC BY HARTMANN VON AUE
Translated, with an introduction and commentary, by
MICHAEL RESLER

EREC by Hartmann von Aue is a new translation, by Michael Resler, of the earliest example of the German Arthurian legend and the beginning of the golden era—1170–1240—of Middle High German literature. An extensive introduction to this translation establishes *EREC* within its historical and cultural setting, and detailed notes to the text refer to the pertinent philological, literary, and historical scholarship that has, during the past century, dealt with this important romance.

Inspired by the activity and cultural cross-fertilization engendered by the Crusades, knight-poets used Arthurian legends and characters as literary models to help shape their own experiences into poetry and myth. These works, written in the vernacular, were immensely popular in court circles and, to some extent, among a common audience hungry for stories of knightly heroism.

Using an earlier French version of the Arthurian legend as a source, Hartmann von Aue introduced into German literature the celebration of knights as a new order of elite fighters and the elevation of courtly behavior and gentility into virtues. In addition to their ability to entertain, Erec's series of adventures are offered as moral instruction, illustrating the importance of moderation in the chivalric code and a delicate balance between action and restraint.

Resler's new translation attempts to strike a balance between its faithfulness to the original in terms of accuracy and nuance and its appeal to the modern reader.

EREC by Hartmann von Aue will be invaluable to students and scholars of Germanic and medieval literature.

MICHAEL RESLER is Adjunct Associate Professor of Germanic Studies at Boston College.

A new volume in the Middle Ages Series.

UNIVERSITY OF PENNSYLVANIA PRESS

FRONT COVER ILLUSTRATION: From the *Dichterminiatur* of Hartmann von Aue in the Manesse Song Manuscript [*Manessische Liederhandschrift*] (1300–1330). By permission of the Universitätsbibliothek in Heidelberg.

COVER DESIGN: Adrianne Onderdonk Dudden   ISBN 0-8122-1247-9